DEBUSSY: IMPRESSIONISM AND SYMBOLISM

STEFAN JAROCINSKI

DEBUSSY
Impressionism and Symbolism

Translated from the French by
ROLLO MYERS

EULENBURG BOOKS
LONDON

This edition first published in 1976 by
Ernst Eulenburg Ltd
48 Great Marlborough Street, London w1v 2bn

Reprinted 1981

© Ernst Eulenburg Ltd 1976

isbn 0 903873 09 5 paperback
0 903873 20 6 hardback

Music examples are reproduced by kind permission
of Editions Durand et Cie

Printed in Great Britain by
Page Bros (Norwich) Ltd

Originally published in Polish as
Debussy, a impresionizm i synmbolizm
© 1966, Polskie Wydawnictwo Muzyczne

French edition
© 1970, Editions du Seuil

CONTENTS

PREFACE

TO THE FRENCH EDITION

by VLADIMIR JANKÉLÉVITCH

Is it necessary to 'introduce' to the French public a musicologist of such eminence as Stefan Jarocinski? We need only recall that after taking part, in the war against the German aggressor, he took a philosophy course at the Sorbonne, and worked under Nadia Boulanger. At the present moment he is Head of the Department of the History of Music at the Institute of Art at the Polish Academy of Sciences in Warsaw, and also Vice-President of the Association of Polish Musicians. He is the author of six works: *Mozart* (1954); an *Anthology of Polish musical criticism* (1958); *Orpheus at the Crossroads* (1958); *Polish Music* (1965); *Witold Lutoslavski* (1967); and the present study on *Debussy*. He is already known to French readers for his remarkable contribution to the Debussy Seminar (*Colloque Debussy*) organised by Professor Jacques Chailley in 1962: 'Some aspects of the sound-world of Debussy'. In 1971 he completed a *Chronicle of Debussy and his epoch* and, in collaboration with M. François Lesure, a *catalogue raisonné* of Debussy's works. M. Jarocinski may, in fact, be considered as being, essentially, the leading representative and most erudite authority among the Polish musical *avant-garde*.

Debussy has always aroused a passionate interest among foreign musicians, whether German, English, Spanish or Italian. Apart from the often biased work of Arnold Alchvang (Moscow, 1935) we would mention especially the magnificent special number of the *Approdo musicale* (1959) edited by Alberto Mantelli, and above all the two volumes of *Debussy: his Life and Mind* by Edward Lockspeiser (London, 1962–1965), which is today the most important study of Debussy. In order to understand the importance of Debussy in twentieth-century music one has only to re-read the moving *Tombeau de Claude Debussy* which *La Revue Musicale* published in 1920 as a supplement to the special issue devoted to the Master two years after his death. There will be found, among many others, the names of Béla Bartók, Manuel de Falla, Eugene Goossens, Francesco Malipiero and Igor Stravinsky; other tributes from European musicians included a *Meditation* by Zoltán Kodály on a theme from Debussy's *String Quartet* and the moving melody which Joaquin Nin, in honour of Debussy, composed in the form of a tribute from the birds of Catalonia.

It is the destiny of all great works of art to be exposed to the often contradictory interpretations placed upon them by successive generations. After the 'impressionist' Debussy of the earliest musicologists, Jean Barraqué sees in him the true originator of the serial music of today; while in her important *Comparative study of the harmonic languages of Fauré and Debussy*, Françoise Gervais paradoxically stresses the pre-eminence of the melodic as compared to the harmonic elements in their music. All these interpretations are equally valid and justifiable; they all throw light on one aspect or another of the inexhaustible treasures which these works contain. And, indeed, the genius of Debussy is so all-embracing that it already contains in itself all the elements of the future anti-Debussyist reaction. Debussy in fact embodies both Debussyism and its opposite. In the incisive, corrosive style of *Ibéria*, the *Epigraphes antiques* and some of the *Etudes* one can sometimes discern the asceticism of the last works of Satie; on the other hand, it would be difficult to recognise in the violence of the Study *Pour les tierces*, or the Study *Pour les accords* those ecstatic subtleties for which Debussy was sometimes taken to task by his academic critics. It is Stefan Jarocinski's aim to explain Debussy in terms of Symbolism rather than Impressionism. And, on a first analysis, this idea seems astonishingly right and fruitful. The care with which Jarocinski distinguishes Debussy from the Impressionists will help us to be suspicious of any misleading analogy between music and painting, and to resist the temptation to confuse the temporal order of auditive sensations with the visual order of spatial coexistence, or vice-versa. Jarocinski denies the right of either the listener or the performer to conceive music in terms of the three dimensions of optical space; while, on the creative side, he questions the possibility of translating a landscape in terms of temporal succession.

Jarocinski is not deceived by the picturesque titles Debussy gave to his *Images*, his *Estampes* or his *Préludes*. But while the literal and, in a sense, juxta-linear correspondence between sounds and colours is of a purely metaphorical nature, the universal correspondence between qualities, through the intermediary of memories and associations, is the whole essence of Symbolism. It was in accordance with this symbolical and spiritual interpretation that Skriabin in his *Prometheus* envisaged the correspondence between sounds and colours. In this context the symbolic function is a particular attribute of music. It is for this reason that music, a language at once ambiguous and ambivalent, and even capable of meaning more than one thing at a time – a language which is, in fact, the opposite of a language – music never has to make a choice between one meaning rather than another, as is the case with rational speech. It lends itself to a great variety of interpretations, all of which are valid, and any of which we can choose to suit our own mood or feeling. But the apparent indeterminacy of music is in reality a proof of the infinite richness of the innumerable meanings and interpretations which it harbours within itself. When the Czech composer Zdenko Fibich wrote his *Etudes de peinture* he was not really trying to translate in terms of music the solitude of the forest which Ruysdael had expressed in colours and forms; what he did was to create a state of mind which would leave the interpreter free to imagine as he pleased the distant horn-calls, the murmur of the brook and the rustle of the wind in the trees.

Similarly, what characterises the music of Debussy is not its descriptive function, but its suggestion of hidden energy; and the power of this suggestion has a magical force which is irresistible. Jarocinski says that *La Mer* symbolises the awakening of life and the expansion of the forces that lie dormant in the depths of Nature. As Skriabin says at the beginning of his Fifth Sonata: 'I summon you to life, O mysterious forces'. This applies even more aptly to Viteslav Novak's admirable *Pan*, in which the association of mountains, sea and forests, and women introduce us to an equivocal world, halfway between real and figurative meaning – meaning in its literal or grammatic, as opposed to its pneumatic sense. The second movement of *Ibéria* ('Parfums de la nuit') has nothing to do either with our olfactory sense or our visual imagination. And yet it disturbs us profoundly, creating in us a kaleidoscope of images, sensations and qualities: 'sounds and scents which pervade the evening air', and filling us with that sensation of 'dizziness and languor' of which the poet speaks. Moreover, its 'evocative' quality, as at the beginning of Albeniz's *Iberia*, always has a distant and almost dream-like quality. Above all dream-like: this liquidity, this 'diffluence' of sensations and of images explain what Tristan Lhermite meant when he spoke of the fascination of 'the slumbering water's dreams'. The wonderful *Promenoir des deux amants* is full of this dream-like quality. Bachelard, with whose works Stefan Jarocinski is familiar, would find the right words in which to express this. Not only water and its dreams, but the brooding air and the sighing wind and the 'marvellous clouds in the sky' – everything that is ethereal, allusive, unsubstantial, forever changing and perpetually transformed, is a part of Debussy's universe.

Moreover, and for the same reasons, this universe is inhabited, not by solid and tangible presences, but rather by things absent – the far horizon, the immensity of the sea, the distant sky and the wind that comes from afar, swift bearer of messages from beyond, sweeping over the vast plains and always coming from elsewhere. Think of the shepherd in the *Boîte à joujoux* playing on his pipe far away, and Mélisande in the First Act when she says: 'Je ne suis pas d'ici' ('Where were you born? – Oh! far away from here, far away'); and the midsummer fairies dancing in the night air; and the girl with the flaxen hair; they, too, all come, not from the East, but perhaps from the West; for the West is the great Beyond in the magical world of Debussy. This is where Mélisande resembles the wind in the plain, which is a 'ponent' wind that is not from here. Better still: the distant inhabitants of this faraway world belong nowhere; and the word 'here' has for them no meaning. In other words, none of them are what they are, or where they are. In this sense, at least, Debussy, like Manuel de Falla and Déodat de Sévérac, seems to be attached by some secret thread to Jaufré Rudel, the nostalgic poet of far-off things. Owing nothing to the 'naturalist' school, Debussy is portrayed by Jarocinski as the poet of a no-man's land, a country that does not exist.

As to this music which takes us beyond what exists, I see no reason why we should not compare it in this respect with the irrealism of Fauré: did not Fauré himself, à propos of his Second Quartet, speak of a desire for non-existent things? In the incomparable poetry of Maeterlinck, with its mysterious symbols and correspondences, it is easy to see where Debussy, Fauré and Chausson discovered their own language. And yet Stefan Jarocinski has clearly understood that, although Debussy's music is by no means confined to the description and transcription of the sounds in Nature, nor to a *pointilliste* representation of waves, it cannot on the other hand be reduced to a purely psychological subjectivism: Debussy may not be a landscape painter, but this does not mean that his works are a kind of 'Symphonie Pathétique'. Jarocinski makes this quite clear. Debussy's music is marked by a harmonic sensuality, and above all, a craving for new sonorities which make it impossible to attribute to him any kind of inner unhappiness or introvert subjectivity.

His sensitivity with regard to instrumental timbres, the inimitable ways in which he renovates them and uses unusual combinations to produce the most uncommon effects, his precise knowledge of the limitations of auditive memory, and the refinement of his perception, border on the miraculous. I would recall here that a feeling for pure sound in itself is one of the distinctive characteristics of French music in general. Liszt and Chopin are, in this respect, the true sources from which modern music has developed. We are so profoundly in agreement on all points with Jarocinski that I am sure he would not object to my mentioning the following details: César Franck, with his taste for voluptuous sonorities, could not be more anti-German. As to Chabrier, he is not only the author of *Gwendoline*, but above all the composer of *Le Roi malgré lui* and *La Sulamite*, every bar and every note of which delight the ear with the most ineffable and entrancing sounds. And need one mention in this context Chausson – the fore-runner of Satie and Debussy? His *Serres chaudes*, almost contemporary with the *Proses lyriques*, are without any doubt one of the sources of *Pelléas*. Nearer to our time, every variety of the most refined forms of pure sonorous delight are to be found in the piano works of Déodat de Sévérac, and in all the works of Ravel. The austere musicians of today, devoured by a kind of ambivalent and suspect rancour against musical pleasure, and who try to make us feel guilty by employing too often the virtuous and moralising term of 'anti-hedonism', would be wise to avoid citing Debussy in this connection. Was it not Debussy who wrote: 'French music desires, above all, to give pleasure', and 'Music must humbly seek to give pleasure'. M. Jarocinski quotes on three occasions the article in *La Revue bleue* in which these statements occur. Maurice Ravel, for his part, headed his *Valses nobles et sentimentales* with this quotation from Henri de Régnier: 'Le plaisir délicieux . . . d'une occupation inutile.' The pleasure produced by the ravishing sonorities of Ravel can be so acute as actually to cause pain, and sometimes produces a kind of passionate ecstasy. Ravel and Debussy were, in this respect, the direct heirs of Scarlatti, who would not have considered it an insult to be accused of 'hedonism', and was not afraid of forbidden delights. Debussy detested boredom, abstractions, pedantry, austerity and the complications of polyphony: 'I detest all doctrines', he used to say. Among the well-chosen texts which Stefan Jarocinski has assembled here and commented on, I have selected this: 'Music becomes "difficult" when it's no longer music.' In other words, music becomes complicated when the composer has nothing to say. Debussy would probably be horrified by certain aspects of the aridity and moroseness of some contemporary music. Debussy thought that music was not made to be written down on paper, but for the organ we call the ear; and, indeed, the doctrinarians, absorbed by the problems of how to write it, are sometimes inclined to forget the existence of that organ; for music is not a graphic phenomenon, but an aural event; it needs above all to be heard – certainly not merely to be read!

Stefan Jarocinski admirably describes the spontaneity of what he calls 'trans-discursive music', which has nothing in common with the conceptual, coded variety favoured by the disciples of Wagner. 'It develops spontaneously, ignoring those long-winded introductions and lengthy *finales* so dear to the hearts of the romantic school. Such music has no beginning and no end. It emerges from silence, establishes itself without any preliminaries, *in medias res*, and then, interrupting its progress, continues to weave its way into our dreams.' One has the impression here that Jarocinski will make some reference to *Boris Godunov,* which has hardly any introduction and which is almost unfinished, deploying its successive scenes between the monodic cantilena of the prologue and the final lamentation of the Idiot, and thus, like the eternal song of the wind in the plains, has no beginning and no end. One would have liked in the admirable pages of this book, in which so many other names are cited, to find some mention of Mussorgsky: not only because he is one of the greatest geniuses of all time, but more especially because Debussy has a fraternal relationship with him, and because Mussorgsky was himself the living incarnation of the anti-rhetorical spirit. One has only to recall the wonderful passage in which Monsieur Croche, having routed the philologists and the pedants, sings the praises of *The Nursery*. This 'innocent grammar of art' of which Debussy speaks in unforgettable terms in a' passage which Jarocinski, with his usual perspicacity, has not failed to notice, is the grammar of Mimi Brigand and of the Nikolka in *Boris Godunov*. No doubt both Mussorgsky and Debussy would have preferred *The Beggar's Opera* to the *Tetralogy*, and Satie's *Messe des pauvres* to the Masses of millionaires. 'To see the sun rise', observed Monsieur Croche with his usual irreverence, 'is more important than going to hear the *Pastoral Symphony*.'

At this point we are again moved back from Symbolism to Impressionism, and Stefan Jarocinski finds himself in agreement with the excellent Russian musicologist, Jules Kremlev, who stresses the realist tendencies in Debussy's aesthetic; and, in his own way, he too may be right. This only goes to prove – and Jarocinski would certainly agree – the relativity of the various categories and headings under which we were hoping to classify Debussy. He himself had a horror of 'concepts', and would no doubt have been the first to express astonishment at being thus bandied about between various conflicting 'isms'. Jarocinski, with irreproachable honesty, quotes the well known passage in which Monsieur Croche speaks of that 'music in the open air' where one hears nothing but the ocean, the wind in the leaves, the shrill chirping of the swallows and the sound of far-off bells. 'All the air from all the seas!' cries Pelléas on emerging from the caves. 'Feel how fresh the wind is; fresh as a leaf which is just unfolding.' And remember Jean de la Ville de Mirmont in that *Horizon chimérique* in Gabriel Fauré's poignant and unforgettable setting: 'All I want is the sea, all I want is the wind.' One recalls, too, the words which Gabriel Dupont inscribed over the door of his *Maison dans les dunes*: 'Alone with the clear sky and the sea so free.'

We should remember, too, how Gabriel Fauré and Déodat de Sévérac at the beginning of this century fulfilled the wishes of Debussy; for did not the open-air theatre at Béziers provide the two orchestras of *Prometheus* and the instruments of the Catalan 'Cobla' in *Heliogabalus* with that free and open sky of which Debussy dreamed? At the risk of reverting again to professional abstractions, I would be bold enough to say that we find in Debussy all the elements of the phenomenology of the immediate. However, this immediate would seem to be more static than genuinely temporal: this immediate is the immediacy of a minute in suspense, an instant of immobility. Think of *Des pas sur la neige*, *La Sérénade interrompue*, *Ce qu' a vu le vent d'ouest*. The west wind has no story to tell; it is merely a minute in the history of the world. We put the following remark to

M. Jarocinski: it is not Debussy who is Bergsonian, but Fauré. Jarocinski writes in a language remarkable for its originality and profundity: 'Thanks to the incessant movement of sonorous particles, whatever their size, something is always happening in this music; something is living or dying, taking shape and incessantly being renewed.' To this I, for my part, would add only a slight nuance: this continual deformation is neither an evolution nor a becoming, but a succession of instantaneous 'fluxions'. It is this succession of infinitesimal discontinuities which makes a continuity. Thus, for example, *Mouvement* (Book 1 of *Images* for piano) is merely turning round on itself: the movement of this *Mouvement* does not 'go anywhere', does not link one point to another, but is eternal, like the wind in the plain. And so something is always happening in this music while absolutely nothing is happening at all – which, paradoxically, comes to the same thing! Nothing happens during the eternal dialogue of the wind with the sea, or in the motionless whirling of sounds and scents in the twilight; there are no events, no progress in time. Nothing but patches of duration, rather like the stagnant and sluggish water we can see mirrored at the bottom of a pond.

A great deal of thought-provoking material is still to be found in the pages of this book, so rich in aesthetic and philosophical insight and perception; moreover, the importance the author attaches to social and historical aspects does not exclude, but on the contrary implies, a very high degree of speculative culture and an obvious taste for theoretical problems. And we have still not mentioned the humour which is never absent from these illuminating pages. But there is no need at this stage to emphasise these features; the reader will soon discover them himself without any further prompting. But before finally leaving Stefan Jarocinski to speak for himself, I would like to point out once more the extent to which Symbolism, in the profound sense in which Jarocinski understands it, is still linked with Impressionism through the paradox of certain elusive external similarities. It is not easy to explain how this contradiction between sensorial discontinuity and the continuity of dreams – between scattered and disparate qualities and the fluidity of a dream can ever be resolved. Yet, in fact, it is resolved, in the way that music sings, in the mystery of the inexpressible and the 'je ne sais quoi'. One again it is Debussy who said – and Jarocinski repeats it several times: 'Music is meant to express what cannot be expressed.'

'Words fail', wrote Janáček at the head of one of the pieces which make up the album *On an overgrown path*. When speech 'can express nothing' – when words fail us; when the infinite ambiguity of a meaning cannot be expressed in ordinary language – then it is time to sing. It is then, when speech is silent, that the oboe d'amore of *Gigues* and the divine music of *Parfums de la nuit* can express, no one knows how, what they alone can express, and whisper in our soul's ears unutterable things.

INTRODUCTION

THE main purpose of the author in this work can be summed up under the following three headings:

1. To explain what is meant by the terms 'Impressionism' and 'Symbolism';

2. To verify whether, and to what extent, the term 'Impressionism' can be applied to the music of Debussy;

3. To show that the aesthetic movement which influenced Debussy's artistic personality most strongly, and with which his works are most deeply impregnated, was 'Symbolism'.

The notion of Impressionism, which was borrowed from painting and became fashionable at the beginning of the twentieth century – that is to say, at a time when impressionism in the arts had at last begun to be appreciated – certainly helped Debussy to win recognition with his early works. It enabled him to establish himself without meeting too much opposition; but at the same time prevented the true nature and significance of the novelties in his work from being properly understood. This was the time when people saw in the music of Debussy a kind of 'sound-painting'. Every work of art, music above all others, is an 'inter-subjective aesthetic object' (1)* which depends on the way in which its characteristic features are understood by audiences in various countries at various times. The formula 'Impressionism' has thus been universally accepted, and has even entered into official terminology.

It was not long before difficulties began to arise. In the first place, many of Debussy's works could not be fitted into this formula, and furthermore, the composer himself always refused to accept it. He thought, quite rightly, that by placing too much emphasis on the external features of his music, this would lead to over-simple interpretations, thereby obscuring its deeper meaning. Some critics, too, were reluctant to accept the term, on the grounds that, being too narrow, it reduced the aesthetic experience of the listener to a feeble and restrictive formula.

* Notes, indicated by numbers in parenthesis, will be found at the end of the book.

Those who favoured the label 'Impressionist' as attached to the names of Debussy, Ravel and other composers, were soon reinforced by the general tendency to extend the meaning of the word (a tendency due to various historical and philosophical conceptions) and to apply the term to all forms of art. The moment had at last arrived when Impressionism was to define the style of living of a whole epoch, and leave its mark upon its general culture.

Thus the term 'Impressionism' had made extraordinary progress in less than half a century. Used at first ironically (in 1874), it had become the password of a group of painters and later the title of the artistic movement which they represented; and, finally, that of an aesthetic category embracing wider and wider spheres of culture (Hamann), and extending even to artistic movements in other epochs (Weisbach). And yet its primitive meaning has remained unchanged. Semantic developments have not affected the etymological roots of the word, and its various applications have not deprived it of its original meaning, associated with the movement that made its first appearance in French painting during the second half of the nineteenth century.

The history of the term 'Impressionism' is an example of the changes that occurred in both the individual and social conscience of succeeding generations. For it is a fact that every epoch not only has its own ideas and particular art-forms, but its own special language and vocabulary as well. In the case we are concerned with here, the meaning it came to acquire was only evolved in the consciousness of an intellectual élite. For the general public it still retained its etymological sense, and only in connection with Impressionist painting.

This is also true of the ordinary music-lover, who would have interpreted it in the same way if he had come across it in some musicological publication where the writer would seldom take the trouble to explain it. It could even be said that audiences today still only appreciate Debussy's music in the same narrow way as those who heard it in the first thirty years of the twentieth century, despite the fact that the new perspective opened up by the most recent advances in music have radically changed our attitude towards his work. For the general public, the label 'Debussy-Impressionist' is associated with the product of a certain artistic activity: good music, no doubt, but of a kind unlikely to arouse any deep emotions, and lacking the 'gravity' of the works of Bach or Beethoven.

As to the importance of the music of Debussy, we find the same misunderstanding that prevailed, for other reasons, in the nineteenth century with regard to the music of Mozart. After Beethoven and Chopin, and above all Wagner, Mozart seemed frivolous and trivial. No one ever thought of wondering why this so apparently disingenuous art had inspired Kierkegaard, or how the philosopher had come to see in *Don Juan* the source from which it seemed to him his whole work had been derived.(2)

Compared with the vital force of Stravinsky and the hysterical expressionism and ecstatic rhapsodies of Bartók, Debussy's music, like that of Mozart before him, was accused of being hedonistic and lacking in profundity. The label 'Impressionism' merely confirmed this opinion, and to such an extent that even to this day the musical public finds it hard to believe that in the eyes of the avant-garde the importance of Debussy in twentieth-century music is being more and more widely recognised. It seems to us that the time has come to abandon a definition which presents the work of this composer in a false perspective.

We do not pretend to have exhausted all the problems touched on in the development of our thesis. More than one of the theories put forward is likely to meet opposition or doubt. But in writing this book we have taken the risk of shocking some readers; and it has been our intention to repudiate the isolationism of musicology which (perhaps owing to the intrinsic nature of its subject) has taken no part in the inter-disciplinary researches undertaken in all the other departments of science and the humanities. Our work was motivated originally by the distrust, so common today, aroused by dogmas and generally accepted formulae; the conflicts surrounding the development of the arts in the twentieth century show that such preconceived ideas tend to hamper and retard our progress in the various fields of art, and prevent us from understanding the changes that have occurred. It is to be hoped, therefore, that this book, which deals with various aspects of the arts in a deliberately polemical fashion, will encourage aestheticians and those concerned with the theory of music – and not only music – to make a thorough study of the problems it raises. If this object can be achieved, then we would consider that it has succeeded in its purpose.

In conclusion, I would like to express my deep gratitude to Professor Josef Maria Chominski for all his valuable advice and encouragement in the course of my work. My thanks are due also to

Professor Juliusz Starzynski, Professor Maciej Zurowski and Dr Wlodzimierz Pozniak who have read my book and offered me their comments. I am also deeply grateful to the doyen of music critics, M. Aloys Mooser of Geneva, for his efficient and disinterested help in placing at my disposal a number of books, and for giving me valuable information about people who were close to Debussy. Finally, my thanks are due to the librarians of the Library of the Art Institute of the Polish Academy of Sciences, and especially to Mmes Elzbieta Szczawinska and Janina Jaworska who helped me particularly in collecting material for this book.

1

IMPRESSIONISM IN NINETEENTH-CENTURY PAINTING

THE term 'Impressionism' is commonly used to describe the artistic movement represented by a group of French painters (Monet, Renoir, Pissarro, Sisley, Degas and others) who, having agreed that their aims and methods of expression were very similar, organised between 1874 and 1886 eight collective exhibitions of their works, although they had all worked more or less independently, and had only met infrequently since 1860.

Their aesthetic and their technique were founded on an empirical basis. The painters had abandoned their studios in order to study the effects of sunlight in nature; and it was this that gave them the idea that in art fidelity to reality could only be achieved by representing what the artist sees, and not what he knows. In other words, they were concerned with seizing the image of a reality which had not yet been deformed by the intervention of the intelligence, and transmitting the pure impresion in the form in which they had actually experienced it. And since the reality which surrounds him always appears to the artist in a different light, according to the time of day and the weather, what he is able to capture is only a momentary impression, the reconstitution of a phase in an ever-changing reality. Edouard Manet expressed the essential principle of this aesthetic when he said that a painter did not paint a landscape, or a seascape or a figure but only created the impression of a certain hour of the day in a landscape or a seascape or a figure (1). It was the play of light on water that suggested to the Impressionists their new pictorial technique. In seeking to render the phenomenon of the fusion and decomposition of colours on the rippling surface of water, they juxtaposed on their canvas touches of colours which had not been mixed previously on the palette, using only the colours of the

5

prism, and excluding all the neutral chiaroscuro tones. The combination of these colours created an impression of vibration, obscuring the outlines of objects, and giving them the form of an imprecise and 'open' sketch.

Impressionist painting appeared to embody the principles laid down by Eugène Delacroix in his *Journal* dated 13 January 1857: 'There are no more outlines than there are "touches" in nature. One must always stick to the means appropriate to each art, which are the language of that art' (2).

But it was precisely this that aroused the most violent opposition. The Impressionists rehabilitated the senses and spontaneous sensations. They revolted against the impersonal art of academic 'naturalism', as well as against its cult of technical skill and its insensibility to colour which made every picture look, as the saying went in those days, as if it had been painted with 'tobacco juice'.

It was the same with Impressionism as with every other revolutionary movement; the public was struck by the destructive elements it appeared to contain, contradicting existing habits and standards and undermining the hierarchy of accepted values. The supporters of traditional realism, who believed in the static reproduction of 'reality', accused the new movement, by attaching so much importance to fleeting impressions, of replacing knowledge through the intellect by knowledge through the senses, and dethroning rationalism in favour of a purely sensuous approach. Certain consequences of the Impressionist method did, indeed, seem to justify this conclusion; but this did not apply to the epistemological principles on which the movement was based. The Impressionists had only the two dimensions of their canvas on which to express all the mobility in the world, perceived through the senses in its primitive essence, almost without any conscious participation. Their methods and their ways of thinking changed as they gradually gained experience.

Nothing could be more interesting in this respect than to follow, for example, the evolution of Monet, exhausting every possible line of research in the direction he had chosen, only to arrive in the end at Symbolism. One could apply to his work the same reproach that Bergson applied to empiricism – namely, that of multiplying one's points of view of an object in the vain hope of being able to reconstitute the object itself by piecing them all together afterwards. This objection applied especially to the theory that it might be possible to arrive at an instantaneous notation of changes undergone by phenomena in time. But can one possibly dismiss as an unsuccessful effort the series of pictures completed by Monet, after 1891: e.g. *Les Moulins, La Gare St Lazare, La Cathédrale de Rouen* etc? Soon after, in 1895, the cinematograph was to make its first appearance. Monet was well abreast of the spirit of the new age. Seurat and Signac, with their 'scientific' theories which were to 'perfect the Impressionist empiricism through a scientific rationalism' (3) were ahead of Monet only in so far as they had understood that an impression received in the course of observing reality was already an act of consciousness (which incidentally is the basis of Bergson's philosophy); in other words, that it would never be possible to exclude the part played by the intelligence.

While academic realism blamed the Impressionists for their excessive distortion of reality, the synthesism preached by Gauguin accused them on the other hand of a blind worship of nature which caused them to lose sight of the artist's essential aim: The Idea. These two attitudes, though based on opposing aesthetic conceptions, in reality concealed an embarrassment common to both sides: What would become of Art if the great mythological, historical and human subjects were excluded from painting, where there would no longer be any gods, or emperors, neither love nor death, but only 'the coincidence between the thing contemplated and the act of contemplation itself' (4)?

The joy with which the Impressionists explored the richness of the colours which their 'naive' vision discovered in nature irritated those who were still weighed down by the romantic tradition they had inherited. Hence the accusations of Narcissism, Hedonism and Aestheticism which they showered upon their opponents. The works of Monet, which were rightly considered the purest examples of Impressionism, were certainly more open than any of the others to interpretations of this nature. It was they which were most frequently cited, by both public and critics alike, as an example of what they called 'the gratuitous interplay of forms and colours'. But if we examine his work more closely, and consider the progress achieved by Monet from the Honfleur landscapes of 1865 down to *The Waterlilies* of 1907 (which André Masson has called 'this Sistine Chapel of Impressionism' (5) we would hesitate to see in them any 'hedonist' motivations.

Ever since *Véteuil – soleil couchant* (1901), and perhaps even before that, in his *Femme à l'ombrelle* (1886), Monet had broken away from the 'naturalism' of the Impressionists. His colours appeal less to the senses than to the imagination and sensibility, as was the case with the Synthetists and, later on, the 'Fauves'. The narrative element is replaced by lyricism, and the poet decidedly takes precedence over the chronicler of events provoked in nature by the sun. With the ardour of an explorer, and a desire to discover the very essence of (natural) phenomena, Monet progressively decomposed the shape of matter, petrified ever since the days of Heraclitus. He pulverised it in a series of pictures; transformed its substance into energy – a lyrical form of energy not dissimilar to music – and finally encapsulated it in a universal symbol, the water of the *Waterlilies'* pond – a magical mirror of the world, 'a subterranean heaven', the very substance of substances of which all the others are only attributes (6) and thereby prophetically forecasting 'Tachism'. It was the Impressionists who started the 'de-materialisation of matter', and who understood that the world was not 'being', but 'becoming'. As A. Hauser has pointed out, they transformed the representation of nature into a process, 'en naissance et passage'.

Marcel Proust was one of the first to give a perfect definition of this aspect of their art – as when, in discussing the pictures of Elstir (i.e. Monet), he spoke of 'boats as if vaporised by an effect of sunlight'; of 'the confused mass of houses stacked together in the mist by the banks of a flattened and disjointed river'; of 'rocks reduced to dust, volatilised by the heat'; of a sea 'which was nothing but a whitish vapour devoid of all colour and substance.' In his desire to 'purge himself, in the presence of reality, of all ideas suggested by his intellect', Elstir succeeded in painting churches 'which, seen from afar in a shimmering haze of sunlight and waves, seemed to rise out of the water, as if moulded in alabaster or foam, and enclosed within the arc of a multi-coloured rainbow, formed a picture of mysterious unreality'; he had learned 'to accustom his eyes not to recognise any fixed frontier, or absolute division between earth and ocean on this day when light had, as it were, destroyed reality' (7).

The contribution of Impressionism to the culture of its time was not merely an improvised device to get rid of the old visual approach; its aim was to point the way to a new conception of reality. After years of controversy concerning the value of its discoveries, a contemporary historian has paid tribute to its merits; a work of art can best be explained, not in terms of the artist's affective impulses, but of his mental approach: 'The new school soon abolished the tradition of "scenographic" space on selected planes and a monocular vision of disparate elements, advocating instead the representation of space by stressing some characteristic detail – a representation which implies a scientific and disrespectful analysis of everyday life. The Impressionists formed a new conception of space, not only because they had abandoned the 'noble' subjects and all the material accessories of the Renaissance, but because they had begun to analyse scientifically the qualities of light. Thus they destroyed simultaneously not only the social distinctions, but the corresponding categories of the theoretic representation of the world' (8).

It would certainly not be wrong to say that the art of the Impressionists reflects a happy optimism which may prevent us from gaining an insight into not only the atmosphere of their epoch, but their own personal griefs. But the spectator who is able to cross the frontier between the old world and the new will be able to understand these things and, when looking at their pictures, feel the same enchantment as Proust did in the presence of the landscapes of Elstir – an enchantment so intense that he could think of nothing but 'exploring the whole wide world in order to recapture the fleeting day with all the immediacy of its somnolent grace' (9). But this does not authorise us to accuse the Impressionists of futility. Are they to be blamed for having with an indomitable faith prepared the way for a new art, instead of lamenting the miseries of the times in which they lived?

Because it affected a large number of aesthetic and philosophical problems which had been germinating for a long time, this art, which was considered frivolous, introduced elements which for many years to come were destined to contribute usefully not only to other branches of art, but also to various other areas of knowledge. If looked upon solely as a manifestation of an exuberant form of sensuality which threatened to undermine the supremacy of reason, Impressionism might indeed have been considered a typical example of the decadent tendency which, according to Spengler, foreshadowed the imminent decline of Western culture, whereas, on the contrary, it was actually making a constructive contribution of the greatest importance.

Wishing to represent the world in all its mobility, the Impressionists progressively became aware that the real nature of objects can only be observed in their reciprocal relationships with one another – relationships in which, clearly, the question of knowledge plays some part. Thus Impressionism introduced a new vision of the world about us, as well as a new intellectual approach representing the world as a system of interdependent forces, man being at the same time both an observer of and a participant in those forces. This gave rise to the school of thought which refuses to make a distinction between the world and the world as seen by man for, as Merleau-Ponty has pointed, out: 'The world is wholly within me, and I am wholly outside myself . . . The world is the field of our experience, and I am a field, I am an experience' (10).

Without dwelling upon the epistemological premises of the Impressionists' aesthetic and technique, it is not possible to understand the role which this artistic movement was destined to play in the culture of its times by preparing the way for the theories of Bergson and creating, together with them, the 'methodological climate' which led to developments in pure mathematics, 'freed from the bonds of realism' and, at the same time, in relativity physics. During the cultural tensions and crises which marked the generation which was to follow, the Cartesian principles of knowledge were obliged to give way to more flexible methods, more conducive to a better understanding of the dynamic and dramatic character of both the natural and the historical developments that were taking place.

2

THE MEANING OF IMPRESSIONISM IN MUSICOLOGY

THE term 'Impressionism' was applied for the first time to the music of Debussy in the report of the Secretary of the *Académie des Beaux-Arts* at the end of the year 1887. Used in a pejorative sense, it was applied to Debussy's second 'envoi de Rome' namely, the Suite in two parts for female voices (chorus 'à bouche fermée') and orchestra, entitled *Printemps*. 'M. Debussy' – I quote from the report – 'certainly cannot be blamed on the score of either platitude or banality. He has, on the contrary, a marked – perhaps too marked – tendency to cultivate the strange and the unusual. He clearly has a strong feeling for colour in music which, when exaggerated, causes him to forget the importance of clarity in design and form. It is very much to be hoped that he will be on his guard against that vague 'Impressionism' which is one of the most dangerous enemies of truth in any work of art' (1).

This early opinion as to the Impressionism of Debussy (which, incidentally, attracted very little attention in musical circles) has a certain importance in so far as, by emphasising in this work the supremacy of musical colour over form and design, it enabled conclusions to be drawn concerning the composer's aesthetic theories and made it possible to compare these with his actual intentions.

Why did the members of the *Académie des Beaux-Arts* try to find in *Printemps* analogies with Impressionist painting, and why did they denounce these alleged 'Impressionist' tendencies? No doubt in order to stress the 'shocking' nature of the innovations it contained. Unfortunately the original score is lost. All we have is an extract arranged for voice and piano which clearly cannot give us any exact idea of how the work sounded in its original form. The orchestral version, omitting the choral parts, based on this extract which Henri Busser made in 1913 does not help us very much. Nevertheless, this important work, monothematic in character, with variations, does reveal for the first time the fundamental characteristic of Debussy's artistic personality: his rejection of conventions whenever they hinder the realisation of his aims. It is obvious that this was bound to offend the members of the *Académie*. The winner of the Grand Prix de Rome, to whom they had just awarded the prize, was in fact defying all the generally accepted rules. Not content with having disregarded Saint-Saëns's recommendation to avoid the key of F sharp major when writing for the orchestra (2) he allowed himself to use melodic themes whose tonality could not be classified as either major or minor; sequences involving four or five different keys; whole-tone scales; plagal cadences; common chords, sometimes combined with chords of the seventh; sequences of ninths and major thirds; and, to crown all, he even used the human voice as if it were an instrument in *vocalises* with widely-spaced intervals and complicated rhythms.

We may ask, then, whether all these devices, most unusual in those days, helped him, as one might expect in the case of an 'Impressionist', to capture the fleeting sensations he experienced in the presence of Nature? His biographers maintain that his *Printemps* had been inspired by Botticelli's *Primavera*. He himself, however, in a letter to the Parisian bookseller Emile Baron, dated Rome, February 1887, defined his intentions in the following precise terms: 'I have decided to create a work in a very special colour which will give rise to as many sensations as possible. It is entitled *Printemps* – not Spring in its descriptive sense, but seen from a human angle. I would like to express the slow and painful genesis of objects and living creatures in nature, followed by an upsurge of expansion and development culminating, as it were, in the overwhelming joy of being born again to a new life. All this, of course, has no "programme", as I have a profound contempt for music which has to follow some silly little story, a copy of which is handed to you as you enter the concert hall. So you see how powerfully the music will have to evoke what I have in mind – and I don't know whether I shall be able to carry out my project to perfection.'

There is nothing in this commentary by the composer himself (very exceptional in the case of Debussy) that would suggest the attitude of an 'Impressionist' convinced of the need for spontaneity and blindly trusting the evidence of his senses. His conception of artistic creation is, indeed, of a definitely literary nature and very similar to the standard ideas about a musical work entertained by certain romantic composers. Yet in his case there is no suggestion of *Tonmalerei*; he does not attempt to describe what he sees, but to convey, by purely musical means, the idea of the awakening to life, and the expansion of the somnolent forces of nature and of one of its creations – Man; he is seeking to isolate the purely abstract idea which for us is symbolised by the word Spring. In other words, Debussy's aim is not to suggest a particular day or a particular spring, but Spring as such – the essence of the phenomenon to which we give this name.

Therefore, since it would be difficult to discern any signs of 'Impressionism' in Debussy's aesthetic conception of spring in his *Printemps*, the only feature in this work which could have justified the disapproval of the members of the *Académie des Beaux-Arts* who were afraid that their candidate was coming under the 'baleful' influence of the Impressionist movement, was the actual musical language and the technical means employed by the composer in organising his material. But the mere fact that he had adopted a personal technique of his own to achieve his purpose was not enough to prove that he belonged to any particular artistic 'movement'. Similar means could be used to serve a variety of ends; moreover, we know that nearly all the procedures which at the time were thought to be Debussy's own 'innovations' had already been employed by others, or were derived from exotic sources. The choice of procedures is not a valid criterion by which to judge or define the style of a work of art unless due account is taken of the artist's aesthetic aims and of the general situation of music and other branches of culture at any given time in history. It was the novelty of Debussy's music, and especially the way in which he exploited his innovations which, in the eyes of the members of the *Académie*, constituted a phenomenon totally unlike anything they had experienced in contemporary music at the end of the Romantic epoch. It was this that caused them to warn the young man of the danger of coming under the influence of Impressionism which, in those days, was synonymous with 'Revolutionary art' and contrary to all the laws of common sense. Many years later Emile Vuillermoz was to declare: 'If the word "bolshevism" had been invented at that time, it would most certainly have been applied to this unruly youngster who dared to write in a key with six sharps. But the French language had not then been enriched by this convenient term, and one of Debussy's judges, M. Camille Saint-Saëns, was then innocently engaged in writing an overture in honour of *Spartacus* without ever suspecting that the day would arrive when he and "Spartacism" were unlikely to get on very well together.'

The pejorative interpretation attaching to the term 'Impressionism' was part of the ideological campaign being waged in conservative quarters on all artistic fronts against the movement which was thought to be responsible for the changes which were taking place in the world of art both in theory and practice. But as Impressionist painting gradually began to gain ground, the incriminating label ceased to be merely an expression of hostility, and was soon being used in a favourable sense. It is interesting to observe how this change of attitude came about, because it helps to explain how the concept of 'musical Impressionism' came to be adopted by Debussy's contemporaries. Naturally we shall cite only the most significant opinions expressed on the subject at that time.

With the exception of the report of the Secretary of the *Académie des Beaux-Arts*, the term was first applied to the music of Debussy in 1894. The occasion was a performance in Brussels of the cantata *La Damoiselle élue*, the text being a French translation of the poem by the English Pre-Raphaelite, Dante Gabriel Rossetti, and two other works: the song-cycle *Proses lyriques*, with words by Debussy himself, and his *String Quartet*. Despite the generally courteous attitude of the Belgian critics towards an unknown composer, M. Kufferath, in the *Guide musical*, blamed Debussy for his 'pointillisme', and compared the style of the Quartet with what he called the 'neo-Japanese pictures of the Montmartre painters'; as for the *Proses lyriques*, they seemed to him to be 'pure cacophony'. An anonymous critic, writing in the *Patriote* praised the 'Impressionism' of the Quartet. Only Octave Maus – a Belgian man of letters, promoter of the avant-garde, and founder of the weekly review *L'Art moderne* (1881) and the association known as *Libre Esthétique* – avoided using the term, and emphasised the 'classic' character of the Quartet, seeing in it, nevertheless, 'a torrent of youth, and of audacious harmonies and unexpected resolutions' (3).

The first performance on 22 December 1894 in Paris of the *Prélude à l'après-midi d'un faune* did not inspire the critics to make vague comparisons of this kind, although the writer of the programme note seemed to invite them to do so; but the three *Nocturnes* for orchestra, first performed in Paris on 27 October 1901, provoked a torrent of extra-musical associations. One of the most interesting commentaries came from the pen of the critic of *Le Courrier musical*, Jean d'Udine who, before becoming a disciple of Dalcroze, had been seeking to establish a connection between sounds and colours, and had even published several studies dealing with this question (4).

He said, among other things, in his article: 'It is impossible to imagine a more subtly impressionist symphony. Consisting entirely of sound-spots, it does not evolve within the framework of any precise melodic pattern, but the way in which the chords and different *timbres* are blended and manipulated – what the painters would call its "harmony" – gives it a kind of very strict homogeneity in which beauty of line is replaced by an equally plastic beauty resulting from the skilful way in which orchestral sonorities are distributed and logically sustained.' Of the three *Nocturnes*, d'Udine preferred the second, *Fêtes*, because this music suggested to him a kind of 'Verlainisme à la Fragonard' (5).

First introduced by a few critics, the idea of a correlation between Impressionist painting and Debussy's music gradually came to be adopted by the public who by now had had time to get accustomed to the art of Monet, Pissarro or Sisley, and even with Post-Impressionist painting. Proof of this can be found in an article which Camille Mauclair, a critic always prepared to cater for his public's tastes, published in 1902 in *La Revue Bleue*. Mauclair – who thought he was entitled to express an opinion on any artistic problem, and who was denounced by Gauguin for his dangerous incompetence in all matters pertaining to the avant-garde movement (6) – had nothing much to add to the formula of 'Impressionism by means of sound-spots' in the music of Debussy; but the title alone of his article, 'Musical painting and the fusion of the arts', showed the direction in which the arts in general were evolving at that time (7).

The conservative composers were more demanding, and were the only ones to reject the imprecise stylistic formula transposed from the domain of painting to that of music. They would have preferred to possess a key better adapted to provide a clue to these works which were a source of perpetual embarrassment to them. The consternation into which they were plunged, for example, over the *Nocturnes* is reflected in a letter from Vincent d'Indy: the Director of the *Schola Cantorum* was trying to find a formula which would be applicable to these pieces, but found, to his annoyance, that in fact they could not be fitted into any accepted scholastic category: 'Sonata? Definitely not. Suite? Equally out of the question. Symphonic poem? Despite the titles, *Nuages, Fêtes, Sirènes* – all very vague denominations – there is no literary programme, or suggestion of any dramatic content which would justify the erratic key changes and agreeable, but uncoordinated meanderings of these three pieces . . . But they exist, and we have got to classify them somehow. But where? Under the heading "Fantasia" – I don't see where else we could place them' (8).

The rigid opinions of d'Indy, who had once somewhat rashly been considered Debussy's equal, were soon to be transformed into open hostility after the production of *Pelléas et Mélisande*. He did not hesitate then to declare that: 'This music will not live because it is without form' (9). His opinions were to become still more virulent in his *Treatise on Composition*; but there, too, although the notion of 'impressionism' had by then penetrated into his mind, d'Indy abstained from using the term: 'Debussy's aesthetic', he wrote, 'is an aesthetic based on sensations, and that is a principle which is scarcely compatible with the true aims of great art . . . Debussy has been an apostle of harmonic "sensationism", just as Rossini was in regard to melody. Yet his harmonies have done no more to uplift the minds and hearts of his hearers than the cavatinas of *The Barber of Seville*, which were written merely to display the charm and agility of the human voice. On these grounds, this kind of art must be judged inferior' (10).

After about the year 1905 the term 'Impressionism' was commonly applied in France to the music of Debussy. The public was beginning to get accustomed to the idea of a new musical style thus designated by the critics, but this idea was still far from being as precise as it was to become later on. In the course of the ideological battles in the art-world, before the heavy artillery of a scientifically inspired literature on the subject came into action, the critics were attacking their opponents with weapons of a lighter calibre. It was the French critics who, generally speaking, had launched the term 'musical Impressionism'; but it was above all the Germans who had founded their structural analysis of Debussy's works on a scientific basis.

This does not, of course, mean that no one in France had studied Debussy's musical procedures (cf. for example René Lenormand's book on *Modern Harmony* which for a long time was the basic work in this field (11)); but these studies were too superficial to serve as a basis for aesthetic speculations of a more general order. Debussy was not a unique case in France of an artist who had a real horror of treatises packed with technical analyses; he believed that, so far as the beauty of a work of art was concerned, it would 'certainly never be possible to discover "how it was done"' (12); consequently, what need was there for detailed analyses? The tendency to classify the human sciences into rigidly specialised compartments, with the result that their common aims and awareness of the bonds uniting closely related disciplines were often lost sight of owing to linguistic distinctions and peculiarities, had always been contrary to the French way of thinking. Being entirely free from the 'scientific complex' characteristic of men and countries endowed with a less rich cultural tradition, French humanist thought never enclosed itself in ivory towers or cultivated science for its own sake or for the sake of a limited *élite*. On the contrary, indifferent to the risk of incurring the reproach of superficiality, it had always shown a desire to maintain contact with the 'consumers' of culture and to serve their interests rather than overwhelm them with its own erudition. This may account for some of its weaknesses perhaps, but also for its undisputed merits upon which, however, it is unnecessary to dwell at this point.

As we have just seen, it was thanks to the Germans, and especially to their *penchant* for classifying artistic phenomena, that the concept of 'musical Impressionism' became firmly established, outwardly at least, and found a permanent place in the vocabulary and literature of musicologists. It all began with a study of the correlations existing between various forms of art and Impressionist painting – a study which had become fashionable thanks to Richard Hamann's book, which had a great vogue at that time, *Impressionismus in Leben und Kunst* (1907). Although by extending the stylistic category of Impressionism to include all paintings of that period, including the pointillisme of Seurat and Signac, Hamann reached some apparently paradoxical conclusions (e.g. he found 'impressionist' features in the works of Wagner, Liszt, Bruckner, Wolf, Reger and Strauss, without even mentioning Debussy), he was nevertheless the first to attempt to extend the concept of an Impressionist style by means of structural analysis. Thus, for example, in loud and frequently dissonant chords he saw a parallel with the technique of juxtaposing little spots of colour; while the disappearance of tonality reminded him of the lack of perspective in the Impressionists' pictures (13).

Hamann's work has contributed to the specification and extension of the use that has been made of the new stylistic category. As early as 1911 Werner Weisbach saw in Impressionism not just a movement which started in the second half of the nineteenth century, but one which in a much wider sense is exemplified in the art of old masters such as Tintoretto, Fragonard, Goya and Hokusai (14).

A year later E. Koehler published his work on the Goncourt brothers as pioneers in the Impressionist movement in literature (15), soon to be completed by detailed analyses of the style and syntax of the Goncourts (16). The theses of Hamann and Weisbach were to find a striking echo in Oswald Spengler's famous book announcing the decline of Western culture. It is noteworthy that Spengler, like Hamann, when speaking of musical Impressionism, also went no further than Wagner and Bruckner (17).

The reason why German musicology before the First World War had not made much progress in the direction indicated by Hamann and Weisbach (and this may be due to certain shortcomings in Hamann's work – he was not a musician) is above all because the works of Debussy were at that time very little known in Germany. It was only in the post-war period that numerous analytical studies began to make their appearance with the object of proving that Debussy's 'Impressionism' was not a mere superficial label, but a stylistic procedure based on scientific laws. The long series of works on this subject opened with Ernst Kurth's book on Romantic harmony and its culmination in Wagner's *Tristan* (1920) (18); this book was destined to play a decisive part in musicology, even outside Germany, thanks to the wealth of ideas it contained, and the very convincing use made in it of analytical methods. It would be no exaggeration to say that developments in musicology during at least a quarter of a century were due to Kurth's ideas, whether the conclusions drawn were favourable or not.

Kurth's views on the music of Debussy have contributed greatly to a proper understanding of his rôle and his importance in the history of the music of our time. Starting from the principle that developments in musical form depend largely on an immanent psychic energy which is constantly disturbing, and even disrupting and destroying the rationalised and functional harmonic system, Kurth showed how the kinetic energy represented by melody had attained its peak with the music of the Romantics gradually transforming itself, since *Tristan*, into a potential form of energy easily assimilated by pure sonority combined with colour; this tendency reached its climax in the music of Debussy. Kurth arrived at the following conclusion: 'The path of Debussy follows Wagner's, even though he himself . . . had declared that his aim was to liberate music from the influence of Wagner.' By coupling Debussy and Wagner together in the same decadent movement, and insisting that harmony was the almost essential ingredient of Debussy's method of composition, Kurth seemed to confirm the thesis of Hamann, and to indicate the chief direction in which future researches would have to be pursued if they were to lead to the discovery of the 'true image', of Debussy's music. Could S. von Hausegger have been right when, ten years earlier, having agreed to contribute, along with a couple of Parisian hack writers, to a pamphlet attacking Debussy, he spoke of his music as being effeminate, bizarre, decadent and without any future, and devoid of melody, rhythm or form (19)? The article was mischievous and caricaturist; but neither the 'objective' studies of L. Fabian, affirming that for Debussy harmony was his primary creative impulse with melody in second place (20), nor those of W. Harburger, who thought that the sole criterion of musical Impressionism was the negation of any constructive principle (21), contributed anything to the basic question. Ever since the first writings of Werner Danckert recognising Liszt, together with Wagner, as the co-founders of musical Impressionism (22), not forgetting the various studies by H. Kölsch, Otto Wartisch, Heinz Günther Schultz, Jakobik and many others who mentioned in passing the name of the composer of *Pelléas et Mélisande*, all these authors invoked especially and almost exclusively the question of harmony as the link which connected Debussy with Impressionism.

Many years later, in a lecture on dodecaphonic music which Arnold Schoenberg gave at the University of California at Los Angeles in 1941, he said that 'it was the harmonies of Richard Wagner which had disrupted the logic and constructive powers of harmony. One of the consequences of this state of affairs was the use of what were called "impressionist" harmonies such as we find especially in Debussy. Devoid of any constructive significance, these harmonies are often used to produce effects of "colour"; their object is to express atmosphere and pictorial images. In this way, however, atmosphere and images, though of extra-musical origin, do become constructive elements, and in the end take their place among other musical functions' (23).

The phenomenological method of musical analysis which, in

Kurth's case, took as its starting point the work as a field of conflicting energies, and in the case of Mersmann, as an 'organism' activated by 'tectonic forces' (24), was an attempt to reconcile analysis with a unique kind of 'hermeneutic' *sui generis* and create a bridge between a work and its perception; and this is the explanation of its success in musicology. But so far as Debussy was concerned, the conclusions arrived at by the adepts of this method did not differ noticeably from the results already obtained by the French critics following their intuition. The image of musical Impressionism and of the music of Debussy as presented by the musicologists seems very similar to that which Emile Vuillermoz offered to French audiences, pointing out that 'the mechanism of the theory of Bergson corresponded exactly to that which inspired the researches of Claude Monet or Debussy: substitute for the word "conscience" the word "perception", and you will have discovered the philosophical basis of both pictorial and musical Impressionism. . . The Impressionist seeks to translate and transpose into the vocabulary of lines and colours, volumes and sounds, not the external and realistic aspect of things, but the impressions aroused by them in our own sensibility. It means responding to their most secret language and most intimate confidences – capturing their irradiations and listening to their inner voices. For things see, things speak, things have a soul . . . Impressionism is a mode of expression which more than any other can claim to illustrate this truth, since it can grasp it *behind* and *beyond* outward appearances. . . . *Tristan* already foreshadowed a kind of sentimental impressionism, transforming love into an enchanted landscape, and then describing amiably all its most subtle nuances and, so to speak, its most mysterious rays of illumination' (25).

Speaking of individual works, Vuillermoz gave, for example, the following description of the second series of *Images* for piano: *Cloches à travers les feuilles, Et la lune descend sur le temple qui fut* and *Poissons d'or*: 'These titles, which suggest to our imagination definite objects, apply in reality to very advanced technical studies corresponding to the pointilliste techniques of the painters. Debussy is undertaking here what is almost a scientific demonstration of Impressionist composition, especially in the first tableau. . . . What the musician wishes to represent is the passage of the sound-waves through the air, opening and closing like a fan – clashing and mingling, giving off an iridescent glow as they meet, and suffusing the air with an atmosphere of poetry and dreams. The bells of Claude

Monet's vibrant cathedrals also play their part in this quivering tissue of sounds, every delicate nuance of which is disseminated, decomposed and muted, as it were, by the foliage through which they pass. And it is through his skilful use of the whole-tone scale that Debussy has succeeded in realising this spectral analysis of sound which is almost a laboratory experiment, but is still from beginning to end an astonishing and enchanting musical experience' (26).

One might simply ask to what extent such an explanation, based on a long-standing tradition and a large number of important studies, is justified, and to what extent it represents the truth. But before attempting to answer this question, we must first consider a problem which cannot be avoided whenever one wishes to verify opinions which have become firmly embedded in the social conscience.

THE SYMBOL IN ART

Seeking a definition

ALL the various forms of human activity, including art, are conditioned by the system of actions and reactions peculiar to each epoch. By taking as an example the way in which developments in the theory of perspective were connected with similar developments in the mathematical theories concerning space, Erwin Panofsky, in the 1920s, had already shown that new attitudes and conventions in the arts correspond exactly with the concepts and trends of thought in any given epoch. In the case of works of art, there are two functions to be considered: on the one hand the relation between reality and imagination, and on 'the other the relation between the artist and his public. It is for this reason that an analysis of the structure of artistic communication is essential if we are to study and learn about the structure of ideas, as well as the structure of society.

One of the chief means employed by an artist in order to arouse our sensibility and communicate his experience is the *symbol*. The broad sense in which Cassirer interprets this concept renders it inappropriate in the context of aesthetics. For, according to Cassirer, the symbol is 'the vehicle perceptible to the senses of spiritual values' (1).

This definition, however, does away with one of the essential features of the symbol, especially as regards the arts – namely that which distinguishes it from a sign or a signal in the sense that it is the *indirect* 'vehicle of spiritual values'; moreover, it is the vehicle of a content which is not completely realised. Among other modalities of the symbolic function (expression, representation and pure meaning) Cassirer does not mention the primary function of art, namely, that of suggestion, which cannot be confused with the expressive function (combining an appeal to the senses and a spiritual content) which is characteristic of the myth, but not of art in general, as

Cassirer would have us believe. It would be more fitting to speak of its representative function (which could be defined as an element perceptible to the senses representing an ideal concept), especially if we admit a distinction between direct and indirect representation.

F. W. Leakey's definition of the symbol, correct in other respects, again, in our opinion, does not go far enough. He calls it 'a metaphor of which the first term is abstract and the second concrete' (2). In point of fact, this entirely fails to take into account the richness and originality of all the efforts to achieve immediate communication made recently in poetry and the arts since Mallarmé and Gauguin. Moreover, if we accept this definition, we make no distinction between a symbol and an allegory – which can after all be considered as a semantically equivalent method. The poets themselves were not always conscious of this distinction. This why we get so many swans and sirens, fauns and virgins, in the poetry of so many French Symbolists. A contemporary writer who had made a special study of this school was right when he said that its followers were more closely allied to the painters than to the musicians (3).

Though the difference between the allegory and the symbol is less clearly defined in the minor poets, the need to make a distinction between them was nevertheless felt in certain quarters. Proof of this can be found in an article by an indifferent critic that has been rescued from oblivion by Guy Michaud. 'The allegory', says this writer, 'is always didactic; its double meaning is only a coquettish disguise; it is not spontaneous, but calculated, and deliberate – the daughter of reason and not of inspiration, appealing to thought rather than to sentiment' (4).

Already Goethe had made a clear distinction between these two modes of direct communication; and no doubt he was also the first to define the Symbol in terms very similar to those which we should employ today: 'The allegory transforms the phenomenon into a concept, and the concept into an image, but in such a manner that the concept can only be stated, confirmed or expressed in the image in a way that is always limited and incomplete. The symbol transforms the phenomenon into an idea, and the idea into an image, and does this in such a way that the idea in the image has infinite repercussions, and remains intangible; even when expressed in every language it will always remain unexpressed' (5).

Two main features of the symbol have been defined as follows: it conveys an imprecise meaning which can be interpreted in various ways; the transposition of its meaning has a dynamic character. The simple meanings contained in the word-units are multiplied and enlarged by the poetic diction charged with a symbolic function. 'The poets', said Bergson, 'suggest to us things that language is incapable of expressing' (6). They succeed by avoiding using words in their literal sense, by arousing our sensibility through not only the meaning of the words, but also their sound, their arrangement and their movement when spoken, and by the placing of stresses in a sentence, the alternation of strong and weak syllables, metrical structures and rhythms, rhymes and assonances – in a word, by all these different means the result of which is to make poetry sometimes sound like music.

'Ambiguity', as von Sydow insists, 'is the essential atmosphere of the symbol' (7). Baruzi expresses the same idea when he says: 'since the symbol is never a translation, this means that it can never be translated' (8). Blanchot also points out that, unlike the allegory, the symbol represents nothing concrete, and expresses nothing: 'it merely makes present – by bringing us into its presence – a reality which cannot be grasped in any other way, seeming to emerge suddenly, prodigiously far away, like some strange apparition' (9). The symbol is, in fact, what Merleau-Ponty calls 'the speaking word' (as distinct from the 'spoken word') where 'the meaning intended to be conveyed is still in an embryonic state. . . . Existence is polarised in a certain direction which cannot be defined by any natural object' (10). Its dynamic and ambiguous character resembles Jung's symbol of the 'archetype'.

The symbol in art is, then, if one can so express it, a 'vehicle of meaning' that indicates the direction of thought and feeling. The process of 'symbolisation' differs from a simple association of ideas by analogy because it is spontaneous, and because the artist is bringing to light a non-conventional analogy, intervening either between phenomena exterior to himself, or between the external world and his own experience. What T. S. Eliot understood by an 'objective correlative' corresponds to the concept of the symbol: 'The only way of expressing an emotion in an artistic form is to find for it an 'objective correlative'; in other words, a group of objects, a succession of events which will constitute a formula for this particular emotion – with the result that, when the external facts which will give rise to an emotion in which the senses are involved are present, then the emotion is immediately evoked' (11). As it is understood today, the symbol is not an expressive sign, but a concrete and dynamic system of signs activating the intelligence and stimulating one's sensibility.

Ferrero divides symbols into two groups: he calls those which are intended to create images and ideas 'intellectual', and those whose mission it is to arouse emotions 'emotional' (12). This distinction is not convincing, since every work of art appeals to both our intellectual and our affective faculties. A better proposition is that put forward by Fiser, who speaks of 'static' symbols, which could include the allegory and its semantic substitutes, and 'dynamic' symbols with which we are more particularly concerned in this context (13). Ossowski defined the latter as 'needing no explicit interpretation' (14). According to Eliot, they take shape in the poet's imagination, not under the influence of violent emotions, but are the result of an intense artistic effort.

For Bayer, the essence of the symbol is 'conceptualisation in its formative state – the meaning of the work translated by the artist into a perceptible form before being fully realised' (15). This explains why the symbol arouses that state of tension and expectation which is one of its characteristics. Its charm is due to the fact that it is polyvalent; it allows different interpretations, while everything it contains is left to the imagination of the spectator who must respond very actively if he wants the work of art to yield up all its secrets and all its values.

And yet, if formulated in these terms, could not the notion of a symbol be applied to any authentic work of art? In other words, is not every work of art symbolic, and is not the language of art always essentially symbolic? Developments in the arts, which have been so rapid since Impressionism, would seem to bear out this conclusion. But before adopting it as final, let us now cast a quick glance at the rôle of the symbol throughout the ages.

Genetic considerations

The origins of the symbol are lost in the mists of antiquity. Research into primitive cultures has thrown a little light upon its function in the conscience of primitive man. We can begin by affirming that it was a means of action, and not of evocation or representation. In magic, sounds were directed towards the phenomenon on which they were intended to produce their effect, their aim being to discover the phenomenon, to render it apparent and to provoke it. In this sense, magic had an initiatory value. The sound-formula which had succeeded in provoking a phenomenon (and not, it must be emphasized, in re-creating its image) assumed the significance of a symbol; it was considered to be the expression of the clan's totem. These were genuine 'sound-symbols', not 'symbolic' sounds; the latter were to appear later in music, their function being to be a vehicle for ideas or images. The symbol in primitive cultures contained, in a condensed form, the kernel, the essence of (all) incomprehensible phenomena. Magic intervenes where science can do nothing. With the help of symbols man dominated through his magic powers everything that seemed to him supernatural. In this way, the symbol's action was always directed towards the phenomenon, never towards man himself. It was the bridge connecting the microcosm to the macrocosm. But the basis of magic thinking was lacking in any analytic conception of reality; there was only a synthetic form of thought – the conviction that all life-forces were united and inter-connected between themselves.

Symbols and Symbolism have their origin in magic, and find a propitious climate when reason is unable to answer the questions which men ask themselves. Not only the Kabbala and the ancient cultures of Egypt, India and Greece, but also medieval Christianity, are all impregnated with Symbolism. 'In God', wrote Huizinga, 'nothing is devoid of meaning ... The conviction that everything has a transcendental meaning gradually takes shape. The person of the divinity is soon surrounded by an imposing system of symbolic figures, all relating to him because everything has meaning only through him. The universe is conceived as a vast assemblage of symbols, a towering cathedral of ideas. This conception of the world is not only the most profoundly rhythmic, it is also the polyphonic expression of eternal harmony'(16).

The Platonic doctrine of Ideas recurs in the earliest stages of Christian thought. As an explanation of the development of Symbolism in Christianity, one need only recall the saying of the pseudo-Denis the Areopagite: 'The truth is that visible things are the image of things invisible' (17). The philosophy of St Bonaventure, says Gilson, reveals to us a world where everything speaks of God – a world perceptible to our senses which constantly reminds us of God (18).

Medieval symbolism was based on the belief that Nature is only a symbol of a reality of a superior kind. Whatever inspiration an artist may draw from nature and express in a work of art can direct men's thoughts towards the supernatural. This is why cathedrals, full of the vibrations of the intense spiritual life of medieval man, are so rich in symbols, allegories and objects of every kind charged with metaphysical meanings.

Gradually, as the human conscience began to free itself from religious domination and come under the influence of 'causal thinking', formal symbolism degenerated, and the quest for symbols and allegories became 'a futile intellectual exercise, a superficial fantasy based merely on analogy' (19). Ancient philosophy which, like mythology, survived in the Middle Ages under the guise of various symbolic images, also contributed to this decline (20). By equating salvation with a rational existence, Protestantism directed men's minds towards more terrestrial goals, and opened the way to a civilisation based on a rationalist conception of the world and life in general. Consecrated by the philosophers and economists of the 'Enlightenment', this civilisation, after the Revolution, was to spread throughout Europe.

But reason was not able to solve all the problems, or elucidate all the mysteries. Whatever in the world and in man himself is judged to be irrational, or whatever cannot be satisfactorily explained and is repressed in the subconscious, goes against man's natural inclination to be in perfect harmony with the world. Tjutchev says in one of his poems:

> 'Il y a en tout un ordre solennel
> Et la paix règne dans toute la nature,
> Nous seuls, dans notre liberté illusoire
> Sommes avec elle en désaccord éternel.'

(A solemn order governs all things, and throughout Nature peace reigns supreme; we alone, in our imaginary freedom are with Nature eternally at war.)

Throughout the nineteenth century this lack of harmony between man and the world in which he lives underlies all poetry, all music, all philosophy and all painting until, in the century's last years, came a great spiritual and intellectual awakening. Poetry, the most semantic of the arts, was the first to play a compensatory role; and this explains why 'the need for a full and complete existence took

the form of a metaphysical revendication' (21). This change was embodied in the German Pre-Romantics (Novalis, Jean Paul, Hoff-
mann, Arnim) and soon appeared in English poetry (Blake, Cole-
ridge, Shelley, Poe) and finally reached France with Baudelaire.

In order to appreciate the significance of this new development we
must remember that the metaphysical aspirations of the Romantic
poets and their successors no longer have anything in common with
Christian metaphysics. Therefore the purpose of the symbol changes
too, although its function remains the same. It no longer serves to
transfer human thoughts from nature to God, but to concentrate
them on a particular kind of human being, the poet. Mme. de Staël
was among the first to point out that this was especially noticeable
in the poetry of the German Romantics, who tended to look upon
the entire universe as a visible sign of the aspirations of the human
soul.

This union with Nature, its enigmas and its secrets, compensates
the poet for his isolation in a world deprived not only of God, but
also of social harmony. From now on he will seek in nature for
symbols, subtly allusive correspondences, to give the reader the impression that 'Nature' in his work in only a pretext, his real subject
being the soul of the poet. Frederick Schiller said that the inanimate
world can symbolise human nature in two ways: it can represent
either feelings or ideas. By means of symbols the poet can suggest
ideas and make allusions to feelings, provided he is not too precise,
'because the charm of aesthetic ideas of this kind lies in the fact that
when we examine them it is like looking down into a bottomless
abyss.' Again: 'we expect every poetical composition, in addition to
its actual content, to be able at the same time, through its form, to
imitate and express feelings, and produce in us a musical effect.' J. L.
Austin rightly observes that this remark of Schiller's contains in
germ the whole Symbolist aesthetic (22).

It is in the poetry of Baudelaire and his aesthetic theories that the
desire to re-discover our lost unity with the world is most forcefully
revealed. By reviving the doctrine of Universal Resemblance, and
the correlation between all the psychic and physical phenomena in
the world – a doctrine which goes back to Plotinus and the ancient
esoteric traditions, more recently developed by Swedenborg –
Baudelaire created his own theory of *Correspondances* which he
expounded in *Les Fleurs du mal,* and which was later to be incorporated in the Ten Commandments of the Symbolist poets. The

doctrine of the universal analogy linking all phenomena could have restricted the role of the poet to that of a scribe recording certain resemblances between things he happened to have noticed. But Baudelaire escaped this limitation by allotting a very exalted place to the creative imagination: 'this queen of all our faculties . . . at once analysis and synthesis and sensibility . . . It is imagination that has taught mankind the moral significance of colour, outlines, sounds and scents' (23). 'The entire visible universe is nothing but a store of images and signs to each of which imagination will assign its proper place and relative value; it is a kind of nourishment which imagination must digest and transform' (24). 'By describing what is, the poet degrades himself and is reduced to the rank of schoolmaster; by telling us what is possible he remains faithful to his vocation; he is the collective soul who questions, who weeps, who hopes and who sometimes guesses right' (25). In order to communicate to others 'the vision produced by intense meditation' the poet must choose the means he will employ to do so with an almost sacerdotal solemnity, because 'there is something sacred in a word, in a phrase, which forbids us to leave anything to chance. To use language skilfully is to practise a kind of evocatory witchcraft' (26).

The rarely quoted passage in which Baudelaire explains what an art that is really 'pure', in the modern sense of the word, ought to be seems like a revelation: 'A kind of evocatory magic containing simultaneously both object and subject, the world outside the artist and the artist himself' (27). Baudelaire was too closely attached to the tradition against which he rebelled to be able to attain this cherished ideal with which poets will never cease to be obsessed. Arthur Rimbaud, that wonder-child of poetry, with his tortured spirit, torn by the convulsions of the times in which he lived and by the contradictions in his own character, was the first to attempt to embody this ideal in his art. It was he who, in *Les Illuminations,* by rejecting formal verse-forms and adopting in their place the automatic notation of the violent explosions which racked his imagination, revealed for the first time the full magic of a poetic form in which the distinction between 'self' and 'non-self' has ceased to exist. It may be recalled in this context that the same problem of overcoming this ontological dualism had been troubling philosophers since Fichte, finding at last its most complete solution in Hegel's famous *dictum*: *Sein und Denken sind identisch,* in which subject and object, 'self' and 'non-self' are assimilated.

Edgar Allan Poe also deserves a mention, however brief, less on account of his poetry and of certain tales in which the symbolism of various sonorous and significant structures must provoke a 'metaphysical thrill', than because of his attempts to reconcile metaphysics with science – note the contrast between the irrationality of his visions and narrative technique (in the *Tales*) and the extreme rationality of his poetic style. Even the famous 'musicality' of his poetry which caused him to be hailed, at any rate in France, as a pioneer (although of course it was Dionysius of Halicarnassus who had achieved the same effects centuries before) was not the result of inspiration, but of a conscious procedure in accordance with the principle that an artist must not put his trust in intuition or chance; a work of art must be executed 'with the same precision and rigorous logic as a mathematical problem' (28). This attitude, apparently in contradiction with the tendencies of the poetry and art created in protest against the scientific dogmas of their epoch, is however often adopted by poets, painters and critics; it was to influence in a very special way the aesthetic thinking of the Symbolists' chief protagonist, Stéphane Mallarmé.

The notion that a work of art is a symbol, and the language of art a symbolic language, firmly implanted in men's minds from time immemorial, was later to become far less widely accepted. As soon as the arts began to lose their artisanal status and became a profession, thereby exposing themselves to the economic pressures of a bourgeois society, the problem arose as to how the independence of the artist and the special nature of a work of art could best be protected. The slogans of 'Art for Art's sake', which circulated periodically during the nineteenth century, were nothing but a protest against the mission which bourgeois patrons of the arts, whatever their political beliefs, sought to impose upon the arts; in addition to the defence of bourgeois morality, the eighteenth century had introduced political and philosophical, and the nineteenth, scientific considerations. The naturalist movement in literature (Zola) had its origin in the aspirations of the scientists. The doctrine of 'Art for Art's sake' only seems absurd or reactionary when detached from its historical context. Even if it sometimes suited the policies of the ruling classes (at times when they preferred art to be neutral rather than critical) this aspect of the question did not alter their general attitude.

Formulated in slightly different terms by the first generation of

French romantics, the slogan reappears during the Second Empire (Baudelaire, Gautier, Flaubert, Théodore de Banville, Leconte de Lisle. It is worth noting that, as Cassagne pointed out in a work that was excellent in its day (29), the majority of its supporters had difficulties with the censorship and were prosecuted in the law courts for 'offending public morality'. The Symbolists adopted the slogan together with the ideological and artistic heritage of the Romantics, Baudelaire, Poe and the Parnassiens. But in the eyes of these new supporters of autonomy in the arts, it would be used to impede the progress of Naturalism rather than as a way of showing their scorn of the 'bourgeois Philistine'. They were to concentrate on issues that were far more serious.

The end of the nineteenth century marked the beginning of a revolution in thought. Important empirical discoveries in the various branches of science led to a transformation of the empirical theories that were preventing rapid progress. This temporary crisis – which affected methodological principles rather than science in the true sense of the term – was nevertheless felt to be a threat to the authority of rationalism, and it gave rise to a powerful wave of irrationalism which affected all the arts.

It would be to over-simplify the question to say that this situation was due merely to the fact that art was faced with fundamental spiritual problems which were all part of the general *crise de conscience*. We have also to consider the new values which were now being generally accepted and which were destined to determine the nature of future developments. It is true that there was a widespread cult of 'decadence'; an unwholesome form of aestheticism was becoming popular; and various forms of mysticism were gaining adepts all the time. These symptoms of decadence and of the de-naturalisation of certain forms of thought and action always appear when social structures and human relationships are going through a process of transformation – and still more so when these transformations affect the whole field of culture. No one was more conscious of these changes in the world which were troubling and unsettling men's minds than Stéphane Mallarmé: 'In a society which lacks stability and unity it is impossible to create an art which is stable and well-defined. It is this incomplete social structure which not only creates an atmosphere of general intellectual unrest, but is also the cause of this inexplicable craving for individuality which is reflected directly in the literary manifestations of today' (30). Consciousness of a rupture has rarely been accompanied, where creative artists are concerned, by so firm a determination to re-establish unity.

Mallarmé's whole aesthetic creed sprang from his faith in reason and absolute knowledge – a faith which often led him to the brink of a metaphysical abyss. How, he asked himself, can a poet understand the meaning of the world – in other words, the Idea – and penetrate to the heart of phenomena, if the language he employs remains attached to tradition and conventions? If he is unable to create his own language, he must at least rid words of the dust with which they have been smothered, and correct the deformations which language has forced them to undergo. Thus, for example, in order to give a darker shade to the clear sound of the word 'nuit' (night), which does not correspond to its meaning, he can precede or follow it with words which have a darker sound. On the other hand, even if the poet uses words which suggest an image, he can, if he does not want an image to take shape in the mind of the reader, deceive him so cunningly that no images will appear. It would seem that Mallarmé has given convincing proof of this in *Le Nénuphar blanc*, which is impossible to describe and leaves the reader in a state of unsatisfied expectation. And yet procedures of this kind are not enough when the poet's object is to unveil the pure essence of the thing which the word represents. What then is there left for him to do? It is here that Mallarmé expounded his famous theory of *suggestion*.

If the poet cannot arouse the idea of the pure essence of something that lies dormant within us either by naming it or by selecting the right word to convey its meaning, then all he can do is to suggest it: 'To evoke, in deliberately shadowy terms, an un-named object, using only allusive, never direct words, the equivalent of silence, is something like an act of creation' (31). Again: 'To name an object is to suppress three-quarters of the enjoyment of a poem – enjoyment meant to develop gradually: but to *suggest* it – that is the ideal. To make a perfect use of this mystery is the function of the symbol: to evoke gradually an object and discover in it a state of mind – or, inversely, to choose an object and discover in it a state of mind by a process of de-coding' (32). As early as 1864 one finds a sentence in his correspondence which shows that the language of poetry was, and had always been, the principal, if not the unique passion in his life: 'A verse, then, must not consist of words, but of intentions; and all words are unimportant when compared with sensations' (33).

A quarter of a century later he returns again to the secrets of his verbal alchemy: 'Verse which, with only a few syllables, re-makes a complete new word, a stranger to the language, and possessing an incantatory quality, achieves this verbal isolation; destroying at a stroke the chance-element inherent in words despite the artifice of alternately emphasising their meaning and their sound, and giving you the surprise of having never heard some quite ordinary expression, while at the same time your memories of the object referred to are bathed in a new atmosphere' (34).

And so in this way, by a combination of meanings, colours and sounds the poet can overcome the obstacle presented by the fact that words have a material quality; by circumscribing and isolating the pure 'idea', he succeeds in the end in communicating to us the mystery. It is only in this way that one can be brought 'face to face with the inexpressible' (35) – with pure Truth, which is Beauty. This is what could be achieved by poetry which would not make use of isolated words but of their associations – poetry based on suggestion and allusion, excluding all description, a 'poetry without words' (though making use of words), a poetry of emptiness and silence – poetry that evokes the apparition of the Idea. Cattaui remarks that, according to Mallarmé, the poet must not try to express in words an idea, but the Idea which itself creates the Word (36).

Mallarmé wanted to liberate poetry from 'subjectivism'; he avoided lyricism in order to escape from 'psychologism'. In his desire to seize the objective Idea, outside time, he dreamed of an extra-temporal language, rejecting subjective deformations. His imagination seems to have revived memories of a language such as had actually existed in ancient Greece. In his book on Greek music and rhythm (37), Georgiades has shown the essential structural difference between the ancient Greek language and modern languages. In the latter the length of the syllables is, in effect, indefinite: the syllable can be either long or short according to the temperament of the speaker – thanks to which fact it is easy to set to music a poem written in any modern language. In ancient Greek, however, the length of the syllables was fixed and, so to speak, pre-determined; consequently the emotional state of the speaker could not in any way affect the structure of the verses. The language was unaffected by any human intervention, and its structure impervious to any subjective attitudes. 'The words are there, rigid and mysterious, like pieces of mosaic fitting one into the other. They form immovable patterns which are independent of the subject and never identified with it. The Greek language is a language of masks. It does not evoke a living physiognomy. Such languages do not exist today except in certain exotic cultures. One cannot guess the speaker's thoughts; one does not know whether his intentions are good or bad, or whether he is happy or in a bad temper. The faces of men, the product of these cultures, are indecipherable; they are like masks. The Greek language is like the masks used in Greek tragedy. There, too, the lack of facial expression does not diminish the expressive force – on the contrary, it enhances it. In this way the Greek spoken word can have a powerful, animal-like, demoniacal and sombre sonority and not, as in modern cultures, one that is subjective, dynamic and internal. The actors' "manner" of speaking, with different shades of expression and so on, is not important; the pathetic note, stemming from the subject and often reflected in the speeches, is quite foreign to the Greek language.'

Mallarmé obviously could not resuscitate language of this kind; but he believed he could create a work which, in a very different and much more complex social and cultural situation, could have achieved what Greek tragedy aimed at doing – namely, to reveal to men the will of the gods. Throughout his entire *oeuvre*, of which the crowning achievement should have been, had he not tragically failed to complete it, *Le Livre* – a total work of art in which the entire personality of the man found its fullest expression – he had striven to achieve the auto-objectivisation of the Idea: 'Pure poetry can dispense with the elocutionary presence of the poet who allows the words to take the initiative through the clash of their mobilsed inequality; they are illuminated reciprocally by the bright lights they engender, making them sparkle like jewels, and in this way replacing the respiration perceptible in the lyrical effusions of bygone times when a sentence could reflect the personal enthusiasm of the poet' (38).

He believed that he could restore the unity of culture in a world deprived of divinities, by abolishing the separations between the arts and achieving their integration in his *Livre*. Whereas Wagner, with the same integration in view, succeeded only in adding one art to another, Mallarmé, realising the failure of the German composer, cherished the hope of succeeding in bringing about a real synthesis between the arts. Even today it is impossible to remain indifferent to the still surviving evidence of his vain efforts – a noble reminder of the grandeur of the mission he had set himself to achieve alone and unaided (39). Claudel was one of the first to attempt to penetrate the true significance of Mallarmé's work: 'Poetry for Mallarmé was the means above all others of transferring reality from the domain of the senses to that of the intellect – from the realm of fact to that of definition – from time to eternity – from chance to necessity, and to substitute this creation (of the mind) for the image we perceive through our eyes' (40). It would, of course, be possible to interpret as a gesture of defence on the part of the artist against the schematisation of thought this rejection of 'normal' speech, and adoption of a hermetic language – a form of self-defence which we find again as the basis of the philosophy of Bergson. And yet this explanation does not seem to us quite adequate. Thibaudet has pointed out: 'the constant aim of Mallarmé was to reduce literature to its absolute opposite – to turn it into a kind of mathematics [under the influence of E. A. Poe who thought a poet should be 'a mathematician of beauty' – *Author's note*] a lofty intellectual game, and to abolish all surface clarity, replacing it by a real clarity, the equivalent of a hyperbolical probity (41). Thibaudet's conclusion was very much the same as that of Rivière who had said earlier that 'Mallarmé's syntax is an important step towards expression and clarity [*sic!*] because its aim is to make the order of the words adhere closely to the order of the poet's thoughts and to reproduce the true continuity of his thinking' (42). Nevertheless, neither the one nor the other explains why Mallarmé had undertaken this task.

It would seem, however, that like the Romantics and like Baudelaire, Mallarmé's aim was to bridge the gap between the 'self' and the 'non-self'; but, whereas the former had immersed themselves in pan-psychism and pantheism, he wished to remain on the neutral territory of knowledge: by seeking through his poetry the intentional structures of acts of conscience he hoped to reveal in the symbolism of his work the meaning of the world, because basically he believed that nothing happened in the universe that was not intentional. He was approaching that ultimate state in which 'the eye is looking at itself.'

The various elements on which the concept of the symbol, in the accepted modern sense of the term, is based have been present in art throughout the ages; but it was not until the Symbolist movement took shape that all these elements were combined to form a whole and the work of art was identified with the symbol.

The quest for musical effects, often considered to be an essential feature of the Symbolist aesthetic, has played an important part throughout. It was Paul Valéry, whose attitude to Symbolism was somewhat guarded, who said: 'What has been called Symbolism is in reality merely the result of a desire, common to several schools of poets, to borrow their material from music ["reprendre à la Musique leur bien"]' (43). What was it in music that attracted them?

In a book published shortly before the advent of the Symbolists and quite forgotten today, there is a passage which, better than the works of Schopenhauer or Wagner which the Symbolists absorbed so passionately, explains what it was in music, as a form of expression, that had appealed to them so strongly: 'If from the world of visible forms and ideas peculiar to poetry and the plastic arts we enter the world of sounds and harmony, our first impression is that of a man passing suddenly from the light into deepest darkness. In the former everything can be explained, follows logically and creates an image; in the latter everything seems to spring from un-plumbed depths where darkness and mystery reign. In the one we find fixed outlines and the inflexible logic of immutable forms; in the other the flux and re-flux of a liquid element, perpetually in motion and metamorphosis, and containing an infinity of possible forms. In this impenetrable night-darkness into which music plunges us, we feel strongly the vibrations of life, but it is impossible for us to see or distinguish anything. But as the soul gradually becomes accustomed to this strange region, it begins to acquire a kind of second sight, rather like a somnambulist who, sinking deeper and deeper into his sleep, becomes submerged in his dream until real objects disappear from sight. But while the outer aspect of things is effaced, their inner content is revealed in a marvellous light' (44). As an 'a-semantic' art *par excellence,* music seemed to fulfil the ideal conditions of the 'work-as-symbol' to which the Symbolists aspired.

As regards painting, Delacroix was the first painter in the nineteenth century to speak of a picture's 'music', and of a 'magic chord of colours' (45). Gauguin later was to adopt this expression for himself (46), while Baudelaire was certainly thinking on the same lines when he spoke about a picture's 'melody'. Another sign of this tendency can be found in the use of musical terms in the titles of poems and pictures pioneered by Théophile Gautier (*Symphonie en noir et blanc*) and by Whistler in his landscapes and portraits (*Harmony, Symphony, Nocturne* etc.) which soon became the general fashion.

Browning took a lively interest in both painting and music, responding more deeply to the latter of whose technical problems he had some knowledge. Thus, in poems such as *A Toccata of Galuppi's*, *Master Hugues of Saxe-Gotha*, *Abt Vogler* or *Parleying* he was endeavouring to transpose into poetry certain musical forms – or, rather, the character of these forms: toccata, fugue, improvisation on a theme, and march. The most successful of these perhaps was *Master Hugues of Saxe-Gotha* (fugue), whereas *Parleying* speaks about music rather than suggesting a particular form, although it is supposed to be in the form of a march. In any case, Browning achieved his best musical effects, without speaking directly about music or trying to imitate its forms, in those poems which were inspired by an inner necessity and not based on any pre-conceived principle or theory (47).

The fact remains, however, that it was Poe who was the first to formulate the principle in which we are interested here – namely that the poet must be attentive to the musicality of his verse, because this is his only means of communicating to others aspects of his poetic emotion which could not be expressed in any other way (48). After Poe we have to wait for Verlaine to provide the Symbolists with a motto: 'de la musique avant toute chose' of which he himself provided a most felicitous example in his own poetry. Having discovered the secret associations between language and sensations, he transposed with an astonishing facility all the sounds in nature into an extraordinarily musical poetic language, which, however, owing to its lyrical character, was deeply rooted in its 'period'.

In 1886, a crucial date since it was in that year that the Symbolist doctrine was firmly established, René Ghil published his *Traité du verbe*, with a preface by Mallarmé. Inspired by Rimbaud's *Sonnet des voyelles*, René Ghil arrived at the following conclusion: 'If sound can be translated into colour, colour can also be translated into sound, and even into instrumental *timbres*'. All that was necessary was to define, in accordance with 'scientific methods', certain principles governing the 'instrumentation of verse', which was the object of Ghil's researches: 'In this way, the "Poem" becomes an actual piece of suggestive music providing its own instrumentation: a music of words evocative of coloured images, but in no way detrimental to ideas' (49). Mallarmé, who had encouraged Ghil's campaign, himself proclaimed that 'the acme of the intellectual Word must . . result in Music', and that 'Poetry, most nearly approaching the Idea, is Music *par excellence*' (50).

In painting, in the new movement instigated by the creative efforts of the Impressionists, similar tendencies were spontaneously making their appearance under the influence of the prevailing atmosphere. Odilon Redon, for example, who called himself 'a musicalist painter' had the same kind of conception of a work of art as a symbol as that of the Symbolists themselves: 'My drawings inspire and cannot be defined. They determine nothing. They place us, in the same way as music does, in the ambiguous world of the indeterminate . . . They are a kind of metaphor' (51). And in one of his letters Gauguin wrote: 'And then think of the musical role that colour will play from now on in modern painting. Colour, which like music is vibration, is capable of attaining what in nature is most universal and consequently most elusive – namely its internal force' (52).

In commenting on *D'où venons-nous* he wrote: 'My dream cannot be pinned down; it doesn't need any "libretto", as Mallarmé said. [No doubt he was thinking of Mallarmé's reply to J. Huret's questionnaire, quoted above; 'To name an object is to destroy three-quarters of one's enjoyment of the poem.' *Author's note*.] Consequently the essence of a work of art, on the highest and immaterial plane, lies precisely in 'what is not expressed'; it is implicitly contained in its lines, without colours or words; it has no material substance' (53). One of Gauguin's disciples, Sérusier, expressed it differently: 'Sounds, colours and words have a miraculously expressive value which has nothing to do with representation or even with the literal sense of the words' (54). Redon, Gauguin and others make the impossibility of copying nature (which was the conclusion to be drawn from the analysis of the Impressionists) the starting point of their theory that painting must aim at the creation of symbols – in other words, a synthesis of the formal elements of the visible world (lines, surfaces, colours) and the subjectivity of the artist. In his interview with Gasquet Cézanne spoke of 'arbres sensibles', and also of his desire to understand what there was in common with trees and ourselves. Later, Debussy was to use the same expression although he was not present at the interview (55). As we said just now, in pursuing the path of Impressionism Monet was to arrive at a similar conclusion: in his latest works (e.g. *Nymphéas*) Impressionism rejoins Symbolism.

Thus the subjectivity of modern Symbolism, which has replaced the impersonal Credo of medieval symbolism, allows for an evolution towards 'pure art', devoid of the element of representation contained in the subject of the work. Impressionism has been the first important step in this direction: it rescued art from the stranglehold of a sterile naturalism. The second was the syntheticism sponsored by Gauguin. From now on the right of the artist to distort Nature will be recognised; the liberation of painting from its imitative role, from mimicry of any kind, will now only be a question of time (the time required for it to be absorbed in the collective conscience). Art will become the creation of the artist as a magician seeking to force Nature to yield up her secrets.

The poets and painters wanted their art to be like music so that they could communicate their creative experience in all its fluid mobility before it became embedded in pictures or in the moulds of language. They wanted to use their art as a symbol, a mode of expression that would favour the free interplay of resemblances, associations, or far-off echos and tensions, and thus result in an 'open' form capable of receiving various meanings without having any definite meaning in itself.

The Symbolists were convinced that all the elements in the world were somehow inter-connected: whatever string one touches in any sphere of life it will certainly find an echo in all the other spheres. No doubt this attitude was the product of a revival at that period of esoteric traditions, and not of a materialistic monism; but that need not affect us who are trying now to discover the actual sources of the Symbolists' activities, and not their ideological motives.

Raymond sees in the Symbolist movement 'the dream of a magical universe in which man would feel himself at one with material things, and where the spirit would reign, without the need of any intermediary, over all phenomena, outside all rational channels' (56). The Symbolists' ideas would find, then, their fullest expression in the philosophy of Bergson who believed that by penetrating to the depths of our 'self' we shall at the same time come closer to the essence of the world. However, in our opinion, it was Maurice Denis, who was himself closely associated with the Symbolist movement, who had the deepest understanding of their aims and had analysed the results: what the Symbolists were aiming at was 'the triumph of the synthetic over the analytic approach, of imagination over sensation and of man over nature' (57). One of the leading exponents of the movement, Charles Morice, was expressing the essential ambitions of his generation when he spoke of 'the intense contemporary desire of the human spirit to see united in one large and vital stream of Beauty allied with Truth the currents of mysticism and science flowing together.' He added that these ideals could only find fulfilment in an "integral art" maintaining the equilibrium of human nature (58).

The real motive force of Symbolism was the consciousness of a break – of a new way of looking at the world (mobility, relativity, dynamism) – an awareness of the collapse of Cartesian rationality, and of the need to prepare humanity to accept new rules and methods. It was not difficult to perceive this force; it was only necessary to free it from the sometimes rather dense layer of metaphysical phraseology under which it was concealed.

In the ancient cultures the symbol helped to reveal the great mysteries of Nature and of life; in the Middle Ages of the Christian era it directed mens' thoughts towards God; in the Romantic era it expressed the subjectivity of the artist. Thanks to the Symbolists, who had become conscious of the specific nature of the language of art and of the ambiguity of the meaning attached to all the values with which it was concerned, the symbol became identified with art. If today we are able to say that art is not meant for contemplation only, but that it must take a part in the creation of life, penetrate all its forms, and become, not only the daily nourishment, but also the daily instrument of man – a manifestation of his need to create – it is to Symbolism, despite its aestheticism and affectations, that we owe this state of affairs.

Expression and the symbol in music

If today one assimilates the symbol with a poetic or plastic work in the modern acceptance of the term, one is still more entitled to do so in the case of a musical work: being unencumbered by semantics, music is by its nature 'ambiguous'. Before we can assert that music has any signification – in other words, that it has a meaning to convey – we must ask ourselves, in order to avoid misunderstandings, whether this implies that its meaning is 'in itself' or 'for us'; when we say that it 'means' something, are we thinking of the work as the product of the creative effort of the composer, or as an aesthetic object perceived by the hearer? The lack of distinction between these two aspects of the problem accounts for most of the controversies this question has aroused (59).

If music *per se* has a content, this is not, in any case, as Hegel pointed out, 'in the sense in which we speak of the "content" of a poem or a picture, or any of the plastic arts; for what is lacking in music is an objective realisation either of forms representing real external phenomena, or of conceptions or representations of a spiritual nature which are also objective' (69). The composer does not function in a social vacuum. For him music is raw material out of which he must form an organised *ensemble* which he will then communicate to the hearer. His work contains an accumulation of experiences which will be communicated to the listener. The composer is linked with his hearers, not only by the *rapport* which the work will create between them, but also by a common social and cultural background which influences them both, but in different ways. The composer only *appears* to enjoy an unlimited freedom in his choice of means. In reality, he depends on the musical climate of his epoch and his audience, even though it may exist only in his imagination.

In the musical system sound exists in several forms: it can be a note, a sign, or a static symbol. It is transferred from acoustic reality into a world of abstractions governed, just as poetic language is, by the strict rules of grammar and syntax which are not necessarily the same as those which govern acoustics or logic. With the help of this system the composer can give several different 'meanings' to his works. Even when the problem of expressing extra-musical values does not arise, the composer in his manipulation of sounds is not acting on an 'absolute' theoretical plane; he relies on the judgment of his own ears – that is to say of himself as a listener, and not as an acoustical specialist trusting blindly in the laws of physics. In his consciousness there is a perpetual conflict between what his unlimited invention dictates to him and what his theoretical audience may be considered capable of understanding. In this sense it could be said that in the process of creation there is no gulf between speculation and the act itself, because it is only in the process of creation that the composer fully understands his work. As Jankélévitch has observed: 'The meaning of a piece of music becomes clear to the composer only while he is creating it, and to the interpreter or hearer, only during its performance' (61).

Thus a musical work which has been defined as 'an intentional object' (Ingarden), 'the conscious auto-objectivisation of the artist' (Ducasse), or 'the expression of the tendencies or subconscious re-

41

pressions of the artist' (Parker), is always the result of its dialectic significance 'in itself' and 'for us'. The composer does not create for himself alone, but for himself and for his audience. He may be mistaken in his estimation of their perceptive faculties, or even not take them into account; yet he must be aware that only a relative state of equilibrium between these two antithetical poles – the sounds existing in his own unfettered imagination and their perception by his audience – will enable the latter to grasp the 'meaning' of the music, the construction both external and internal of the work as a whole, and to experience that 'meaning' in terms of 'beauty'.

What we call 'beauty' is, like the work itself, determined by certain specific cultural standards; beauty does not exist outside time and space, and the hearer can only experience it when there is no fundamental divergence between what the work means 'in itself' and 'for us'. Beauty is the guarantee of authenticity of a work submitted for public approval. By coming into contact with the work the hearer admits *a priori* that it will arouse in him some aesthetic reactions. But before deciding that it is beautiful he must verify, through his perception of it, whether his confidence in it is justified. In other words, in its external form, as perceived through its sound during performance, a musical work promises an aesthetic experience; but whether this promise is justified or not depends on the hearer's perception. It is its form, then, which is the symbol of an entity of a superior order, which reveals to us that entity as it really is, and thus ensures that we experience it as an aesthetic object. If the hearer's reaction is unfavourable, this may be due just as much to the immaturity of the hearer as to that of the work itself; in any case it proves that the hearer does not perceive the work in question as an aesthetic object.

Beauty does not exist outside our perception. Nor is there such a thing as intentional beauty, because in that case it would have to precede the creative act. It descends on the work like an act of grace. It may perhaps illuminate the creative artist's intuition, but it is visible only when the artist's work is finished. Rilke said that beauty cannot be 'created', and that the artist ought not to think about it at all. His only concern should be to know under what conditions, when he has fulfilled them, it is possible that 'beauty might perhaps deign to descend upon the work he has created' (62). For the creator, beauty is the result of his work; for the hearer, the work is the source of beauty. J.-C. Piguet is therefore justified in affirming that the perception of a work of art in its perfect unity is the point at which art and aesthetics are indissolubly linked (63).

'Music in itself' does not signify anything concrete outside itself, or anything that could be transposed into the language of images or concepts. It is the region of non-existent things that can nevertheless be brought to life through the imagination of the creator and his audience with the help of a definite musical system. As soon as that system collapses, the musical formulae which were based on it are no longer valid; eventually they cease to exist, or else are incorporated in some other new system in which they may sometimes be invested with expressive functions completely different from those for which they had originally been created.

All semantic explanations of music are based either on the indications of the composer himself (titles, programmes etc.), or on associations or, maybe, conventions. One cannot speak of a 'musical language' being used to convey extra-musical meanings except in the context of a specific cultural background. Western audiences today are already accustomed – as the extensive researches of R. Francès have recently confirmed (64) to seek in music something more than a mere manipulation of sound structures; this 'supplementary value' which they have introduced undoubtedly improves the quality of their aesthetic experience. But we must not attach an exaggerated importance to this way of approaching music. If the value of a work of art depended on its extra-artistic content, then in the event of its subject-matter, or whatever it was supposed to symbolise, falling out of fashion and ceasing to be of interest to an audience, its value would cease to exist. The Baroque period has bequeathed to us a great many works '*à clef*' which still appeal to us even though it is impossible for us today to decipher their secrets.

The problem of music's 'content' and how to communicate it with the aid of various symbols is too vast and too complicated for us to try to expound here, even briefly – especially since, despite many attempts to do so, this question has up to now never met with any satisfactory theoretical solution. The names of Kretzschmar, Schering, Kurth and Mersmann and of some Soviet musicologists (among them Assafijev and Kremlov) together with those of Gisèle Brelet and, in Poland, Mmes. Lissa and Lobaczewska, represent various stages in the abundant literature on this subject. Starting from different principles, their writings contain numerous methodological propositions which have led to the adoption of the system used by musicologists during the last fifty years to describe a musical work. But the crisis in musicology caused by recent advances in contemporary music, which has affected especially the field of aesthetic research, seems to confirm doubts that have already arisen in other departments of science and the arts: is there a place in our culture for the traditional aesthetic approach? The study of aesthetics, now practised in both psychology and sociology, and divided by ideological differences, today enjoys a certain prestige only in the sphere of phenomenology (Merleau-Ponty, Ingarden) thanks to the 'neutrality of knowledge' confined uniquely to the description of intentional structures. Another issue appears to have been raised by the science of cybernetics and the theory of information now used to describe every acoustical phenomenon in terms of aesthetic communication. It is too early to say whether the study of aesthetics is going to be pursued along those lines. In any case, as soon as the system of correspondences comes into play, as for example in the field of expression, we encounter insurmountable difficulties. Proof of this can be found in the attempts to revive the 'semantic', neo-Kantian aesthetic of Cassirer which seem to have found favour in America – for example, in Mrs S. K. Langer's theory of a 'non-discursive symbolism' according to which all works of art are considered merely as a symbol of 'affective values'!

This failure to provide any satisfactory solution to these problems has been recently demonstrated by N. E. Ringbom who, in his *Über die Deutbarkeit der Tonkunst* (Helsinki, 1955) has subjected to a critical analysis the methodological principles of the science of musical symbols propounded by A. Schering, while being equally critical of the methods of Kurth and Mersmann, and also of Gisèle Brelet's theory of a 'musical time'. Ringbom attempts to make a precise distinction between the functional and the expressive aspects of a musical work, since it is only the first which can be actually verified and measured. Ringbom establishes the principle of a strict separation, both in practice and in research, between 'functional analysis' and 'hermeneutic expression', which are two totally distinct methods which can only in the last resort be judged by their results.

We can only consider here the historical aspects of the problem in so far as they throw light on our subject. The general conception of a work of art considered as a symbol, which we have accepted, provides in our opinion a sufficient basis for the considerations which follow now.

From the ethical to the pathetic

At every stage in its history music acquired various 'meanings' more or less easily transposable into the language of speech. Schering has already observed that the history of music was an arena in which certain symbols were continually dying and others being born (65). The tradition of attributing to music psychagogic and expressive faculties goes back at least as far as the Pythagoreans for whom rhythms were the symbols of psychism, and who 'used music to purify souls' (66). We find the theory of the *ethos* of music throughout the whole period of Greek antiquity; neither the Sophists nor the Sceptics were able to check its progress. It was revived again in the Christian Middle Ages. The symbolic character of music seemed obvious and indisputable, and it was the subject of a great deal of subtle research. Let us take, for example, this quotation from St Augustine who traced the descent of music from the human soul [he was speaking of course of vocal music, the only form current at that time – *Author's note*] in these words: 'A man when he is happy does not speak – his joyous song is without words; it is the voice of his heart which melts for joy and tries to express its feelings without even understanding what they mean' (67).

Fourteen centuries later D'Alembert declared (he was no doubt thinking also of instrumental music) that music was becoming progressively a form of speech, even a language, which made it possible to express all sorts of states of mind, from whence he deduced that it might well also be used to convey visual impressions (68). Rousseau goes further: he declared that 'natural music', which gave only pleasure to the senses was inferior to 'imitative music'. In his opinion; 'music paints everything, even objects that are only perceived by the eye; by an almost inconceivable miracle it seems to put a man's eye in his ear.' Rousseau was not thinking only of onomatopoeic effects (which abound in French music ever since Jannequin's *La guerre* (1528)); a composer himself, he understood how limited this imitative formula was. 'Music' he said, 'must not represent things directly, but must arouse in the mind the same impressions that we receive on seeing them' (69).

In the eighteenth century the growing pressure of the 'bourgeois mentality' became apparent in all the arts, and also in aesthetics. For bourgeois audiences, not yet truly 'enlightened' and on the brink of acquiring power, pure music, such as that of Bach, Mozart and

Haydn, was on too high a level. D'Alembert had good reason, in his *Discours préliminaire de l' Encyclopédie*, to wonder who would be able to teach this new audience how to listen to music. But generalities such as: 'music brings joy or sadness' or 'it gives pleasure or causes pain' could not satisfy an uninitiated listener who demanded a more precise definition of the scope and potentialities of this art. Hence the advent in the eighteenth century of the first musical criticism, its role being not to limit the freedom of the composer, (which alas! was all too often the case, as can be seen from some of its less reputable examples) but to explain the music. 'The Revolution', wrote Grétry in a letter to the Director of the Brussels Opera, 'is driving us to respect truth in all things, regardless of prejudices' (70). The cult of rationalism had inculcated in bourgeois audiences the conviction that everything could be expressed in concepts – an idea which, when applied to music, sometimes produced the most absurd results. One has only to recall the project of creating rules for symbolism in music propounded at the end of the eighteenth century in Germany by D. Schubart, and a little later, in France, by Sudre. These naive ideas may amuse us today, but at the time they masked a desire, by no means naive, to discipline an art which, until then, had had nothing to do with common sense.

In this way the eighteenth century had taken a big step forward on the road to understanding the ways in which music could be used as a means of expression. Not only bourgeois audiences, but composers themselves now became convinced that not only opera and vocal music in general, but pure instrumental music could also represent emotions, ideas and visual impressions. This had various consequences that influenced future developments in music.

Although the early Romantics were still looking back to classical models, the changes that had taken place in their social status and ways of thinking were too important for it to be possible for them to write the same kind of music as their predecessors had done. A new content called for a new symbolism, and breaches of the old classical rules were inevitable. In the works of Haydn and Mozart, it wasn't their language that most impressed the first bourgeois audiences (founded on functional harmony it had merely found in those masters its final consecration), but the 'pure beauty' that emanated from their music and from the perfect balance between the 'in itself' and 'for us' formula – a kind of beauty which audiences until then had never experienced, because it had always been reserved for the *élite*. Soon it was to become everyone's ideal, and the musical language which had accomplished this miracle was to maintain its prestige down to the present day.

At the basis of all great art there lies an ethical problem. Like any other human being conscious of his *raison d'être*, the artist seeks the truth – that is to say, unity with the world around him. So long as the Romantic creative artist cherished illusions with regard to the liberating mission of his class, there was no fundamental contradiction between his artistic aims and the requirements of his bourgeois audience. The conflict, which was to become more and more acute, became apparent when artists realised that they could no longer hope to find themselves in harmony with 'reality' as they saw it in the world around them. Being unable to accept reality, there were only two ways left to them in which to assert their individual liberty: either to try to transform reality, or else to turn their backs on it in scorn, and express their most intimate thoughts and experiences in an art which would be inaccessible to the masses.

The situation in which the artist found himself at the end of the eighteenth and beginning of the nineteenth century can only be described as paradoxical: no sooner had he achieved social emancipation – no sooner had he gained, at least in appearance, his independence as regards morality, politics and science – at the very moment when he abandoned the classical ideal, the artist, willy-nilly, was now falling into a new form of slavery – that of 'psychologism'. The fact is that all his efforts to escape from a life in which he felt he had no definite place, and take refuge in an art in which sublime thoughts and feelings could be expressed, had been in vain because the music critics, who had been the first to fulminate against the extravagances of any form of musical expression that did not conform to classical ideals, were now beginning to realise its expressive potentialities, and were teaching bourgeois audiences how to penetrate the apparently hermetic symbolism of the new music. Threatened in his 'splendid isolation', the artist now began to employ more and more recondite methods of expression, and arrogantly to expose his most intimate emotions. Berlioz was a striking example of this 'theatrical' attitude towards music (71), while Wagner, of course, provided a 'stage setting' for everything he did, in his art as well as in his life. In order to express as convincingly as possible Tristan's passion for Isolde, Wagner made himself fall in love with Mathilde Wesendonck.

Szymanowski, who had suffered from the pressures of this

romantic trádition, defined it perfectly when he discovered already in Beethoven the supremacy of the ethical element over the aesthetic; it was this, said Szymanowski, that led to exhibitionism and to 'theatrical attitudinising' not only in Wagner, but also and especially among minor artists 'drowned in insipid sentimentality ... or inflating with pathetic gestures their uninteresting personal problems to raise them to the level of an universal catastrophe' (72). Was it not Richard Strauss who showed up most effectively this type of artist in his *Heldenleben* in describing, not without humour, it is true, his own, typically bourgeois, life?

Nietzsche was right when he said that, in music, intelligence would only be able to represent 'the will' (allusion to Schopenhauer) and the 'thing in itself' (allusion to Kant) when the entire field of the inner life was open to musical symbolism (73). The triumph of 'psychologism' and of the conception of 'expressionism' were to influence the future of music for hundreds of years. In the light of what we have just said, the 'autonomist' aesthetic propounded by Hanslick seems sensible, and can be seen as a protest on the part of intelligence against excessive emotionalism in music; it would be difficult to look upon it as an attempt to justify a formalism which a passionate admirer of the classics and of Brahms was scarcely likely to admire. Moreover, neither Hanslick nor Théophile Gautier who, almost at the same time, was roundly asserting that art was not a means but an end, refusing the title of 'artist' to anyone who was seeking anything but beauty (74) had met with much support; in any case, they failed to alter the course of events. Musicians fought shy of these ideas, and Saint-Saëns himself, although a staunch defender of *'métier'* and for that reason looked upon by many romantics as a black sheep, thought that music was first and foremost a matter of form. Yet in 1897 he felt obliged to declare that 'Music is not an instrument of physical pleasure. . .. It is not a matter of finding what gives more or less pleasure to the ear, but what dilates the heart, elevates the soul and arouses the imagination' (75). Debussy alone was not ashamed to declare openly, and against all the Wagnerian fanatics that 'French music desires above all else to give pleasure' (76). The 'democratisation' of musical culture in the nineteenth century hastened the process whereby musical symbolism became a conventional language. It was not only the Fifth Symphony 'knocking at the gates of life' with its four notes, or the *Darstellungsmotive* alone which supplied the imagination with concrete images: everything in this system could serve as a vehicle for extra-musical matter – everything became semantic. The invasion of the language of music by concepts, and the growing gulf between musical thought and its actual expression in terms of sound, were often encouraged by the preponderance of the linear element in the construction of a work. The introduction of an harmonic element into the melodic structure, universally adopted in the eighteenth century based on the functional major-minor system, did nothing to change this predominating principle, since it was accompanied simultaneously by the introduction of a system of thematic invention based on the technique of imitation. The 'well-tempered' chord-system generally adopted, through the wide use of the piano, played an equally important role, but it was the triumph of the 'expressionist' conception of music above all that led inevitably to the standardisation of musical symbolism. The dialogue with human experience, embodied by the magic of art in the expressive, if ambiguous form of a work, was thus transformed into the passive reception of the signs of a code of information which did not leave much room for the free play of imagination.

The musical system in common use was outmoded, and Debussy was painfully aware of this state of affairs. This is shown clearly in the account he gave of his meeting with Henri de Régnier in 1893: 'As he was talking to me about certain words in the French language which had lost their original rich overtones through vulgar misuse, I thought to myself that the same thing was happening to certain chords whose sonorities had been cheapened in "music for export". There is nothing startling in this reflection in itself; but I must add that they have at the same time lost their symbolic essence' (77).

'Impressionism': an embarrassing formula

A musical work conceived within the limits of a long-established tradition may be open to all sorts of interpretations; viewed as a whole it may seem to the hearer to call for some sort of semantic interpretation, or even arouse in him associations of ideas or concrete images. It may therefore seem unnecessary to try to discover whether Debussy found his basic inspiration in Symbolism or Impressionism – especially since the public has for a long time opted in favour of Impressionism. Would it therefore really serve no useful purpose to re-open the discussion at this stage at the risk of merely getting involved in sterile terminological arguments? If the problem were merely one of finding a more precise definition of the terms, then in my opinion there would be no point in conducting such an enquiry. But something much more important is at stake. In the case of the music of Debussy (and let us not forget that, even in the eyes of the strongest supporters of 'musical Impressionism' this music appears to be the only music to which the term could properly be applied), the analogy with Impressionist painting was based on false premisses which resulted in the invention of a false stylistic category. Moreover, this led to the distortion of the real lines along which music was developing by preventing a proper appreciation of the innovations introduced by the composer of *L'Après-midi d'un faune*.

In our perception of a musical work the only 'measurable' quality is its functional aspect; on the other hand, everything it represents and expresses can be interpreted in various different ways. Thus the musicologists, and German musicologists especially, have tended to concentrate on Debussy's compositional technique. In their analyses their criteria have been mainly based on historical precedent, and this is why we may often be shocked by the narrowness of their conclusions. As Kant has pointed out, empirical knowledge depends not only on the material to be studied, but also on the categories of concepts among which we include the objects on which we seek knowledge. Despite certain attempts at modernisation, musicologists in the 1920s and 1930s were still using traditional concepts, and were therefore unable to grasp the profound significance of Debussy's work. Their theories about instrumentation were still in an embryonic stage, while their attitude regarding the psychological significance of expression was either based on metaphysical principles, or still conditioned by the 'associationist atomism' theories of Helmholtz, Stumpf and Ebbinghaus, while ignoring both the *Gestalttheorie* and psycho-analytical approach. Research during this period was concerned primarily with tonal and harmonic problems; but no attention was paid to the actual sound of a musical work or its structural features, which were considered to be of only secondary importance. And yet it was precisely those features which were beginning to play an essential role in the music of Debussy: pure sound in itself, was, in his opinion, a no less important creative element in the structure of a work than melody, rhythm or harmony.

When taking as their models the great works of the past, musicologists always had recourse to spatial metaphors which for long had been an essential part of the European cultural tradition, especially as regards the definition of musical phenomena in terms of visual categories. It has often been pointed out (78) that the basic musical vocabulary has been largely derived from the sphere of optics (e.g. interval, design, form, ornament, 'above' and 'beneath', 'high' and 'low', symmetry and a-symmetry etc.). This, no doubt, can be explained by the fact that in musical notation a note is transcribed onto a flat surface, and this was sometimes reflected in the music itself (e.g. the polyphonic figures in a 'crab' or 'mirror' sequence). If we add that in current parlance 'melody' is synonymous with 'line', and 'harmony' with 'colour', it is no longer surprising that in musicological terminology the actual sound qualities of a work resulting from the chosen method of performance, and the ways in which sound was affected by rhythm, dynamics, accent and articulation, were interpreted as manifestations of 'sound-colour'; they were also examined in relation to functional harmony, although in fact they had no connection with the latter or its laws. On the basis of this system of metaphors or, as it has rightly been called, this 'musical topography', as developed by tradition and in more recent times, analogies with painting could easily be established in musicology, and in fact have ever since been increasingly adopted. Any analogy may be useful so long as it is not made the basis of theoretical constructions which create confusion in our outlook upon and knowledge of the world. In their desire for exactitude musicologists were right to concentrate especially on the functional aspect of Debussy's *oeuvre*; unfortunately, their analyses did not cover all the problems inherent in his music. The question of pure sound-quality values escaped their attention; yet these values were no less important than any of the others. One has only to consider the latest developments in music to realise that they were in fact far more important than many of the other features which attracted more attention.

By employing traditional methods in their analysis of Debussy's compositional technique, musicologists only arrived at partial results – on a par with the significant aberrations that characterised their interpretation of the aesthetic aspects of his work; for instead of seeking correspondences between his style and that of the poets and painters who were his contemporaries, they were content to adopt the current formula of Impressionism. It is true that during Debussy's lifetime this formula was generally accepted by the public, but in the field of ideological controversy it had already ceased to play a preponderant part, having been superseded by new movements, such as Symbolism, Synthetism, Fauvism, Expressionism and Neo-classicism, which appropriated its conquests for their own ends. The notion that music was lagging behind other branches of art first took shape at this moment, and that the ground thus lost could not be recovered even by a creative artist such as Debussy who, nevertheless, was more keenly sensitive to what was going on around him than any other musician in history.

Paul Valéry was right when he said: 'There are two kinds of works of art: those that create their own public, and those that are created by their public. Every new "school" tends to create a public of its own; but once this public is created it calls in its turn for works which satisfy its tastes' (79). Musicologists found themselves in the same situation as the public which, having come under the spell of Impressionist painting, sought in it resemblances to the music of Debussy. They were unable to rise above the average level of perception and transcend the boundaries which, especially at moments of deep spiritual crisis, separate the aesthetic experiences of the public from the intentions of the artist. The phenomenology of writers like Kurth or Mersmann did nothing but encourage this approach, since it accepted *a priori* the idea of universal harmony, thus taking its stand on the neutral ground of 'knowing' where the nature or constitution of a work of art's meaning (*Konstituzion*) is seen as identical with its perception (*Sinngebung*), confounding the artist with the public and art with aesthetics (80) – in other words, the phenomenologists confused artistic aims with the objects of aesthetics – and consequently the kinds of language which are proper to both. When a musical system is decomposed, all its expressive functions are changed; the sound-entity which we perceive ceases to be for us a vehicle of meaning (*Sinnträger*) or, as Roman Ingarden would say, of 'sound-values'; the meaning which this entity confers upon itself (*Selbstsinngebend*) cannot be perceived by us because we know nothing about the new system of correspondences. It thus becomes apparent that where the study of works of art is concerned there is no exhaustive method to which we can accord any degree of exclusivity. We are, so to speak, forced to accept a plurality of methods and a plurality of points of view. The thesis of Ludwig Wittgenstein (which has been clarified by Bertrand Russell) has made this clear to us – namely, that there can be no transference from one language to another – in the case with which we are concerned, from the 'normative' language of aesthetics to the 'evocative' language of art – because each of them has its own idiosyncracies and is governed by its own logic (81).

It is true that musicologists had noticed the part played in Debussy's music by pure sound-values, but by treating the latter as of secondary importance compared to the harmonic element in his work, they failed to deduce from this observation a conclusion which would have enabled them to revise their methods of research. Kurt Westphal was not far from the truth when he declared that the music of Debussy 'had discovered pure sound – as an elementary acoustic factor distinct from artistic combinations of sounds grouped in accordance with a purely functional principle'; he added that, in Debussy's case, one could even speak of 'sounds liberated from harmony' – but he was preaching to deaf ears (82). Nobody tried to understand what he was saying; what is more, he himself did not seem to attach much importance to it. After the Second World War, Werner Danckert, the most subtle of all the German experts on Debussy, still thought it unnecessary to pay any attention to Westphal's opinion (83).

Obstinately attached to traditional methods, the musicologists were capable of explaining the decomposition of the system of functional harmony in the works of Debussy, that is to say, its destructive effect; but quite failed to describe the workings of a new system of correspondences, and the preponderant and form-creating role played by sound-values within this system. By attributing to them the same 'colouristic' qualities that they recognised in the harmonic elements (of this music), and at the same time expanding the metaphor by references to Impressionist painting, the musicologists, although they could have availed themselves of the theories of phenomenology, continued to follow the same old paths which could only lead to an impasse. In point of fact, however, these 'irrational' sound-values, whose importance they failed to grasp, were – since they were the only ones to escape from the confines of the existing 'conceptual' system – an admirable adjunct (as Debussy's music proved), which made it possible not only to break up the structure and symbolism of a musical work, but also to build up new structures based on different principles.

The 'Impressionist' formula did not help but, on the contrary, hindered a proper appreciation of Debussy's music. It laid too much stress on the external and formal aspect of his works which, already, musicologists were unable to reveal in their true perspective so long as they continued to employ traditional methods; moreover, the term had first appeared in a specialist literature (not uninfluenced by the writings of Hamann) used in a purely artificial sense by those who claimed that it represented a 'style' (either of a school or of an epoch).

If by 'style' is understood a particular way of creating organised artistic ensembles – a way that is determined by the artists' own character and their social and historical situation, then it is clear that it would be unreasonable to attempt to define an artist's style solely on the basis of his use of formal techniques (84). Account should also be taken of other features, such as the personality of the author, his philosophical and aesthetic opinions, his preferences with regard to subject and *genre*, the epoch he lives in and his social position. What, then, are the features which the musicologists took into account when they invented the term 'Impressionist style'?

Apparently all. But, on closer examination, it is clear that none of them had been sufficiently studied in depth. The type of stylistic analysis favoured by the musicologists has recently been severely criticised by one of our most brilliant Polish musicologists, M. Bristiger in his study *The origins of musical form* as follows: 'It is characteristic of the method adopted in analyses of this kind that they are applied only to fragments of the works being studied – a procedure, it is claimed, that is quite sufficient for the purpose of stylistic description, though very often no attention is paid to other features which can only be defined after studying the form of the work as a whole (85).

There is no doubt that pre-war musicology was lacking in several elements including, among others, familiarity with the sources of information on the period during which Debussy was developing his aesthetic theories, and the fundamental works of John Rewald on Impressionism and Guy Michaud on Symbolism. Other weaknesses were the result of the too close proximity between the cultural phenomena of the end of the nineteenth century and the beginning of the twentieth. It is nevertheless a fact that, almost half a century after the death of Debussy people were still using the same magic formula which, from the beginning already meant too many things at the same time to have any meaning at all. Why, then, should this formula be kept alive by artifices, of which the article by Hans Albrecht in the encyclopaedia *Die Musik in Geschichte und Gegenwart* is a striking example (86)? In order to preserve it the writer cites every conceivable argument: the influence of romanticism, the realistic and naturalistic elements in the language of music and, of course, the correspondence between music and Impressionist painting and poetry (in which, however, he fails to make a distinction between Impressionism and Symbolism) and finally with exoticism and the folk-lore of foreign countries. However, Albrecht is honest enough to recognise the anti-Impressionist elements in Impressionist music, such as, for example, the return to French classicism of the eighteenth century, the emphasis placed on rhythm and melodic line, and the tendency to 'caricature'. The question of wounded national pride is also discussed in this study (a whole chapter is devoted to it), recalling Debussy's bitter campaign against the influence of Wagner and the hegemony of German music. Finally, so far as the artistic procedures of Impressionist music are concerned, one has only to glance at the chapter headings to see that the author will have nothing new to say on this subject. One might have expected that the arguments assembled would be favourable enough for him to be able to tell us what is meant by Impressionism in music; alas! we are presented with only a hybrid explanation, from which the only conclusion to be drawn, so far as the music of Debussy is concerned, is that his refined and 'naturalist' sensuality, tinged with decadence, led to a new 'programme', the principal feature of which was a taste for Far-Eastern exoticism and foreign folk-lore which did not, however, prevent his music from having a very pronounced, even nationalistic character. For a study of several pages, intended to provide a precise definition of the controversial term, the result is meagre in the extreme; even an inexpert and impartial reader, after perusing this article to the end, must wonder whether the point at issue, discussed at such length, really exists at all.

The works of Mme. Stefania Lobaczewska, in which the question of Impressionism is dealt with at some length, provide further proof of the fragility of the arguments on which this musicological theory is based. 'Without taking into account the close connection between music and painting' she writes, 'it would be impossible to define the essence of the Impressionist musical style' (87). Elsewhere she states: 'The programme in the music of Debussy has been sublimated to such an extent by the profoundly musical temperament of the composer that it cannot be accepted here as a criterion of style.'

What criterion, then must we accept? No doubt: 'Above all, harmony' (88). And here we come back to the idea borrowed from Kurth which constantly recurs in Mme. Lobaczewska's studies; it was from Kurth, too, that she borrowed the formula describing Impressionism as 'the last phase of Romanticism'; contrary to Mersmann, she claims that Impressionism was not a reaction against naturalism, since it was itself 'a kind of naturalism [echoes here of Gauguin – *Author's note*] and, in any case, was a product of naturalism' (89). It was not until 1962 that Mme. Lobaczewska changed her opinion under the influence of Jozef Chominski's theoretical articles on *La méthode sonorielle d'analyse de l'oeuvre musicale* (90).

It is regrettable that it took Mme. Lobaczewska so long to take a more favourable view of the idea (borrowed from Westphal but in a more elementary sense) that 'in Impressionist music (especially that of Debussy) the actual sound is both the object and content of the work'; it is not the harmony which plays a decisive part, but the whole sonorous aspect of the work (Mme. Lobaczewska still speaks of 'colour') which is at last recognised as 'the original element that determines the way in which the other musical elements are used', – and that includes harmony (91). Nevertheless the author, in the same article, returns to the analogy with Impressionism – 'more especially pointillism' or, to be more precise, 'tachism' – and to the criterion, already rejected, stating that all the effects of this music 'are still subject to a certain programme, defined in the title, without which neither the author's intentions, nor the forms in which they will be realised, can be fully understood.'

One could multiply indefinitely examples of all the various inconsequential arguments which violate elementary logic – and even gratuitous statements – of which the defenders of Debussy's Impressionism are guilty. But it would be a mistake to believe that this formula which, it was claimed, correctly defined the essence of his music, did not encounter some opposition. Its inadequacy was apparent to many of Debussy's contemporaries, and especially to himself who often made fun of it. Paul Dukas, for example, who sometimes wrote musical criticism, never employed this label. Other friends of Debussy, e.g. Robert Godet, Georges Jean-Aubry and Louis Laloy were very chary of using the term. Laloy, a musicologist and critic who was considered a great authority in his day, foresaw with uncanny accuracy the paths that music would trace for itself in the future (92). It was he who in the same article said, with so much justice, of Debussy, that: 'He combines the logic of the notes with the logic of sound.' Laloy is an interesting case if only because, while not denying the existence of Impressionist as well as Symbolist tendencies in Debussy (which, in his opinion, were proof of the 'anti-cerebral attitude' common to both movements, and of a concern with 'the unknown regions of existence') (93), he had discovered in some of his works (beginning with *La Mer* and even earlier compositions) a third and 'classical' tendency. In accordance with his own personal tastes he welcomed, in 1908, signs of a new style: 'The art of Debussy ... at first wholly Impressionist, is assuming ampler forms today, more clearly defined ideas, more solid constructions and more vigorous rhythms' (94). His hopes were based especially on works like the symphonic triptych *La Mer* (1905); *Children's Corner* for piano (1908); *Trois chansons de Charles d'Orléans* for mixed *a cappella* chorus (1908). But as Debussy's creative evolution became, towards the end of his life, particularly capricious, none of the 'new styles' mentioned by the critic was ever consistently maintained.

Laloy was not the only one to have this experience. D. Chennevière, the author of a monograph on Debussy (the second to appear in France during the lifetime of the composer) had tried to distinguish in his work three periods: the first, up to and including *Pelléas et Mélisande*, dominated by Symbolism with a tinge of Impressionism; the second marked by a 'naturism' culminating in *Ibéria* (1908); while in the third period the composer's art became 'idealist' and 'essentially melodic, tinged with an Attic simplicity and clarity' which reached its climax in *Le Martyre de Saint-Sébastien* (1911) (95). This classification, like all the others, seems to correspond with the wishes of the author rather than with reality.

Nevertheless, the term 'classicism' launched by Laloy, probably under the influence of Busoni (96) and automatically repeated by Chennevière, was for many years to be applied to the 'last period works', despite the fact that the true representatives of 'classicism' (Satie, 'Les Six', Prokofiev, Stravinsky and Hindemith) never recognised Debussy as their precursor.

Although many were of the opinion that it was time to renounce the Impressionist formula (Setaccioli, Perrachio, Koechlin) their arguments were never sufficiently convincing. As often as not a compromise solution was sought. Thus, for example, Fabian maintained that *La Mer* had closed the Impressionist period and opened the way to Expressionism. He looked upon the years 1904–13 as the period of the 'simplified melodic style', parallel to Expressionism. He also included in the 'neo-classic period' (1913–17) *Le Martyre de Saint Sébastien* and *Jeux* (97). Andreas Liess in his earliest works followed Kurth closely, although from then on he found it difficult to explain certain peculiarities in Debussy's musical language (98); then, following Laloy, he tried to prove in a full-length study that the music of the composer of *L'Après-midi d'un faune*, 'Symbolist in spirit and Impressionist in technique' showed a definite trend towards 'absolute music', 'pure music', and marked the beginning of the 'neo-classic' period (99). It was Werner Danckert who made the most profound study of Debussy's work in his monograph, no doubt the best that has appeared to date; but so far as the composer's musical language was concerned, he still adhered to the accepted point of view and did not dare openly to take his stand along with those who defended the Symbolist theories about Debussy.

But of those who did dare there were very few. One would never have expected that one of these would be Kandinsky, the creator of abstract art. Yet in a small book written in 1910, *Über das Geistige in der Kunst*, we find the following: 'The most modern musicians, such as Debussy, give us impressions, often borrowed from nature, which they transform into 'spiritual' images in a purely musical form. For this reason Debussy has often been compared with the Impressionist painters . . . But it would be going too far to pretend that this observation is enough to account for the scope and significance of the work of Debussy. Despite his affinities with the Impressionists, he is so deeply concerned with the *internal* content (of what he experiences) that one finds in his works the tortured spirit of our time, vibrant with passions and nervous convulsions. Moreover Debussy, even in his impressionist images, never confines himself to the notes perceived by the ear – which is the characteristic of pragmatic music – but, over and beyond the notes, aims at making an integral use of the internal values of his impressions' (100). Considering the date at which this was written, it must be admitted that it would be difficult to pay a finer tribute to the music of Debussy.

Among the critics, the English were the first to recognise the links between Debussy and Symbolism. Arthur Symons, for example, in 1908 affirmed that 'Debussy is the Mallarmé of music' (101); while T. E. Clark amplified this comparison by adding that 'Debussy uses chords like Mallarmé uses words, as mirrors which concentrate the light from a hundred different angles upon the exact meaning, while remaining symbols of that meaning and not the meaning itself. These strange harmonies ... are not the end, but the point of departure of the composer's intentions; they are the loom upon which the imagination must weave its own fantasies' (102).

Debussy saw that that the superiority of music over the other arts is precisely because of its ambiguity, and the fact that it is not subjected to 'the same necessity for precision and other contingencies as are colours and words' (102). He does not order his army of sounds like a general who follows rigorously drawn-up tactical plans. He is more concerned with strategy. He trusts his intuition and does not hesitate, at the critical moment, to allow the sounds themselves alone to take the initiative; he joins conscious action with the action of fortuitous forces – or, at any rate, appears to do so. If he attracts the attention of the hearer to details, this is in order to multiply the points of view in the latter's perception. He either assembles the sounds in more or less homogeneous groups, or else allows them to create disorder in combinations which have long been considered respectable, and in this way throws a new light upon both momentary and more durable associations of sounds, continually changing their expressive values, and preventing them from establishing themselves or assuming an 'identity'. By diversifying metrical values, he forces the hearer to become conscious of their importance in a musical work; he blurs or stresses rhythmic impulses, divides or merges sonorities – nothing in his music can be foreseen in advance. It develops spontaneously. It ignores those long introductions, those endles *finales* so dear to romantic rhetoric. His music has no beginning and no end. It emerges from silence, imposes itself without any preliminaries, *in medias res*, then interrupting its course, continues to weave its pattern in our dreams. Its form is not closed; it does not indulge in static images – unless for the sake of showing it can do this too. Why should it be 'a window opening on the world' (as, according to Alberti, a picture is), creating the illusion of three dimensions if it is already in three dimensions itself? Debussy does not, like the Impressionists, hope to see the truth and reveal it. He knows very well that all we can do is to experience truth and then at most, *suggest* the nature of that experience. Thanks to the incessant movement of particles of sound, whether large or small, something in this music is always happening; something lives and dies there – takes shape, renews itself continually and flashes in every direction without ever having any *definite* meaning. It seems the very incarnation of the Bergsonian 'Being and Becoming', but it is more than that: it is a cathedral full of symbols that traverses Time.

4

DEBUSSY AND SYMBOLISM

The climate of the period

THE last fifteen years of the nineteenth century and the first years of the twentieth – a period of intense activity in Debussy's life since he was associated with the ideological and artistic movements during that time – were destined to have a great influence on the future of European art and culture. It was this period which witnessed the beginning of one of the greatest cultural crises in history, caused by the rapid strides made in science and technology which the collective conscience of the people was unable to understand. There was a wide gulf between what science and technology had to offer and the extent to which human society was able to assimilate or adapt it to conform with ideas, habits and institutions which were still traditional.

We have already shown (in Chapter One) how this crisis, which affected both science itself and its methodological principles, had provoked a powerful wave of irrational currents. In art these tendencies did not manifest themselves immediately. The names of Darwin, Pasteur, Edison, and Helmholtz still enjoyed a great prestige. It is true that many years had passed since Flaubert had declared that great art should become scientific and impersonal, but Zola was still working up to 1893 on the *Rougon-Macquart* series in which he drew inspiration from the methods employed in experimental sciences, and Seurat was propounding his pictorial 'divisionism' as a scientific theory. The critics were ready to accept this, and one of their most brilliant members, Félix Fénéon, announced in *La Vogue* the end of 'naturalistic' Impressionism (that of Monet and Renoir), and the arrival on the scene of the 'scientific' Impressionism of Seurat (1). He thus won the approbation of Seurat himself and of the Symbolist poet Moréas, who both described him as 'the first scientific critic' of their works. In addition to the 'scientific aesthetic' (1886) of Charles Henry, there appeared the 'scientific criticism' (1888) of Emile Hennequin; while René Ghil, in his *Traité du verbe*, was trying to lay the foundations of 'scientific poetry'.

In their antagonism to the Germanic spirit, the bourgeois, rationalist and nationalist elements in France were violently anti-Wagner. In 1886, on hearing that the Opéra-Comique was preparing to produce *Lohengrin*, the painter Boulanger threatened to bring to the dress-rehearsal two hundred students and models from the Beaux-Arts, dressed in togas and armed with whistles (2). The threat was successful, and the Opéra-Comique cancelled the performance. A year later Vincent d'Indy failed in his attempt to get *Lohengrin* produced at the Eden Théâtre under Lamoureux; after the first performance on 3 May 1887, the project had to be abandoned on account of the disturbances caused by the Nationalist extremists.

Nevertheless the new movements began to gain ground, publicised in the press, in books and through the activities of more or less important artistic groups. Aestheticism, 'Decadentism' and Symbolism were becoming fashionable. Huysmans' *A Rebours* (1884), whose central character des Esseintes – a neurasthenic living in an artificial world in which reality is replaced by dreams and nature by artifices of all kinds – was considered a decadent work. But the impression it made, not only on account of its content, but also by its form, was a profound one, as can be seen by what Oscar Wilde had to say about it: 'The style in which it was written was that curious jewelled style, vivid and obscure at once, full of *argot* and of archaisms, of technical expressions and of elaborate paraphrases that characterizes the work of some of the finest artists of the French school of *Symbolistes*. There were in it metaphors as monstrous as orchids and as subtle in colour. The life of the senses was described in the terms of mystical philosophy. One hardly knew at times whether one was reading the spiritual ecstasies of some medieval saint or the morbid confessions of a modern sinner. It was a poisonous book. The heavy odour of incense seemed to cling about its pages and to trouble the brain' (3).

Despite the intentions of the critics, the epithet 'decadent', far from harming the novel, ensured for it a notable success, and soon became a slogan in numerous artistic circles. Two years later the following passage appeared in the first number of the new Review *Le Décadent*: 'To deny the state of decadence we have reached today would reveal a complete lack of sensitivity. In religion, morality, justice – it is apparent everywhere. An ultra-refinement of appetites and sensations; a taste for luxury and sensuality; neuroses, hysteria, hypnotism, morphinomania, scientific charlatanism, an excessive cult of Schopenhauer – such are the prodromes of our social evolution' (4). The new ideas, infinitely more supple and diverse than hitherto, corresponded to a need for new forms of satisfaction – hence the extravagant vocabulary adapted to the complexity of current sentiments and sensations.

Impressionism, which had for long been a much-disputed subject, banished from the salons and ridiculed, began gradually to penetrate the consciousness of artists and intellectuals, and ended by making a breach in their ways and habits of thinking. We owe to Jules Laforgue one of the most remarkable essays on the subject ever to have been written at that time, summarising in a most striking fashion the essential features of the aesthetic theory on which this revolutionary movement was based (5). The lesson taught by Impressionism to contemporary painting was nevertheless still regarded with a certain suspicion, reinforced by the influence of new movements which, although they still made use of the technical discoveries of the Impressionists, were critical of the 'too humble' objectives of Monet, Renoir and Sisley. Impressionism was attacked from all sides, not only in conservative circles, but also in those of the avant-garde (Gauguin, Seurat); this sometimes disconcerted the public, and even certain critics, starting with the 'hesitant reactionaries', such as Camille Mauclair, who had no personal opinions with regard to these new tendencies (6). Again, in 1905, Impressionism was violently attacked by Burne-Jones (7).

Nevertheless the ideas and the analytical and searching approach of the Impressionists were soon gradually to pervade every department of the arts, and eventually the entire cultural scene. Certitudes thought to be inviolable began to waver and finally collapsed altogether. When, in 1886, after the publication of *Oeuvre* (one of the *Rougon-Macquart* series) Monet, Renoir and Pissarro broke off relations with Zola, despite their long friendship with him, everybody knew that this was not intended as a protest against 'naturalism', but as a manifestation of solidarity with Cézanne, who had recognised himself in the character of Lantier – a caricature to which Zola, his friend since childhood, had added certain features, or at any rate opinions, which could be ascribed to Monet. The following year a group of writers of the 'naturalist' school issued their 'Manifeste des Cinq', which was a direct attack on Zola's aesthetic (8).

Maupassant brought about the final collapse of the 'school' when he abandoned his principles in, among others, his two stories *Le Horla* and *Lui?*; he had some harsh things to say about the 'school' also in the preface to *Pierre et Jean* (1888). Zola did not change his ideas, but Brunetière was right when, in 1887, he declared the 'bankruptcy of naturalism'. Huysmans, who had been one of the first to abandon it, accused 'naturalism' (in *Là-Bas*) of 'having incarnated materialism in literature ... What a musty and narrow system it was – to want to stew in the hothouse atmosphere of the flesh, reject whatever cannot be apprehended by the senses, repudiate dreams, and even fail to understand that art begins where the senses have ceased to be of use ... No, there is no denying that the whole "naturalist" school, in so far as it still continues to exist on a feeble scale, reflects the appetites of an appalling age' (9).

With 'naturalism' relegated to the background, the stories and poems of E. A. Poe, in the admirable translations of Baudelaire and Mallarmé, enjoyed a great success, while in the last years of their lives Villiers de l'Isle-Adam and Barbey d'Aurévilly enjoyed a belated triumph. Born in France, the romantic doctrine of 'art for art's sake' found in England an ally in the 'aestheticism' preached by the American painter Whistler, the poet Swinburne and the aesthetician Walter Pater – also by the Pre-Raphaelites. Oscar Wilde was the personification of this school in the eyes of the public. The following English writers appeared in French translations: Tennyson, Keats, Swinburne, Browning and, later, Meredith, as well as the Scandinavians: Ibsen, Björnson, Strindberg and Hamsun. The poems of Verhaeren were admired; Rodenbach enjoyed a vogue, and later Maeterlinck, who was revealed by Octave Mirbeau in 1890. Hegel, Schopenhauer, Nietzsche and Carlyle also aroused great interest. In 1891, when asked what his tastes in literature were, Maeterlinck mentioned in the following order: Villiers de l'Isle-Adam, Mallarmé, Verlaine, Barrès, Henri de Régnier, Viélé-Griffin and Moréas, and added that he also admired the English poets Swinburne, William Morris, Rossetti, and in France Puvis de Chavannes, Baudelaire, Laforgue, André Gide's *Les cahiers d'André Walter* and Poe (10). Apart from Puvis de Chavannes, included for some unknown reason in this literary company, Maeterlinck's reply gives a list of names which could be considered typical, and representative of the tastes of readers of literary journals – in other words, the educated public.

It was during this period too that Russian literature enjoyed a great success. *Crime and Punishment* and *Anna Karenina*, translated in 1886, were best-sellers. Melchior de Vogüé, who with his *Roman Russe* had greatly contributed to their success, summed up as follows the qualities of the Russian writers: 'The essential feature of these realists is their understanding of the under-side, the "surroundings" of life. They study in depth reality, and yet meditate upon the invisible. Their characters are troubled by the mystery of the universe, and lend an ear to the murmurings of abstract ideas' (11).

In 1886 appeared the famous Manifesto of the Symbolists, drawn up by Jean Moréas. According to him, this literary renaissance was due to the use of methods such as 'an excessive ceremoniousness, unfamiliar metaphors, a new vocabulary in which harmonies are combined with colours and lines. ... Charles Baudelaire must be considered as the true founder of this new movement; M. Stéphane Mallarmé invests it with a sense of mystery and the ineffable; M. Paul Verlaine broke in its honour the cruel fetters restricting poetry whose stranglehold had already been loosened by the prestigious fingers of M. Théodore de Banville' (12).

Three great poets, Baudelaire, Verlaine and Mallarmé were the undisputed masters of the new generation of poets; but there was a fourth, not mentioned in the Manifesto – Rimbaud, who had freed poetry from the tyranny of 'verse', invented the *vers libre*, the 'colour' of vowels and 'a poetic language which sooner or later would be accessible to all the senses' (13); he was revealed when Verlaine had published his poems. 'Whereas Verlaine and Rimbaud had followed Baudelaire so far as sentiment and sensations were concerned', said Paul Valéry, 'Mallarmé had developed it in the domain of perfection and poetic purity' (14). Their aesthetic englobed the whole artistic ideology of this movement to which the name of 'Symbolism' was given.

Correspondances, the celebrated sonnet in *Les Fleurs du Mal*, became the gospel of the new poetic movement. The language of Baudelaire appeals as much to the intellect of the reader as to his physical sensibilities. It does not directly represent things and feelings; it offers a choice of the most suggestive correspondences among the analogies which exist between words, and sounds and their atmosphere – a choice which tends to create a harmonious poetic substance which acts upon the imagination, not only through its meaning, but also through its sound. Having discovered the secret connections between words, sensations and man's spirituality, Verlaine transposes, with an astonishing felicity, the slightest sounds in Nature into an extraordinarily musical poetic language. Take, for example *La chanson d'automne* where a subtle interplay of nasal and oral vowels creates a kind of soothing atmosphere – or other poems from *Fêtes galantes, Les Ariettes oubliées* or *Aquarelles* which many composers, especially Debussy, set to music.

'La poésie incantatoire', founded on allusion and the symbol, had been, as we have already said, the subject of lengthy research on the part of Mallarmé. One of its earliest examples can be seen in *Apparition* (1863) – a poem which the young Debussy was later to set to music under the same title. In 1864 Mallarmé wrote: 'I have at last begun my *Hérodiade*. Full of terror, because I have invented a language which must of necessity emerge from a very new kind of poetry, whose aim I might define briefly as being to paint, not the thing itself, but the effect it produces' (15). Here we have come a long way from 'naturalism', and very near, it would seem, to the moment when, this time a philosopher and not an artist, was to write: 'Words with well-defined outlines, crude words . . . obliterate or, at any rate, obscure the delicate and fugitive impressions recorded by our individual consciousness' (16).

It is equally easy to see the connection between Mallarmé's early poetic theories and the Impressionist aesthetic into which Proust gained his initiation through the paintings of Elstir – Monet. Elstir's aim, said Proust, was 'to portray things, not as he knew they really were, but in accordance with those optical illusions created by our first view of them. . . . If God had named the things he created, then it was by depriving them of their names, or giving them new ones that Elstir re-created them. Names which describe things always imply the notion of intelligence, which has nothing to do with our real impressions . . .' (17). This is exactly what Mallarmé did in his *Après-midi d'un faune* (1876) where, despite his use of the alexandrine, that well-worn metre, all the images evoked by his dreaming, inert Faun, when 'tout brûle dans l'heure fauve', seem actually to disport themselves in the air, as light as the memories that rise to the threshold of our consciousness.

The ideas of the Impressionists and the Symbolists were in the air and pervaded everything – literature, music, philosophy and painting. Gauguin, who thought that the role of art was to translate thoughts into purely plastic images, advised painters to 'aim at suggestion rather than description, just as music does'. Instead of a 'likeness' they should seek a 'subjective correspondence' (and here he was thinking no doubt of the growing vogue of photography which guaranteed a picture identical with its model). 'Why', asked Gauguin, 'should we not succeed in creating different harmonies (in colour) corresponding to our mental and emotional state?' (18). Van Gogh also sought for a symbolic meaning in colours through which to express his feelings; while in an article that attracted a lot of attention, entitled 'Symbolism and painting', Aurier laid down the principles which in essence foreshadowed the future theories of the Nabis: 'A work of art must be *idéiste* . . . symbolist . . . subjective . . . decorative' (19). It is clear that the ambitions of the Impressionists and 'Divisionists' were soon to be realised.

Impressionism and Symbolism had had a strong influence on Bergson's philosophic thinking. The Impressionists were trying to capture phenomena in full flight, as it were, at different hours of the day and in all their complexity and mobility. Their ambitions found an unexpected justification in Bergson's philosophy, with his new definition of reality, his 'critique' of the nature of intelligence, his intuitionism and especially his theory of the continuity of consciousness. Published in 1889, *Essai sur les données immédiates de la conscience* expounded this theory for the first time; it was also the first violent attack on the 'associationist atomism' which was then popular among psychologists. When Bergson declared that there was no psychic state, however simple, which was not subject to continual change – in other words, that there could be no two identical psychological moments in any one individual consciousness – he was in fact merely formulating the principle on which the Impressionists' practice was based (20).

It is not only life of which the essential characteristic is its constant mobility. According to Bergson, nothing 'is' but 'is becoming'; everything is in a state of becoming – an uninterrupted succession of new events. This is why our intelligence, with its fundamental tendency to simplify and systematise, is unable to grasp – and therefore cannot ever know – reality. The formulae created by our intelligence falsify reality. The names and words it uses are rigid moulds applied to what is essentially fluid and perpetually in motion.

By extending in this way to the whole of reality the theory that our psychic life is in a continuous state of becoming, Bergson, at a time when 'scientism' was not yet dead, was entering the field of metaphysics; he was the first to have so boldly examined its problems once again. It was less than thirty years since Amiel, deploring the narrow-mindedness so prevalent in France, had noted in his Journal: 'What the French lack is initiation into the mystery of Being' (21). And now, and in France too, someone had arrived who was about to renovate metaphysics. A disciple of Boutroux, he had far out-distanced his master whose only courageous action had been to open up the way to all sorts of irrational trends through his criticism of scientific objectivism.

A metaphysical *Angst* was spreading among the *élite* and was almost a mark of prestige among writers. For example, Jules Lafor-gue, the poet who died at the age of twenty-seven and whose writings were gradually attracting readers because they satisfied the needs of the age on account of their bitter irony, veiled pessimism and philosophical thought, felt himself to be 'a blade of grass', 'an atom in the Infinite' (22); from Vienna, as a far-off echo, came the voice of Hofmannsthal proclaiming that: 'We are surrounded on all sides by incertitude, ambiguity and formlessness; and beyond lie the bottomless gulfs of existence' (23).

The reign of 'scientism' was nearly over. It was no longer fash-ionable to be an avowed atheist; this was the era of conversions when the Catholic Church took to its bosom its prodigal sons (Bourget, Lemaître, Huysmans, Jammes, Morice, Claudel and many more). Jacques Rivière, however, was highly sceptical of these conversions. Concerning Huysmans, this is what he wrote in a letter to Alain-Fournier: 'It is art and art alone that has converted him. He has been converted to the Christian art of the Middle Ages, not to Christianity' (24). At the same time esotericism, occultism, spiritism and Satanism were attracting converts all the time.

Philosophic Positivism had proved a deception; the intellectual *élite* in France were going through a period of profound spiritual disillusionment. Albert Aurier described it in somewhat dramatic terms as follows: 'The nineteenth century, after having for the last eighty years proclaimed, in its childish enthusiasm, the omnipotence of scientific observation and deduction, and maintained that all mystery had been abolished by the microscope and the surgeon's scalpel, at last appears to have realised that all its efforts and its boasting had been in vain. Mankind is still surrounded by the same enigmas, still confronted by the same formidable "unknown", now more obscure, more disturbing than ever since it has become the fashion to ignore it. Many *savants* today are giving up in despair, having at last understood that this experimental erudition of which they were so proud is a thousand times less "true" than even the most bizarre theogony, the wildest metaphysical visions, or the most improbable poetic dreams; they realise now, that this lofty science which in their pride they described as positive, is perhaps nothing more than the science of relativities, of appearances, of "shadows" as Plato called them, and that they themselves have nothing with which to replace, in the old Olympuses, the gods whom they have dethroned and the stars they have extinguished.' No better description could be given of the anguished state of mind prevailing at that time (25).

Spiritualist movements, too, were springing up on all sides. In 1893 Marcellin Berthelot spoke of a 'counter-attack' in the sphere of mysticism. Within the space of ten years France – or rather the highest levels of French culture – had been so completely transformed that Bourget's proclamation of the 'bankruptcy of science', which in 1888 had been received with open scepticism, was no longer treated as a paradox in 1895. Brunetière himself, that eminent academic, while summarily announcing the death-knell of 'naturalism', and openly admitting that science had lost its prestige, went on to proclaim the renaissance of Idealism (26).

All authentic art is, in one way or another, however difficult it may be for ordinary people to realise this fact, closely related to the experience of human society. Art may well be the connecting link between a high and a low level of 'initiation' (either scientific or religious according to the level of civilization in any given society). Did not the young Valéry remark: 'Poetry seems to me to be a fine and delicate explanation of the World . . . a lofty symphony uniting the world which surrounds us and the world by which we are haunted' (27).

The Symbolists, the Nabis and other artistic groups were moved by the same desire to grasp the inexpressible, and to be immersed in this atmosphere which heralded the epoch of profound transformations – disturbing because they were unknown. Although their talents may not always have enabled them to comprehend all the complicated problems of that new era – can they be blamed for that? Charles Henry interpreted correctly the transformations that had taken place in the very structure of civilisation. In his reply to J. Huret's questionnaire (28), he wrote as follows: 'It is impossible to believe in the future of "naturalism" or of a "realist" school of any kind; the advent of an art that will be truly idealist, and even mystical, based on new techniques, is inevitable. It is impossible to doubt it when one considers the developments in scientific methods and industrial progress. The future belongs to an art which will have got rid of methods of any kind, whether logical or historical, because men's minds, exhausted by purely rational thinking, will one day feel a need to penetrate into completely different regions of thought.'

Nevertheless the revolution in ideas during the years 1885–1895 was not accompanied by a revolution in forms. The latter were incapable of expressing all the richness of the new movement's intellectual content, and were soon infected by all the new mannerisms of every description which began to be fashionable around the year 1900. The artists involved in the movement seemed to be united so long as their leaders (Mallarmé and Gauguin) were alive; but when they were no longer there, groups which until then had appeared to be working together in harmony began to break up.

Gauguin, who had been obliged to leave Europe in order to 'find himself', and who did not realise his full potential until he settled in Tahiti, issued, but in vain, warnings and encouragements to defend the new forms: 'We must fight, body and soul, against all "schools" of every description, not by disparaging them, but in other ways, attacking not only the official Establishment, but also the Impressionists and the Neo-Impressionists, the old public as well as the new; tackling the most extreme abstractions, doing everything that is forbidden, and re-constructing everything to the best of our ability without fear of exaggeration, or even with exaggeration. We must learn afresh, and then, after what we have learned, learn still more. All timidities must be crushed, regardless of the ridicule we may incur. In front of his easel the painter is the slave neither of the past, nor of Nature, nor of his neighbour' (29). It was only the generation that followed that was to heed his appeal.

Wagnerism and French Music at the end of the nineteenth century

While Symbolism was all the rage, painters and poets had elevated music to the dignity of an art which would govern the imagination. They all wanted to take music as a model for their creative work, because it alone was capable of suggesting and communicating to man what was inexpressible in any other medium. Did not Schopenhauer declare that music alone, the noblest of all the arts, was the direct expression of the Will, that is to say the Essence of the Universal Being, and that music alone could give direct expression to the affective life of the soul (30)? Even so 'positive' a thinker as Taine recognised that music 'was better able than any other art to express floating thoughts and formless dreams, object-less and limitless desires and all the painful and grandiose emotions of the troubled spirit with boundless aspirations and no permanent attachments' (31). And what other art could express the Bergsonian concept of reality as 'becoming'?

Music had regained the esteem of the French intellectual élite; a few years earlier it had been possible for Berthelot, without shocking anyone, to explain the relatively high percentage of madmen among musicians by saying 'These are people who feel but don't think.' At the same time there was a painter who accounted for the alleged extraordinary protection afforded to musicians by the State on the grounds that 'all the Jewish bankers are mad about music.' We would never have heard of these *bons mots* which were fashionable at the time if the Goncourt brothers had not taken the trouble to make a note of them, while confessing at the same time that, so far as they were concerned, 'the only kind of music they could bear was the military kind' (32).

The cult which the Symbolists professed for music was partly a reaction against the lack of musical appreciation shown by the preceding generation, of which Delacroix, Gautier and Baudelaire were praiseworthy exceptions. Never before had music found so many fervent supporters among painters and men of letters. It was something more than a passing taste: it was a religion. They all tried to outdo one another in their zeal so as not to be accused of being insensitive to music; and nearly all of them were passionate admirers of Wagner.

Edouard Schuré, Catulle Mendès, Houston S. Chamberlain, Théodore de Wyzewa and many more were all ardent propagandists for his music. Catulle Mendès tried to find a compromising formula which, without irritating the Nationalists, was calculated to please the 'Wagnerites', declaring that: 'Music-drama in France would produce works whose inspiration, although profoundly French in essence, would be developed according to the principles laid down in the Wagnerian system' (33).

Théodore de Wyzewa, one of the pillars of *La Revue Wagnérienne*, wrote that since the role of the poet or writer was to suggest rather than to describe, literature was therefore basically music, because music has developed the powers of suggestion more than any other art, and is able to evoke, far better than words, the mysteries of life. In his view the master of 'word-music' *par excellence*, and the true representative of 'Wagnerian art' in France was Villiers de l'Isle-Adam; at the same time he placed in the category of 'Wagnerian painting' the works of Puvis de Chavannes and Odilon Redon, as well as those of Monet, Degas and Cézanne (34).

What attracted the poets in the 'synthetic' art of Wagner was the union of words and sounds, the symbolism of the musical *Leitmotifs*, and especially the element of mysticism which particularly appealed to their imagination. It was the Wagnerian conception of art and its philosophy, as Edouard Dujardin, Editor of *La Revue Wagnérienne* was to point out many years later, that really inspired the Symbolist movement (35). Thus, in their enthusiasm for Wagner the artists were more concerned with his aesthetic theories than with his actual music, of which they had only heard fragments in the concert hall, or had heard about from those few who had made the pilgrimage to Bayreuth. Léon Daudet admitted frankly that: 'The vague, incestuous mysticism, the preoccupation with genesis, the ethnical horizons and the excessive, sudden and quasi-miraculous emotions which characterise the Wagnerian drama seemed to the weary youth of France like a promise of deliverance from their fatigue ... I find it amusing today – it seems stupid to have to confess it – but what we admired most were the legends. We studied with an almost crazy enthusiasm the most fantastic characters, as if Wotan was the answer to the riddle of the Universe, or as if Hans Sachs had been the first to reveal the secrets of a free, natural and spontaneous art' (36).

Mallarmé's critical approach was in contrast to the adoration with which Wagner was surrounded in this small world of 'littérateurs'. Though disclaiming any right to judge his music himself, Mallarmé took it for granted that it was excellent, but found it all the more difficult on that account to conceal his embarrassment at the aesthetic and poetic content of the works. Perceiving their shortcomings and weaknesses, he was unable to share the enthusiasm they aroused among his entourage (37).

The tide of admiration for Wagner did not begin to ebb until after the *première* of *Pelléas et Mélisande*; but already, in 1899 (three years after his break with Pierre Louÿs, who was a whole-hearted Wagnerian) Gide had the courage to confess, in a letter to Paul Valéry, that 'Wagner's music seems to me to be a terribly coarse form of art . . . an art of artificial flowers' (38).

It was from 1885 onwards that the influence of Wagner began to make itself felt more and more – and there were many reasons for this. After the defeat of 1870, Nationalist feelings ran high. The principal aim of the *Société Nationale de Musique,* founded in 1871 on the initiative of R. Bussine and Camille Saint-Saëns, was to propagate the works of French composers. Nevertheless, at the heart of the movement whose noble task it was to cultivate *Ars Gallica,* serious differences of opinion on questions of aesthetics soon began to appear.

Eminent 'masters', enjoying a widespread reputation were safely installed in the various academies and other musical institutions to which they had been elected in recognition of their merit and high qualities. Nevertheless, even the most gifted among them, such as Saint-Saëns, Gounod and Massenet, were too ready to follow the line of least resistance, and were content to go on repeating endlessly the same trick or stylistic formula, which at first had been an original discovery; and by exploiting in this way what had once been an artistic triumph, gradually became bogged down in an academic groove. In the eyes of the more ambitious younger generation their example was scarcely inspiring; and it was not surprising that they turned their attention to other masters and other models. Many years later Debussy was to declare that true fame was 'fortunately reserved for those whose lives are devoted to the quest for a world of sensations and of forms constantly being renewed' (39).

The man who seemed to be the ideal incarnation of the creator perpetually and untiringly seeking more and more perfect forms of artistic expression came from Belgium. César Franck, organist of Ste. Clotilde in Paris, did not attain the summit of his art until he was over sixty with his *Variations Symphoniques,* the *Symphony,* the *Sonata* for violin and piano and the *String Quartet.* His example won for him respect and admiration, and soon there had gathered around him a group of devoted disciples faithful to the principles of his art (Bordes, d'Indy, Duparc, Chausson) the future founders of the *Schola Cantorum.* Nevertheless, the 'school of Franck', though it had caused French composers to take a greater interest in symphonic and instrumental music – an interest which Saint-Saëns had already done much to encourage – was to prove a disappointment to those who had based their hopes on it. It produced neither great works nor great talents and, generally speaking, it did more harm than good to French music, as was already apparent as early as 1906 (40).

It must not be forgotten that Franck himself, 'the son and grandson of Germans, was himself the product of a Germanic tradition. Both in Vienna and in Paris he was conscious only of the Germany of Bach and Wagner, and was for a long time strongly influenced by Beethoven and Schubert. It was his destiny to transmit to the French, after Habeneck and Berlioz, the gift of Germanic music' (41). And so in this way the disciples of Franck, mainly connected with Nationalist circles, became, in spite of themselves, the apostles of the German neo-romantics. It was they, too, who were to help to weaken the resistance of French musicians to the 'Wagnerian virus' if it is permissible so to describe it, – that virus which, by the end of the century, in France had turned into a veritable epidemic.

Even before the Wagnerian fever had overcome the *Ars gallica,* that noble emblem had begun to lose its lustre. Feeling themselves not strong enough to defend it against the invasion of new ideas, even on the platform of the *Société Nationale,* its supporters in 1886 handed over, with scarcely any resistance, the direction of this institution to Franck and his followers. After that, no one objected any longer to the annual pilgrimages made by the official delegates of the *Schola* to their new Mecca in Bayreuth, which was also the meeting-place of the most fervent champions of the Wagnerian cult.

It was a triumph for Wagner, – a posthumous revenge for the deplorable fiasco of *Tannhaüser* in Paris in 1861 when Baudelaire alone – and not even Hector Berlioz who was Wagner's friend – had the courage to defend the work which was being trampled in the mud. At that time the number of 'sorcerer's apprentices' was increasing every year. Anyone and everyone thought that all he had to do to create a masterpiece was to bewitch his imagination with the Master's magic formula. Paris was flooded with waves of unoriginal music, unsuccessful imitations and ill-digested ideas. The situation was paradoxical: on the one hand there was the Parisian *bourgeois* who was scandalised by *Lohengrin,* only accepted *Tristan* in the concert hall, knew nothing about and refused to become acquainted with the Tetralogy, seeing in the legends nothing but the expression of German arrogance; while on the other hand, the intellectual *élite* traded illegally in Wagner's poetic theories and presented them to the public in an idealised form, tinged with their own ideas.

And yet, who other than Franck or Wagner could have served as a model and a source of inspiration for young musicians? They really had no choice. Even a composer as confident of his own abilities as Lalo revealed, in *Le Roi d'Ys,* what he owed to the Wagnerian aesthetic. Chabrier, that volcano of joviality, apparently destined to renovate French *opéra-comique,* instead devoted all his energies to opera, preferring to waste them on preaching the gospel of Wagner. D'Indy and Chausson were unable to free themselves from the influence of Franck and Wagner, which tended to stifle their own personalities, and they never succeeded in doing so, though Chausson did speak of the 'necessity to de-Wagnerise' music (42). Duparc was to offer, year after year, the distressing example of a talented artist destroyed by the Wagnerian 'pressure' ever since 1885, and was only to contribute a dozen songs which, nevertheless, were judged by posterity to be 'works of genius' (Ravel).

The wider the cult of Wagner spread, the more damage it did. Certain perspicacious historians of the following generation went so far as to compare Wagner with Attila, in whose tracks no grass ever grew again (Adler). Only Gabriel Fauré seemed exempt from any hesitation. He followed his own path to attain in the end results which earned for him great esteem in France. But his aims were apparently not clearly understood by his contemporaries since, in 1903, Debussy could not find any other words in which to describe him except, somewhat ironically, as a 'master of charm' (43).

In the company of composers of this (Wagnerian) school the young Debussy, full of doubts and hesitations, could not but feel ill at ease. Hence his preference for painters and poets: the musicians, despite the high esteem in which the art of music was held by artists in other fields, lagged behind the movements of the avant-garde, and confined themselves to copying the models of a past age, or else imitating Franck and Wagner.

Debussy and his environment

With the exception of the last thirteen years of his life which were relatively stable, Debussy's whole existence had been fraught with uncertainty – both in a material and, to a certain extent, spiritual sense. Being by birth of humble origin he was obliged, ever since his childhood to develop on a superior level. Thanks to the protection of patrons of the arts he was able to taste the pleasures of 'gracious living', while his connection with the 'artistes maudits' reinforced his consciousness of being 'different'. It was in these conditions that his tastes and his artistic personality were formed.

His father, Manuel Debussy, the son of a cabinet-maker and an illiterate working woman, had served for five years in the French Marines somewhere in Guadaloupe or New Caledonia. On his return to Paris, he had married Victorine Manoury, the daughter of a carpenter and a cook, who in 1862 gave him his first son, Achille Claude, the future composer (Debussy abandoned his first Christian name in 1893). His father tried his hand at various trades, being succesively a dealer in china-ware at Saint-Germain-en-Laye (where Debussy was born), a business representative, a commercial traveller and a dealer in lithographs, without ever succeeding in ensuring for his increasingly numerous family a decent style of living. The mother loved only her eldest son, and left the others under the care of her sister-in-law Clémentine Debussy, a dressmaker by profession, and a little better-off than the rest of the family thanks to her liaison with a rich broker, A.-A. Arosa, followed by a 'friendship' which was to end in her marriage to a *maître d'hôtel* in Cannes named Alfred Roustan.

We know that in 1864 Achille-Antoine Arosa, and his mistress Clémentine Debussy, stood as godparents to the future composer; and we also know that, like his brother the banker Gustave Arosa, godfather and protector of Gauguin, Achille-Antoine's hobby was collecting works of art (his collection included works by Delacroix, Corot, Daubigny, Jongkind, Gavarni, Pissarro and Sisley), and that the two brothers owned a handsome villa at St Cloud, which had been restored after the ravages of the Franco-Prussian war. It was there that they kept their collections and entertained their friends including, among others in 1885, Pissarro and Gauguin. On the other hand, it is impossible to state categorically whether or not A.-A. Arosa influenced Debussy's intellectual development in any way. We can conjecture that, at any rate during his liaison with Clémentine (but not later than 1868) he gave his godson handsome presents; it may be that he also taught him to appreciate the attractions of wealth by inviting him to his villa at St Cloud. It seems that Arosa was conscious that he owed something to Debussy's parents, since on two occasions he helped his father when the latter was in trouble – first political and then financial. Leaving his biographers to investigate the second of these embarrassments, we shall now consider the first as being more germane to our main subject.

During the siege of Paris, from December 1870 to March 1871, Debussy's father was employed at the commissariat branch of the town hall of the first arrondissement in Paris. Having been dismissed from this post, he joined the National Guard. On March 18th he was promoted lieutenant, and on May 3rd Captain of the 2nd company of the 13th battalion of the federal forces. He took part in the attack on the fortress of Issy, and when the commander of the battalion, after being wounded, gave up the struggle, he took his place. (It is interesting to note that Paul Verlaine, one of the 'disinherited' and 'cursed' poets, was fighting on the same front). After the collapse of the Commune on May 22nd Manuel Debussy found himself in gaol at Satory, where he awaited for six months the sentence of the Court which condemned him to four years imprisonment. Although he was set free after five months, thanks to the intervention of his wife, who was left alone with four children and practically no resources, the family situation did not get any better; it was impossible for a former 'communard' to find a situation of any kind, especially since the civil death sentence passed on him had been upheld. It was at this juncture, it would seem, that Achille Arosa came to his assistance and found for him a modest job as a clerk in the firm of Fives-Lille which Debussy *père* was to hold down, apart from an unexplained interruption of eight years (from 1887 to 1895), from January 1873 to 1906.

In the gaol at Satory Manuel Debussy had struck up a friendship with a musician, Charles de Sivry (we shall come back to him later) who, having been freed earlier, had made the acquaintance of the wife of his fellow prisoner, and in October 1871 had introduced her to his mother, Mme. Mauté de Fleurville, a piano teacher. This event was to play an important part in determining the future of Claude Debussy, then nine years old.

Antoinette-Flore Mauté de Fleurville, *née* Chariat, had, by her first marriage, a son, Charles de Sivry, and by her second, a daughter, Mathilde, the beloved fiancée and unfortunate spouse of Paul Verlaine. She posed as an aristocrat, the victim of misfortune, as a former pupil of Chopin, and at one time the friend of Balzac, de Musset and Wagner himself. In reality she was a false marquise (the name Fleurville is pure invention), a pianist, the pupil of unknown teachers (in any case none of her names are to be found on any list of Chopin's pupils), but nevertheless a piano teacher with exceptional pedagogic gifts. She was the first to discern in the son of Mme Debussy, who had only just begun his piano lessons (thanks to the initiative of his aunt Clémentine, with a violinist in the municipal orchestra at Cannes named Jean Cerutti), a remarkable musical talent which she took it upon herself to cultivate without seeking any financial reward. She must have taken her self-appointed task seriously, for scarcely a year later Claude Debussy, having successfully passed the extremely difficult entrance examination to the Paris Conservatoire, was accepted, on 25th October, 1872, as a pupil in the piano class of the famous professor Antoine-François Marmontel (44). Debussy always acknowledged how much he owed to his teacher; and Paul Verlaine himself also, years later, paid tribute to his ex-mother-in-law: 'She was a charming soul, an instinctive and gifted artist, an excellent musician with exquisite taste, intelligent and devoted to those she loved' (45).

The lessons were given in the apartment where Mme de Fleurville was living with the Verlaines. As is well known, Arthur Rimbaud was a frequent visitor; and since July 1872 his presence had led to dramatic scenes which ended in the separation of the ill-assorted couple. The young Claude had no doubt often met in this house the chief characters in this drama, and he may well have been the unwilling witness of some shocking scenes. There is no evidence that in later life he kept up his acquaintance with Verlaine of whose poetry, however, he was a great admirer. The fact is that, ever since his childhood, he had rubbed shoulders with the world of the 'accursed ones', and this first time was not to be the last.

The reason why we have dwelt in this way upon certain biographical details which only a few years ago were practically unknown (46) is not only because of the light they throw upon certain well-known facts which we do not propose to go into now, but above all because they constitute the first link in a chain of events which were to have a profound effect upon the imagination of Claude Debussy, enriching his inner life, influencing his intellectual development and determining his attitude towards the world. Anything 'strange' had always interested him: people who were outside his own milieu, and arts which were different from his own. Anything unconventional, or which flouted mediocrity, and everything that seemed to violate the rules that were supposed to govern life or the arts – in a word, anything that overthrew established conventions or which savoured of exoticism, of the unknown, or even of scandal, attracted him in the same way that a lamp attracts a moth – except that he never allowed himself to be 'drawn'; while remaining an 'outsider', he indulged his imagination and allowed these experiences to kindle the flame of his art. In the last years of his life, during which he apparently found peace, Debussy became estranged from the friends of his youth, not because he had joined the ranks of the 'bourgeoisie' through his second marriage, but on the contrary, because it was they who could not forgive him for having forsaken his wife, in defiance of bourgeois common sense, in order to take the wife of another and seek his happiness with her. He himself had not changed. His mind, as always, was full of new ideas. His art was to remain to the end a symbol of the rebellious and revolutionary spirit of the twentieth century.

He entered a famous school of music without even having had an elementary education; his only intellectual stock-in-trade was what he had been able to learn from his mother and his friends. His parents' hopes that he would be able to complete his education here, or at any rate learn everything there was to be learned about music, were going to be doubly disappointed. At the Conservatoire nobody taught him grammar or spelling (which was always to be his weak point); while as regards music, this honourable school, obsessed by the spirit of academicism, was unlikely to teach him much more than he already knew, thanks to the 'Marquise' de Fleurville. And so, after the first years during which he won rewards which encouraged those nearest him to 'dream of castles in Spain built on what my future fame would bring in', as he used to say later, (47) the time came when he no longer hid from his companions his spirit of independence and scorn for traditional 'rules', although he concealed these views from his teachers for fear of losing their support (48).

The series of excursions in the former direction started with an invitation he received to stay in Touraine in the magnificent Château de Chenonceaux in the summer of 1879 where he was engaged as pianist in a trio sponsored by the châtelaine, a rich Scotswoman Mme Pelouze-Wilson. After that, he was engaged by Mme Nadjezda Filaretovna von Meck, Tchaikovsky's benefactress, to act as accompanist and tutor to her children. He spent with her three long vacations; from early July to the end of October 1880 in Switzerland and Italy (Interlaken, Naples, Rome, Florence); in 1881 first Russia (Moscow and Gurievo, the Bennigsens' private chateau), then in Italy (Rome and Florence); and finally, in 1882, in Russia (at Plestchievo and Moscow) and then Austria where, in Vienna, it would seem he heard for the first time Wagner's *Tristan und Isolde*. In 1885, while in his second year at the Villa Medici as winner of the Grand Prix de Rome for composition, being unable to return to Paris, as he would have liked to do owing to his love affair with Mme Vasnier, he accepted the invitation of Count Primoli (the son of Charlotte Bonaparte and a relative of Princess Mathilde) and went to escape the heat of Rome, staying in the Count's villa at Fiumincino, a beautiful spot on the shores of the Adriatic.

These relations with influential people, motivated more often than not by financial reasons, were to continue throughout his life. The list of names begins with Arosa, continues with those we have already mentioned, and included in addition the aristocratic titles of Balbiani, Cystria, Polignac, Poniatowski, San Martino. Then there were the bankers (Courty, Dupin); the publishers (Durand, Fromont, Hamelle, Hartmann, Jobert); the theatrical managers, great and small (Antoine, Astruc, Carré, Charlot, Chautard, Gatti-Cassazzi and Lugné-Poë); and finally various patrons among the higher bourgeoisie. Apart from the financial advantages, Debussy acquired, thanks to these social connections, a certain knowledge of the world, a taste for good living rather above his means, and sometimes a knowledge of things that he would not otherwise have had the opportunity of getting to know – for example, the von Meck family introduced him to Russian music, even though this was restricted to Tchaikovsky. He was also able to form some valuable friendships, notably with Dupin, Hartmann and Durand.

As regards his intellectual development, however, by far the most important factor was his acquaintance with the Bohemian world of writers and painters. As for musicians, he had no need to seek their company since he mixed with them daily at the Conservatoire. Apart from music, it was to poetry that he felt most strongly attracted – we do not know how this came about, or what it was that influenced him; but it is a fact that, before his artistic conscience was fully awakened, his infallible good taste guided him to all the best works available which might also be useful to him. One has only to recall his earliest songs (1876–8) on texts by Banville, Musset, Cros or

Bourget. One of his earliest friendships at the Conservatoire, with Raymond Bonheur, had indeed begun thanks to a volume of poems by Théodore de Banville which Bonheur had noticed he was carrying. This was in 1878 (49).

A little later it was the turn of Verlaine, Mallarmé, Baudelaire, Poe and Laforgue – in a word, all the saints of Symbolism. It would be fair to state that the collection of five songs on texts from the *Fêtes galantes* composed in 1881–2 and dedicated to Marie-Blanche Vasnier, his *inamorata,* who was also blessed with a beautiful voice, was not a chance happening, but definitely a manifestation of an already formed artistic taste in a young man of twenty.

Evidence of the extent to which his mind was receptive of the 'spirit of the age' is to be found in a letter to the husband of Mme Vasnier, dated 1886, from the Villa Medici: in it he formulates, unwittingly and in almost the same terms, the ideas which Baudelaire had expressed in a letter of 1862 addressed to Arsène Houssaye introducing *Le spleen de Paris* (50); the only difference seems to be that Debussy was speaking of music and not of art in general. A coincidence, or an excusable plagiarism? Certainly neither the one nor the other, but a lasting impression of Baudelaire's ideas in the memory and mind of Claude Debussy, and so, compared with artists in other domains than his own, he did not seem at all an 'outsider'; on the contrary, he was very much *au courant* with the artistic life of Paris, which was becoming increasingly rich and intense, independently of official institutions, academies and exhibitions. Beginning with nocturnal escapades at the cabaret of the *Chat Noir,* opened in December 1881, he finally reached, by various stages, the famous 'Tuesdays' of Mallarmé in the rue de Rome.

He was probably introduced to the *Chat Noir* by Charles de Sivry, himself a composer of *chansons* and, together with Georges Fragerolle, purveyor of music for the shadow theatre run by the painter and poet Henri de Rivière, aided by the famous caricaturist Caran d'Ache. Debussy took part in the programme as accompanist to the male and female singers who appeared on the little stage under the direction of Robert Salis. He soon struck up a friendship with another accompanist, a little younger than himself, Vital Hocquet (Narcisse Lebeau) to whom, ten years later, he was to dedicate one of his *Proses lyriques*, and thanks to whom he made the acquaintance of Erik Satie. The circle of the people Debussy met at the *Chat Noir* is so extensive that it is impossible to name them all. Among those with whom he was to establish a more or less lasting relationship were Maurice Vaucaire, poet and dramatist, who was later to become Antoine's right-hand man at the Théâtre de l'Odéon; the humorists Alphonse Allais and Raoul Ponchon, the latter being the friend of Verlaine and of Emmanuel Chabrier; and finally another satirical author, Maurice Donnay.

The *Chat Noir* was also the headquarters of the Friday meetings of a literary and artistic group founded by Goudeau which, under the patronage of the poet Charles Cros, the inventor of photography and the gramophone, had undergone three metamorphoses, adopting in succession the titles of 'Hydropathes', 'Hirsutes' and 'Zutistes' before finally breaking up and becoming merged more or less in the main current of the day, Symbolism. Among the song-writers who had belonged to the group may be mentioned, among others, Rollinat, Lorin, Marie Krysinska, a poet of Polish origin and one of the first to use *vers libre* (before Gustave Kahn had claimed to have invented it). Among the personalities directly connected with the *Chat Noir* was Edmond Haraucourt whose 'poèmes hystériques' had caused a scandal (e.g. *La Légende des sexes,* 1882). Like many other avant-garde writers Haraucourt was later to become engulfed in the Parnassian classical movement cultivated by Pierre Louÿs and patronised by Jean Moréas and Henri de Régnier after the collapse of Symbolism. Others to be remembered were Paul Delmet and the chansonnier who made his debut at the *Chat Noir* – Aristide Bruant. The latter was later to open his own cabaret, *Le Mirliton.* Mention should also be made of the two draughtsmen and decorators, the caricaturist Théophile-Alexandre Steinlen, well known for his radical opinions, who was to succeed Bruant at the *Mirliton*; as a fellow contributor to *Gil Blas,* he had made for Debussy the design in Indian ink which had often been reproduced. The second was Adolphe Willette, who turned out a series of Pierrots and Colombines; it was he who illustrated Debussy's *Mandoline* (on a text by Verlaine), first published in 1890 in *La Revue illustrée.*

But pride of place among all these budding artists belongs incontestably to Maurice Rollinat ('a sort of local Heine', as Lockspeiser describes him (51)), the author of a collection of poems bearing a title typical of the spirit of that new generation of artistic Bohemians, *Les Nevroses,* in which one finds, among other things, poems about Chopin and Poe. Rollinat also set poems by Baudelaire to music, which he interpreted himself or else entrusted to the famous

Yvette Guilbert. The *Chat Noir* was at the height of its vogue during the years 1885–95 after the cabaret had been transferred to the rue Victor-Masse. There, an inscription over the door invited the passer-by to be 'modern', and the waiters were dressed in the green uniforms of members of the Académie Française. Among its regular customers were Théodore de Banville, Renan, Maupassant, Verlaine, Villiers de L'Isle-Adam, Paul Bourget, and Jehan Rictus. In their wake came a crowd of bourgeois, eager for amusement and willing to be the target of venomous satirical attacks for the privilege of rubbing shoulders with decadent Bohemians.

We have no proof that after Debussy's escape from his Roman 'exile', which lasted for two years and three months, he still kept up his connection with the cabaret; but the contacts and friendships which he had formed there, as well as at the Conservatoire, were to be for him an ever increasing source of human relationships. It was probably the first years of the *Chat Noir*, during the hey-day of the 'Hirsutes', that saw the beginning of his short-lived friendship with Paul Bourget, whom Debussy mentions in his letters from Rome to Vasnier, and who might well have been the first to introduce the young composer to the poetry of Jules Laforgue. It was probably during this period also that he formed what was to be a more lasting friendship with Charles Morice who was later to become Gauguin's friend, and is referred to sympathetically by Debussy as late as 1912 (52). It should be noted that the 'Hirsutes' had been the instigators of an ambitious though eclectic weekly review, *La Nouvelle Rive Gauche,* founded in 1882, which was to become *Lutèce* four months later, in March 1883. Among its contributors were Morice, Haraucourt, Rollinat, Bourget, and Moréas. In 1883 Verlaine published in its columns his anthology of *Poètes maudits,* including Rimbaud (*Les voyelles* and *Le bateau ivre*), and some unpublished poems of Mallarmé (*Apparition* which Debussy was later to set to music), Laforgue and others.

It was through Maurice Vaucaire that Debussy got to know the Peter family (he was to be for many years a friend of René Peter) and joined the circle of those who enjoyed in varying degrees the friendship of Huysmans (though not always sharing his ideas) – such as Robert de Montesquieu, poet and eccentric who was to serve as a model for both the author of *A rebours* and Marcel Proust; Gabriel Mourey, poet and critic, translator of Poe and Swinburne, who introduced Debussy to the poetry of Swinburne as well as to the paintings of Turner and Redon. It was through Mourey that Debussy had a brief acquaintance with the occultist and Satanist Jules Bois, who had initiated Huysmans into the mysteries of the Black Mass. Erik Satie was the only one to be seduced by the mysticism of Bois and that other 'prophet', who called himself the 'Sâr' Péladan.

Among his fellow students at the Conservatoire, it was Raymond Bonheur, the friend of Charles Cros, Francis Jammes, Albert Samain, André Gide and the painter Carrière (greatly admired by the Symbolists) who was to help Debussy to make friends in artistic circles outside music. It was thanks to him that Debussy met Charles Cros and the satirical poet Gabriel Vicaire, the author, in collaboration with Beauclair, of an anthology of parodies of decadent and symbolist poems entitled *Les Déliquescences d'Adoré Floupette* (1885) which some critics had taken seriously – thereby learning to take a little more interest, perhaps, in Verlaine and Mallarmé.

But it was above all thanks to his own personality that Debussy was able so easily to enlarge his circle of friends. He was certainly not loquacious, but his appearance, as revealed in his first portraits by Pinta and Baschet, could not possibly fail to attract attention. He had, moreover, a sense of humour and of irony which apart from the testimony of his contemporaries, is strikingly apparent in his letters, in *Children's Corner* and in his articles. He knew how to listen, and his intelligence enabled him to grasp in a flash the thought of his interlocutor and meet it with a suitable repartee. It was also thanks to this intelligence that he was able to complete with such astonishing speed his cultural and general education. It was not his talent which gained for him access to the intellectual and artistic *élite* of France, since no one apart from a few musicians was able to appreciate it – or even form any opinion as to its worth – but exclusively his way of thinking and feeling.

He read books and periodicals with avidity. 'His parents are not rich', wrote one of his classmates in 1884, 'but instead of using the money he earns by giving lessons to help them, he buys new books and knick-knacks, water-colours etc. His mother showed me drawers-full of such things' (53). Others of his contemporaries expressed similar opinions, but nevertheless showed a little more understanding of Debussy's juvenile passions. In the first letters he wrote to Vasnier, to Popelin or to Baron that have been preserved, he either speaks of his personal worries and plans for work, or else gives his impressions of musical works he has heard, or of books he has been reading. In his letters to the Parisian bookseller E. Baron, written from Rome in the years 1886–7, he asks Baron to send him all the latest works of Verlaine, the complete poems of Shelley in Rabbe's translation, the *Cantilènes* of Moréas, and the most recent works of Vignier, Morice and Henri Becque; and to crown all – and this reveals him as a passionate bibliophile – a *de luxe* edition of Huysmans' *Croquis Parisiens*.

We know from other sources that during his stay in Rome he immersed himself in Shakespeare, Baudelaire, Laforgue, and the Goncourt brothers. It was through Gabriel Sarrazin's recently published *Modern English Poets* (in translation) that he got to know the Pre-Raphaelites. His interest having been aroused by reading Melchior de Vogüé's *Le Roman Russe,* he read the first French translation of Anna Karenina – though this did not cause him to change his opinion as to the superiority of Flaubert over all other prose writers. Even Schopenhauer and Spinoza aroused his interest, and became the subject of discussions among a small circle of his friends (mostly non-musicians) at the Villa Medici. In those days Debussy admired Whistler's paintings and Japanese art. Among other works he ordered from Baron were: the *Revue Indépendante* and *La Vogue, La Vie moderne* and *La Nouvelle Revue.* Leaving aside the last of these (only one number was printed, containing the *Sonnets* of Paul Bourget), it is interesting to recall the part played by the others during the years 1885–9 when the Symbolist movement was at its peak.

The *Revue Indépendante,* founded in 1884, had had a curious career during the first five years of its existence. Edited first by Félix Fénéon, the celebrated critic, then aged twenty, the defender of new tendencies in poetry and painting, a supporter of anarchism in politics (many years later he engaged Debussy as music critic of *La Revue Blanche*), *La Revue Indépendante* was above all a forum for the 'naturalists'. In September 1886 Edouard Dujardin took over as editor, and from that moment the Review became a famous literary and artistic magazine, entirely devoted to the cause of the latest tendencies in the arts. Laforgue, Kahn and Verhaeren published their poems in its columns, and Charles Henry, Théodore de Wyzewa and Moore their articles; it also contained reproductions of Whistler, Seurat, and Signac. Fénéon also arranged for exhibitions to be held on the premises of works by Manet, Berthe Morisot, Rodin, Pissarro, Seurat, Signac and van Gogh. After the departure of Dujardin, and later of Fénéon, the Review was edited for a time by Gustave Kahn and René Ghil (in 1891 Aurier published his article on Gauguin), only to end up in the hands of the reactionaries who were fighting for the restoration of the Orleans dynasty (54).

La Vogue, a weekly Review edited by Léo d'Orfer, lasted barely eight months – from April to December 1886; but its short existence was a brilliant one: Verlaine caused Rimbaud's *Illuminations* to be published in its columns; Mallarmé, J. Laforgue, Moréas and Gustave Kahn contributed poems; and it was *La Vogue* that published translations of Whitman and Keats; a series of articles by Fénéon on *The Impressionists in 1886* (mainly devoted to Seurat and Gauguin); an article by de Wyzewa on *Mallarmé and Symbolism*; and articles by Henry and Morice.

Finally, the eclectic magazine *Vie Moderne,* edited by Charpentier, that had been in existence since 1879, enjoyed a brief period of glory in 1887 when its contributors included Pissarro, Seurat and Signac.

Among the periodicals which Debussy did not order from Baron, because he could see them at the Villa Medici and certainly read them assiduously, mention should be made of *La Revue Wagnérienne,* edited from 1885–8 by Edouard Dujardin. Reading this magazine had for a time a disturbing effect on the young composer because it fomented his admiration for Wagner. Having only just completed the *Ariettes oubliées* on texts by Verlaine shortly after his return to Paris (1888 and 1889) Debussy yielded to the temptation of a pilgrimage to Bayreuth. Fortunately for him, because it was this experience that was to cure him entirely of the Wagnerian fever, only a few traces of which remained in the five settings of poems by Baudelaire (1887–9).

In March 1887, with his head full of new ideas and tired of a love affair which had imposed upon him an unduly protracted strain, Debussy decided once for all to leave the Villa Medici and return to Paris where he was soon to be caught up in a whirlwind of Bohemian life which made it possible for him to accept without too much distress the loss of the object of his Roman dreams. By contenting himself with love affairs which were not too demanding, he devoted himself entirely to his creative projects and to the exchange of ideas. He did not positively avoid the *Chat Noir*, but he was more often

seen in the bistros and cafés where artists foregathered. Gone were
the days when- Sainte-Beuve, Taine, Flaubert, Turgenev, Renan,
Gautier and the Goncourt brothers used to dine Chez Magny, while
Manet and Zola and their companions occupied the Café Guerbois.
The new generation often changed its meeting places. Almost every
little group, and even individual artists, had their favourite haunts
where they could be found at any hour of the day, so long as they
had not felt an urge to move to other quarters.

From 1887 onwards the meeting-place of the Symbolists was the
little *Librairie de l'Art Indépendant*, a modest but not un-ambitious
publishing house run by Edmond Bailly who occupied the premises
previously owned by *La Revue Indépendante* at no. 11 rue de la
Chaussée d'Antin. Bailly published poetry, philosophical studies and
even music; and it was he who undertook the publication of
Debussy's *Cinq poèmes de Baudelaire* in 1890 and, three years later,
his Cantata *La Damoiselle élue*, on the poem by Dante Gabriel
Rossetti (in a translation by Gabriel Sarrazin) with a cover design by
Maurice Denis. The personality of Bailly himself, occultist and music
lover, and the atmosphere of the place, half library and half old
curiosity shop, full of old documents and bric-à-brac, attracted
Mallarmé, Villiers de l'Isle-Adam, Henri de Régnier, Maurice Denis,
and later Pierre Louÿs, André Gide, Paul Verlaine and occasionally
Whistler. In 1891 Bailly started publication of *Les Entretiens
politiques et littéraires*, a monthly review with anarchist tendencies,
admirably edited by Viélé-Griffin, in whose pages Gide first published his *Traité de Narcisse* and Debussy part of the text of his *Proses
lyriques* (1892). It was certainly in the bookshop in the Chaussée
d'Antin that Debussy had his first close contacts with the leaders of
the Symbolist movement.

Nevertheless, Bailly's bookshop was only one of the meeting-
places frequented by the *éminences grises* of the artistic life of Paris.
Debussy was often to be seen Chez Thommen in Montparnasse,
where he met Charles Cros and Gabriel Vicaire, or again at the
Brasserie Pousset in Montmartre, where Catulle Mendès hobnobbed
with Georges Courteline, and the poet Henri Mercier, translator of
Keats and a friend of Verlaine, could often be seen. There was also
the Café Vachette, the headquarters of Jean Moréas. It was here in
the course of a stormy discussion between Moréas and Mercier on
the subject of Schopenhauer that Debussy made such a pertinent
comment that it left the two adversaries speechless; they never

thought that a mere musician would have anything at all to contribute to such an abstract argument (55).

From 1900 onwards it would seem that Debussy frequented the *Café Voltaire*, Place de l'Odéon, where on Mondays, Charles Morice, whose *Littérature de tout à l'heure* had caused him to be considered as the leading theoretician of the Symbolist movement, was in the habit of meeting members of the editorial staff of the *Mercure de France*. Alfred Vallette, with his wife 'la belle Rachilde', Henri de Régnier, Rémy de Gourmont, Albert Samain, Anatole France and Maurice Barrès went there sometimes; and so did the 'Nabis', with Maurice Denis at their head, and the founder of the sect of the Rosicrucians, the 'Sâr' Péladan. It was here, too, that Gauguin first met Verlaine, and that Carrière painted his celebrated portrait of the poet. It was also at the Café Voltaire that Mallarmé presided over the banquet given in honour of Gauguin on the eve of his first journey to Tahiti.

As regards the cafés frequented by Debussy, mention must be made of the Taverne Weber, rue Royale, and Reynolds' Bar nearby. At Weber's Debussy would meet his closest friends, such as René Peter, Pierre Louÿs, J. de Tinan and P.-J. Toulet; while among its regular customers were Léon Daudet, the celebrated pamphleteer who was later to be associated with the ultra-right-wing newspaper, *L'Action Française*; André Tardieu, journalist and future statesman; the famous 'Willy' (Henri Gauthier-Villars), music critic and first husband of Colette; Marcel Proust with his inseparable Reynaldo Hahn; and finally three satirical artists: Robert, Dethomas, and the most famous of the three, Forain. Léon Daudet has recreated in his *Souvenirs* the atmosphere that reigned 'chez Weber' – with its constant stream of witticisms kept up by a group of skilful players (56).

Reynolds' Bar, where English jockeys, coachmen in domestic service and circus artists used to meet, had quite a different *ambiance*, and Debussy was attracted by a certain exotic atmosphere such as is to be found in the pictures of Degas, Toulouse-Lautrec or Picasso in his 'blue' or 'pink' periods.

So now we see Debussy admitted to private artistic circles which he frequented from 1887 to 1900, and an always welcome guest, whether with the Peter and Chausson families, or *chez* Henri Mercier and Henri Lerolle; or again as the friend of Pierre Louÿs, or wherever he went to introduce his compositions, e.g. to Arthur Fontaine, or for any other reasons, as in the case of Alfred Stevens. But of all these get-togethers, those which took place at 89 rue de Rome, at Stéphane Mallarmé's flat, were particularly important; for to be admitted to these Tuesday gatherings was equivalent to receiving from the hands of his host a certificate of intellectual nobility. Curiously enough, people went there, not to talk, but to listen to the endless monologues of Mallarmé himself. 'Nothing could have been more modest', wrote André Gide, 'than Mallarmé's rooms, or his personal appearance. His salary as a teacher of English at the Lycée Condorcet did not allow him any luxuries, but everything in his house showed an exquisite taste. The little dining-room where he received us could only hold eight persons at a time – ten, at the most – sitting round the table where an enormous jar of tobacco took the place of a meal. The Master himself remained standing, his back propped against a brown enamelled stove . . . Mallarmé was almost the only person who talked. *Les Divagations*, which he published subsequently, give a fairly accurate impression of his conversation. But the tone of voice, the smile which came, not from the lips but from his whole expression – a discreet, veiled and almost timid smile – generally accompanied by a furtive gesture – perhaps a forefinger lifted in a gesture of interrogation or expectation . . . Ah! how far away one felt in that little room in the rue de Rome – far from the empty rumours of the busy town, political gossip, scandals and intrigues. One entered with Mallarmé a supra-sensitive region where money, honours and public acclamation no longer counted . . . As a result of his teaching I have always had a horror of facility, of complaisance and of everything that smacks of flattery or seduction, whether in literature or in life. An uncompromising love and need for sincerity, and integrity towards not only oneself, but mankind as a whole . . . The lessons we learned in the rue de Rome affected not only our minds, but helped to shape our souls' (57).

During the period covered by the 'Tuesdays', which started in 1880, one might have met there Verlaine, Catulle Mendès, Villiers de l'Isle-Adam, Jules Laforgue, Moréas, Mirbeau, Verhaeren, Huysmans, Henri de Régnier, Hérédia, Pierre Quillard, Dujardin, Théodore de Wyzewa, Fénéon, Stuart Merrill, Gustave Kahn, René Ghil, Charles Morice, Mourey, Viélé-Griffin, Hérold, Fontainas, S. George, Oscar Wilde with Lord Alfred Douglas, Symons, Maeterlinck, Rodenbach, Marcel Schwob, Pierre Louÿs, Gide, Valéry, Claudel, the brothers Natanson and the painters Berthe

Morisot, Renoir, Monet, Degas, Whistler, Redon, Gauguin and Vuillard.

The most faithful disciples also went to see Mallarmé at Valvins near Fontainebleau, where the poet had for twenty years spent his summer vacations; but the character of these meetings was not the same as those of the Rue de rome (58).

The famous 'Tuesdays' put all the other intellectual gatherings in the shade. Neither the 'Saturdays' of Jose-Maria Hérédia in the rue Balzac, nor the 'Wednesdays' of Pierre Louÿs in the rue Rembrandt (around 1894), and still less the musical evenings given by the Prince de Polignac in his town house could ever pretend to compete with them.

According to Landormy, it was Edouard Dujardin who accompanied Debussy on his pilgrimage to Bayreuth, and introduced him to the Symbolists' inner circles (59). What we know today about Debussy's youth enables us to state categorically that he did not need a guide to help him find his way. But we still do not know when, and in what circumstances Debussy first met Mallarmé. The visit paid by the latter, and described by Debussy in a letter to Jean-Aubry dated 25 March 1910 took place at the end of December 1894, or perhaps a little later (60); but the Memoirs of André Poniatowski, published after the last war suggest that Debussy must have have known Mallarmé since 1890, and had long been a member of the Tuesday gatherings, since it was in that year that he had dared to introduce his protector, and had even been able to win for him the Master's approval and admittance to these meetings. Present on that occasion were Henri de Régnier, Rodenbach, Pierre Louÿs and Marcel Schwob (61).

In any case, it seems certain that it was not by chance that Debussy found himself involved with the Symbolists. Like all great artists, he refused to go on repeating worn-out formulae, and allied himself with the avant-garde of those days. The contribution of the Impressionists was a lasting one, but their aesthetic, at that time, satisfied no one, including themselves. It had been a powerful influence, encouraging research into all the domains of art; but it had not provided an universal key which would have solved all the problems encountered. To see Impressionism as the main tendency in the literature of that period was the mistake made by the theorists; the notion of musical Impressionism was another. If there were any general categories to be discovered these should have been sought for in every branch of the arts, using the means appropriate to each art. The integration of such means was only possible on the basis that every work of art must be considered as a symbol – ambiguous, dynamic, and uniting the world of ideas with the material world. It was the Symbolists who made this clear to all artists including Debussy; it was they who, under the aegis of Mallarmé, represented the new avant-garde of their era.

The Symbolist movement had begun in poetry and in music: its precursors had been Baudelaire and Wagner. Poetry is nearer music than painting; hence it was poetry which had first inspired Debussy; painting had only been a source of inspiration in so far as it strove to imitate poetry, trying to borrow its expressive qualities, addressing itself to the whole man, and not only to his intelligence or his senses. Feeling himself to be a bit of a poet himself (his *Proses lyriques* and *Les Nuits blanches* bear witness of this, as do also the titles of the Piano *Préludes* and those of the second series of *Images*) Debussy quite naturally tried to establish contact with poets rather than painters; moreover, he did not have to seek their friendship; they came towards him of their own accord, attracted by his personality.

As regards his tastes in paintings, so many erroneous opinions have been put forward on this subject that it may be as well to consider this question here. Contrary to what has often been alleged, there is nowhere to be found in his articles, his correspondence, or even in the recollections of those who knew him best, the slightest proof that Impressionist painting had influenced him to any extent. On the contrary, as we have already pointed out, he repudiated the term Impressionism when applied to his music, and employed it himself only in an ironic sense. Those who use it because they think it seems to describe his work have not only ignored the protests of the composer himself, but have in addition ascribed to him a taste for Impressionist painting which in fact he never had. In order to justify a false supposition (resulting from an inaccurate analysis) use has been made of false premisses. Certain references to be found scattered through the various writings of Debussy and in his letters are enough to reveal his preferences as regards the plastic arts. For example, a questionnaire to which he replied in 1889, reveals that his favourite painters at that time were Botticelli and Gustave Moreau. Later, we find the names of Whistler and Turner – the forerunner of Impressionism and also of Symbolism, and the painter whose pictures had impressed his imagination most profoundly, and whom he described in a letter to Durand in March 1908 as 'the finest creator of mystery in the history of art' (62). His interest in the paintings of Degas and in Japanese art, and also in the work of Toulouse-Lautrec and Goya, dates from approximately 1890. We know, too, that he liked certain paintings by Henri de Groux (*Christ aux outrages*) and did not like Rodin, 'modern style' utilitarian art, or the 'Byzanticism' of Léon Bakst (who was one of Diaghilev's designers). We also have good reason to suppose that he was not indifferent to the Pre-Raphaelites, nor to the 'Nabis', Walter Crane and Aubrey Beardsley, Redon and Gauguin. These few names represent approximately all the painters who, one can confidently assert, had had a definite influence on Debussy's sensibility. Of these, only Degas belonged to the Impressionist group; moreover, he occupied a rather special position, a little outside what we are accustomed to call 'pure' Impressionism, as represented by Monet or Sisley. We do not find in the above list any other representatives of this movement; and it is noteworthy that Monet is not mentioned. Most of the painters we have listed belonged more or less directly to the Symbolist group. Nor can Debussy's personal relations with painters and sculptors, noticeably less close than those that linked him with the poets, lend any support to the theory that he had any connection with Impressionism.

During his stay at the Villa Medici he had dealings with either academic artists, such as Cabat or Hébert, or else with other *Prix de Rome* winners who had not yet decided what line they were going to follow (e.g. Pinta and Baschet to whom, incidentally, we owe good portraits of Debussy, and the sculptor Lombard), none of whom, however, despite all the medals and awards they gathered later, ever achieved fame of any kind. During this period Debussy also met Paul Baudry, another academic painter, who had painted Mme. Vasnier's portrait. From his 'Bohemian' period date his relations with the artists Willette, Steinlen, Dethomas, Forain, Robert and Detouche; a little later, at the time when he first met Mallarmé and the Chausson family, he had sporadic contacts with Whistler and the Nabis. If for a short time, he was often to be seen at Alfred Stevens' house, this was not because he was interested in this fashionable painter of Parisian society and the demi-monde, but rather in his daughter, Catherine Stevens to whom he proposed in 1896 but was politely rejected. She was willing, however, to reconsider the matter 'after the production of *Pelléas*.' He struck up a friendship with the sculptor Camille Claudel, sister of the poet and a pupil of Rodin's, just at a time when an incurable psychic disturbance from which the artist suffered made relations difficult. Debussy kept until his death two little sculptures by Camille, *Clotho* and *La Valse* dating from 1893. Through Mallarmé and Pierre Louÿs he often met the fashionable portrait painter Jacques-Emile Blanche, for whom he also posed on two occasions, in 1902 and 1909.

It was in connection with the design for the title page of *La Damoiselle élue* that he first met Maurice Denis, while the painter Henri Lerolle offered him financial support, and introduced him to the leading artists and influential society people whom he used to entertain. Debussy enjoyed the hospitality of the Chausson, Fontaine and Escudier families, and his attachment to the charming daughter of the painter Yvonne was no doubt one reason for his friendship with the latter. As for Odilon Redon, we only know that he offered Debussy one of his engravings, and that he designed the scenery for Diaghilev's production of *L'Après-midi d'un faune*. An oil painting of Debussy, dated 1909, and a bust are evidence of his relations with Henri de Groux.

The composer probably met Toulouse-Lautrec at the *Moulin Rouge*, through the intermediary of Paul Chansarel, the brother of his Conservatoire friend. According to a tradition current in the Chansarel family, the two artists admired each others' works (63).

Debussy's aesthetic opinions

As we have seen, the *milieu* in which Debussy's artistic personality was developed consisted exclusively of poets and writers – in a word, of men of letters. Paul Dukas was right when he said: 'The strongest influence which Debussy ever came under was that of the writers of his day, and not that of the musicians' (64). It should be noted that this influence made itself felt long before Debussy actually entered this *milieu*, since it began in his early youth as a result of his reading contemporary literature. At the time when, on his return from Rome he began to frequent the *Librairie de l'Art Contemporain* and Mallarmé's Tuesday gatherings, his tastes and his artistic sensibility were already practically formed. All he lacked then was an overall view of the problems which the 'new era' posed for artists, and that flexibility in his thinking and methods of expression which he was to acquire from his literary associations; it is difficult to imagine what his writings, which charm and astonish us today, would have been like had he never come under those influences. Debussy observed the musical phenomena of his day with an extraordinary lucidity, often in much the same way as we view them today. Many of his judgments have had a definite influence on our ways of thinking without our ever being conscious of the fact.

Debussy's literary production consists in the main of musical criticism and general articles written between 1901 and 1915; some attempts at literary composition, and his correspondence during the period 1885–1917. Interviews complete what can be described as his literary output. There he expounds his basic aesthetic convictions – those, of course, which he defended, not those which we might deduce from his music. We shall see, moreover, that between these two aesthetics there is no essential contradiction – the one serves to support the other.

We find in his writings the climate of the period, echos of the controversies which raged at the time – a combative note, even – but above all a lively way of thinking, attractive in its simplicity and, at the same time, irony. In an article in *La Revue Blanche* of July 1901, the first of the posthumous critical essays which constitute *Monsieur Croche*, Debussy outlined in a few strokes the silhouette of his imaginary interlocutor, so full of sly humour, and recalling perhaps at times Anatole France or perhaps, according to some, Bernard Shaw – and no doubt 'Monsieur Teste' – that one is tempted to seek beneath the mask the personality of one of his contemporaries. In reality, Monsieur Croche is not modelled on any one person. It is Debussy himself who speaks every time he thinks it opportune to make his interlocutor assume responsibility for his opinions. 'Discipline', said Monsieur Croche, 'must be sought in freedom, and not in the formulae of an outworn philosophy, fit only for the weak. Do not listen to anyone's advice, but hearken only to the wind that passes and tells the story of the world' (65).

This last phrase seems almost to advise the young not to take too seriously the advice of their elders; it expresses the spirit of revolt which Debussy had already shown a few years previously in a letter to Henri Lerolle: 'Let us cultivate only the garden of our instincts, and trample disrespectfully upon the flower-beds in which ideas are all lined up symetrically in full evening dress' (66). Debussy believed that real talent cannot accept without discussion the teaching lavished upon it, because too great a confidence in scholastic formulae leads inevitably to a weakening of the imagination – that mysterious thing which enables us to find the right expression of a feeling. It is equally dangerous, however, if going to the other extreme, we force the imagination by entering into 'assiduous and obstinate researches.' 'We have to acknowledge the fact that we are only the instruments of a destiny the fulfilment of which we cannot prevent' (67).

Many years later, in his article *Du goût*, Debussy was to develop these ideas which had haunted his youth. 'There have been, and they still exist, despite the disorders which civilisation brings in its train, charming little peoples who learned music as simply as one learns to breathe. Their Conservatoire is the eternal rhythm of the sea, the wind in the leaves, the thousand little noises which they listen to carefully, without ever consulting arbitrary treatises. Their traditions only exist in very old songs and dances to which each one of them, throughout the centuries, brought his respectful contribution. Nevertheless, Javanese music is characterized by an art of counterpoint compared to which that of a Palestrina is mere child's play. And if we listen, forgetting our European prejudices, to the charm of their percussion we are forced to admit that ours sounds like the barbarous noise of a travelling circus. The Annamite theatre is a sort of lyric drama in embryo, showing Chinese influence and based on the tetralogical formula; the only difference is that there are more·deities and less scenery . . . A tempestuous little clarinet supplies the emotion; a tam-tam organises terror . . . and that is all. No special theatre, no hidden orchestra, nothing but an instinctive craving for art and ingenious methods of satisfying it – no traces of bad taste (68). Could it be that in civilised countries it is the professionals who ruin art?'

The 'Faustian' features of our civilisation, which had reached their apogee when 'scientism' reigned supreme, also found their reflection in music – in its conventional symphonic sense – and Debussy saw these as a disturbing element destroying the balance between thought and existence, reason and nature. Hence the particular importance he attached to intuition in the process of musical creation. For what, indeed, is music? 'Music is a mysterious form of mathematics whose elements partake of the Infinite. It is responsible for the movements of water, the pattern of curves traced by the wavering breeze; nothing is more musical than a sunset. For anyone capable of seeing it emotionally, it is the finest lesson of development contained in this book, too seldom referred to by musicians – I mean the book of Nature' (69).

Years later Debussy was once again to harp on this idea: '[Music] is a free art, a spontaneous, open-air art, an art commensurate with the elements – wind, sky and sea. It is a mistake to turn it into a closed, scholastic art' (70). And yet, says Monsiur Croche, 'we make of it a speculative song. I prefer a few notes from an Egyptian shepherd's pipe; he is part of the landscape and hears the harmonies not mentioned in your treatises' (71).

'Who will ever know the secret of musical composition?' was another question Debussy asked himself; 'The sound of the sea, the curve of the horizon, the wind in the leaves, the cry of a bird – all these arouse in us a number of impressions. Then, all of a sudden without our willing it in any way, one of these recollections assumes an outward form and expresses itself in musical terms, clothed in its own harmony, which could never be improved however hard one might try. It is only in this way that a heart destined for music makes its finest discoveries ... I loathe doctrines and their impertinences. That is why I wish to write my musical dream with complete detachment from myself. I want to sing my interior landscape with the naive candour of a child. This will always shock those who prefer artifice and lies' (72).

'Music', wrote Debussy, 'is precisely the art which is nearest Nature. Despite their claim to be expert translators, painters and sculptors can only give us a fairly free and always fragmentary interpretation of the beauty of the universe. They can capture and fix only one of its aspects, only for a single instant: only musicians are able to capture all the poetry of night and day, of heaven and earth, and to re-create their atmosphere and give rhythmic form to their intense vibrations' (73). Evidently it was not a question of direct imitation, as Debussy had made clear long before 1913, but of a 'sentimental transformation of what is "invisible" in Nature. Can one convey the mystery of a forest by measuring the height of the trees? Is it not rather its un-plumbable depth which stirs the imagination?' (74). And this is how he expresses an idea which has much in common with the Symbolist aesthetic: music is not 'confined to reproducing, more or less exactly, Nature, but the mysterious correspondences which link Nature with Imagination' (75).

The young Paul Valéry expressed a very similar opinion when he said that the ideal would be an art which would unite the world in which we live with the world by which we are haunted (76). We find almost the same idea, closely resembling Baudelaire's '*correspond-ances*', expressed by Gauguin: 'If you observe the vast creations of Nature, you will see whether there are not laws for re-creating, under quite different aspects but producing always the same effect, all human emotions' (77). Nothing was more alien to Debussy than a *recherché* kind of music. Did he not often say that 'music must humbly seek to give pleasure. ... Extreme complications are contrary to art' (78). He also explains what he means by this state-ment: 'Music until now has been based on false premises. Too much attention is given to writings; the result is paper music, whereas music is meant to be heard. Too much importance is attached to how music is written – to formulae and craftmanship. Composers seek for ideas in themselves instead of looking for them outside. They combine and construct and imagine themes to express ideas; these in turn are developed and modified to fit in with other themes which represent other ideas: all this is metaphysics. The effect should be grasped spontaneously by the ear without the hearer being obliged to discover abstract ideas in the meanderings of a complicated development' (79).

'Beauty must be experienced directly by the senses' – this was another of his pronouncements – 'so that it can procure for us immediate pleasure, and either impose or insinuate itself in us with-out our having to make any effort to understand it' (80). And again: 'Music becomes "difficult" whenever it does not exist – the word difficult being here only a word-screen to conceal its poverty' (81).

'We must simplify our music', he said in an article. 'Let us try to thin it out. We want our music to be more naked. We must never allow emotion to be stifled under an accumulation of themes and super-imposed designs: how could we ever convey its flavour and its force if we are still worrying about the way it is written, and trying to subject to an impossible discipline the teeming profusion of little themes which jostle and overlap one another in order to bite the legs of the wretched "emotion" which soon seeks salvation in flight ... As a general rule, whenever in art we try to complicate a form or a feeling, it is because we don't know what we want to say' (82). The same importance which he attached to the spontaneity of the artist he accorded to the spontaneous reaction of the hearer. 'One often hears', he said, 'the remark: "I need to hear that piece several times". Nothing could be more untrue. When one listens properly to music one hears immediately what one ought to hear. The rest is only a matter of *milieu* or extraneous influences' (83).

Debussy often spoke about dramatic music, and consequently of Wagner. We must not forget that he was himself the author of one of the greatest operatic masterpieces, that he had to overcome the influence of the Master of Bayreuth, and that he would also have liked to do the same for those around him. According to Debussy, the 'symphonic' element introduced by Wagner into opera does not solve the problem of musical drama; moreover, this formula is open to contradiction. 'Music has a rhythm whose secret force directs its development; the movements of the soul also have a different one, generally more instinctive and subject to a multiplicity of events. The juxtaposition of these two rhythms engenders a perpetual conflict. All this does not happen at the same time: either the music is out of breath after pursuing a character, or else the character settles down on a note to enable the music to catch up with it. There are miraculous encounters of these two forces . . . but this is due to chance . . . The combination of symphonic form and dramatic action might well end by destroying dramatic music instead of helping it' (84).

As to the characters in Wagner's operas, Debussy has this to say: 'Remember that they never appear without being accompanied by their damned *Leitmotiv*; sometimes they even sing it. This is about as crazy as if someone in handing you his visiting card were at the same time to sing what was written on it' (75). And Wagner exaggerated this procedure to an almost caricatural degree. 'I hate the *Leitmotiv* even when, without being exaggerated, it is used with taste and discretion. Can you imagine that in a composition the same emotion can be expressed twice? Either one has never thought about it, or else it is just laziness. Do not allow yourselves to be taken in by a change of rhythm or key; this is only adding to the deception' (86). 'Wagner tends to approximate to the speaking voice; or rather he pretends to do so, while still treating the voices in a very "vocal" manner. His kind of declamation is neither the Italian recitative, nor the operatic aria. He adds words to a symphonic continuum, while at the same time subordinating the symphony to the words. But not always enough. His works only partly embody the principles which he has laid down with regard to this essential subordination. He lacks the courage to apply them. He is too precise and meticulous, leaving no room for any un-expressed implication ... And there is too much singing. There are only certain places where it is necessary to sing' (87).

'What, from our French point of view, is especially false is his conception of the theatre. Four evenings for a play! Does that seem to you admissible? And don't forget that during those four evenings you will be hearing always the same things. The characters on stage and the orchestra go on exchanging the same themes, and then you arrive at the *Twilight of the Gods* which is once again a *résumé* of everything you have been hearing. Well, I can only say once again that all this is inadmissible for those who like clarity and concision'. (88)

In musical drama everything must be subjected to bringing out the lyrical element incarnate in the human voice. It must not be drowned by the orchestra, which expresses the Dionysiac element in the cosmos, and this is just what happens in Wagner. In *Parsifal*, what Debussy admired was precisely the fact that here the music is reduced to more human proportions. 'Here we are spared the frantic portrayal of Tristan's unhealthy passion, the wild animal shrieking of Isolde, and the grandiloquent commentary on the inhumanity of Wotan' (89). And yet the pretentious aspect of this pseudo-religious mystery which was supposed to promote the moral renaissance of humanity, did not escape him. For, in fact, what moral teaching can be found in this 'art of redemption'? 'Look at Amfortas, that sad Knight of the Grail. If one has to pierce one's side with a lance one doesn't exhibit a guilty wound to the accompaniment of melancholy cantilenas throughout three whole acts.' Wagner was more successful with the character of Klingsor. But who is Klingsor? 'A former Knight of the Grail dismissed from the Holy Precincts for having too personal ideas with regard to chastity', spiteful and vindictive, 'a crafty magician', 'a hardened old veteran', he is 'the only "human" character, the only "moral" person in this Christian drama ... in which the most spurious moral and religious ideas are paraded', and where no one wants to sacrifice himself except the sentimental Kundry, 'that old rose of hell'.

The lesson of *Parsifal* – a work both ideologically reactionary and dramatically a failure, although containing several pages of fine music – enabled Debussy to draw a sarcastic comparison: 'Wagner's work provides us with a rather striking image: Bach as the Holy Grail, with Wagner as Klingsor, trying to destroy the Grail and take its place ... Bach reigns supreme over the music, and in the kindness of his heart has wanted us to hear the as yet unknown words of the great lesson he has taught us inculcating a disinterested love of music. Wagner is fading out, a murky and disquieting shadow' (90). These words were written in 1903 at a time when the glory of the great Bayreuth reformer was at its height, and there was nothing to suggest his decline. From this moment Debussy was fully aware that in order to make up for what Wagner had done to retard the development of music it was necessary to destroy his myth which was clouding the minds of artists. Hence his invectives against *Tristan*.

His 'heroic showmanship' and his 'grandiloquent hysteria' were Wagner's undoing, together with 'that German mania for continually hammering on the same intellectual nail for fear of not being understood.' Debussy predicted that Wagner's works would not stand the test of time. 'All the same, some fine ruins will survive in the shade of which our grandchildren will be able to dream of the past greatness of this man who, if he had only been a little bit more human could have been really great.' Wagner had led his followers into a cul-de-sac: 'Wagner has never served the cause of music; nor even that of Germany. And when in a moment of crazy conceit he proclaimed: "And now you have an art", he might just as well have declared "And now I leave you with Nothing; it's up to you to get out of it" ' (91). 'Wagner', concluded Debussy, 'if we may express it in suitably grandiloquent terms, was a fine sunset which might have been mistaken for the dawn' (92).

He had a disastrous influence on French music: 'We must admit that nothing was more melancholy than that neo-Wagnerian school in which the French genius was swamped by the forgeries of a "Wotan" in jack-boots and a "Tristan" in a velvet jacket' (93). 'Generally speaking', observes Debussy, 'music in our time tends more and more to serve as an accompaniment to sentimental or tragic anecdotes, and assumes the somewhat shady role of a "busker" at a fair where the sinister "Mr Nobody" tries to attract attention' (94).

He also criticises Italian *verismo* severely: Verdi alone is spared, despite the encouragement given to this trend by the aesthetic of *Traviata*. 'We go from romance to romance, on a journey where, instead of genuine passion, one finds only light distraction. No attempt is made to strike a deeper note. It's all a façade and, despite the sadness of certain scenes, the sun is always shining. The aesthetics of this art are certainly false, because life cannot be mirrored in songs; yet Verdi has a heroic way of falsifying life which is perhaps finer than the realism aimed at by the young Italian school' (95). 'As to the operas of Leoncavallo and Mascagni, they are a kind of realistic cinema in which the characters fall about on one other, snatching the melodies from each other's mouths, and where in one act the whole of life is represented: birth, marriage and assassination all included. This calls for a minimum of music since, quite logically, one has no time to listen to it' (96). It was for these reasons that Debussy called upon the younger generation of musicians not to allow themselves to be seduced by *verismo*. 'So many efforts to extricate music from the rut of falsehood and restore it to its pristine beauty must not be allowed to moulder in the factory of falsehood known as *verismo*' (97).

Neither 'Wagnerism' nor even less, *verismo* could satisfy the composer of *Pelléas et Mélisande*, whose aesthetic basis certainly owed much to the Symbolists, but at the same time, unlike theirs, was directed above all against Wagner. Recalling the decisive turning-point in his artistic evolution Debussy wrote: 'After a few years of passionate pilgrimages to Bayreuth, I began to have misgivings about the Wagnerian formula; or, rather, it seemed to me that this could only be useful in the particular case of Wagner's genius. It was therefore necessary to seek music that would be *after* Wagner, and not *derived* from Wagner' (98). What he especially disliked about the German composer was the transparency of his symbolism. Shorn of all ambiguity, the Wagnerian symbols (*Leitmotifs*) were, for Debussy, merely a translation of verbal phrases, a cheap intellectual distraction for a listener easy to please. Not calling for any effort of the imagination, they gave the listener no opportunity of enjoying the true value of a genuine aesthetic experience; for 'to pretend that a certain succession of chords can represent a particular sentiment, or a certain phrase a particular character is a strange form of anthropometric fantasy' (99).

What, then, was Claude Debussy's ideal of what music for the theatre should be? He described it, at a very early age already, in 1889, to Ernest Guiraud; and it is interesting to note the close affinity between his ideal and the aesthetic theories of Mallarmé: 'I have no desire to imitate what I admire in Wagner. My conception of music-drama is quite different: music takes over where words fail; music is made for the inexpressible; what I would wish is that it should seem to emerge from the shadows and retire again from

time to time, and that its role should always be a discreet one . . .
Nothing should hinder the continuity of the drama: any musical
development, however brief, is incapable of synchronising with the
movement of speech. 'What kind of poet would be capable of writing
an operatic libretto that would satisfy these demands? 'He who, by
leaving certain things unsaid would allow me to graft my dream on
his; he who would create characters who belong to no time or place,
and would not force me to compose a big scene 'for effect', but
would leave me free, at certain times, to allow my art to take
precedence over his and to complete what he had begun . . . I dream
of poems which would not oblige me to write long and boring acts,
but which would supply me with mobile scenes, of different times
and places, in which the characters would not discuss, but accept
what life and destiny hold for them' (100). These words already
foreshadow *Pelléas*.

In order to free French musicians from their infatuation with
Wagner, Debussy reminded them of their own glorious predecessors, and did not shrink from striking a patriotic note: 'To believe
that the qualities which distinguish one race can be transferred to
another without suffering deterioration is an error which has often
done harm to our music because we are apt to follow blindly
fashions with which the French genius has nothing in common.
It would be wiser to compare them with our own; to see what
qualities we are lacking in, and try to recover them without in any
way changing the rhythm of our own way of thinking. In this way
we could enrich our own patrimony' (101).

'As regards myself', he said, 'I have given free rein to my nature
and temperament to express themselves. I have above all sought to
become French again. The French too easily forget those qualities
of clarity and elegance for which they are renowned and allow
themselves to be influenced by Teutonic heaviness and long-
windedness, (102). And yet, he added, 'we had in Rameau a pure
French tradition of a delicate and charming tenderness, marked by
precise accents and strict declamation in recitatives, without that
Germanic striving for profundity . . . It is all the same to be regretted
that French music has for too long followed paths which disastrously
caused it to abandon that clarity of expression and formal precision
which were the distinctive and significant qualities peculiar to the
French genius' (103). 'Today we hardly dare to be clear-headed for
fear of being thought lacking in grandeur' (104).

As for Couperin, 'the most poetic of all our harpsichordists, whose tender melancholy seems to echo adorably the mysterious backgrounds of those landscapes of Watteau with their sad inhabitants', we owe it to him to study the example set by some of his little pieces for harpsichord: 'They are adorable models of a graceful and natural form of expression which is unknown to us today. Couperin and Rameau – these are really French . . . French music is marked by clarity, elegance and a simple and natural form of declamation; French music desires, above all, to give pleasure . . . The French musical genius is a kind of combination of fantasy and sensibility' (105).

Clearly Debussy was not interested in imitating ancient models, nor in returning to the music of the past. What was important for him was to liberate the art from the Germanic hegemony and direct it along new paths. That this was possible is proved convincingly by his own works; but he felt it was necessary to recapitulate his own experiments and to define clearly the significance of his aesthetic principles.

It was at one of Pierre Louÿs's 'Wednesdays' (at about the time when, having finished L'après-midi d'un faune he was working at the first version of Pelléas – i.e. six or seven years before he had begun to write for the newspapers) that, exasperated by the Wagner enthusiasts, of whom there were many among Louÿs's friends, Debussy gave expression to one of his most interesting theories, in the following terms: 'Already in Beethoven the art of development consists of incessant repetitions of identical phrases. And Wagner has exaggerated this procedure almost to the point of caricature. . . . I would like to see, and I will succeed myself in producing, music which is entirely free from "motifs", or rather consisting of one continuous "motif" which nothing interrupts and which never turns back on itself. Then we shall have a logical development, concise and deductive; there will be no hasty and superfluous "padding" between two repetitions of the same "motif" which will be a characteristic and essential part of the work. The development will no longer be a purely material amplification, a rhetorical exercise performed by a well-taught professional, but will have a wider and, indeed, psychic significance' (106).

Several years later he was to revert to this subject: 'I am more and more convinced that music is not, in its essence, something that can be poured into a rigorous and traditional mould. It is made up of colours and rhythm . . . Bach alone has realised this truth' (107). Elsewhere, in speaking of the chorus which was to play an important part in his projected opera-comique *Le Diable dans le beffroi*, he expressed the following wish: 'What I would like to realise is something more divided, detached and impalpable – inorganic in appearance, and yet fundamentally organised; a real human crowd in which each voice is free, and where all the voices together nevertheless create an impression of a real, living ensemble' (108).

It is clear from the preceding quotations that Debussy envisaged a new organisation of sound-space. But in what direction? There seem to be undeniable links with the Bergsonian theory of duration. But there is something more: the last quotation reminds us of the aleatoric technique as shown, for example, in the way the chorus is handled in Lutoslawski's setting of *Trois poèmes d' Henri Michaux*. On the other hand, what Debussy often said about a 'musical arabesque' throws some light on this problem.

With reference to Bach's G major *Brandenburg Concerto*, he wrote: 'We find here almost intact this "musical arabesque" . . . The primitives – Palestrina, Vittoria, Orlando di Lasso etc. all made use of this divine "arabesque". They discovered its principle in Gregorian plainsong, and fortified its frail traceries with a solid counterpoint. Bach, adopting the arabesque, made it more fluid and more supple and, in spite of the severe discipline to which this great master subjected Beauty, enabled it to move with that constantly renewed and free fantasy which still astonishes us today. In the music of Bach, it is not the character of his melody that moves us, but its 'line'; more often than not it is the parallel movement of several lines whose meeting, sometimes fortuitous, sometimes unanimous, arouses our emotions' (109). A year and a half later, returning to the example of Bach, he wrote: 'Old Bach, in whom all music is contained, make no mistake about it, despised harmonic rules. He preferred the free interplay of sounds, whose curves, whether parallel or in contrary motion, prepared the way for that unexpected flowering which enriches with imperishable beauty the slightest page in his innumerable works. This was the time when the "adorable arabesque" reigned supreme, and music conformed in this way to the laws of beauty inherent in the whole cycle of Nature' (110).

What is generally understood by the term 'arabesque' is that capricious and sinuous line which had its origin in the motifs of stylised plants in Greek, Byzantine, Arabic and Persian ornamental art. But for Baudelaire already 'the arabesque line is the most spiritual of all' (111). It seems that it was viewed in the same light by the second generation of the English Pre-Raphaelites (William Morris, Walter Crane, and Edward Burne-Jones); the latter, with Aubrey Beardsley, the famous illustrator, had largely contributed to making it popular, being influenced in this sense to some extent by certain paintings by Van Gogh and Seurat, and also by Gauguin's woodcuts, certain gouaches by Gustave Moreau, lithographs by Odilon Redon, drawings by Toulouse-Lautrec, Japanese art, paintings by the 'Nabis' and finally the work of Edvard Munch. It is especially prominent in the graphic and decorative arts of the *fin de siècle*; the arabesque thus became an essential feature of the '1900 style' in which the epoch tried to express its universalist and spiritualist aspirations. Influenced by the tendencies of this period, Oswald Spengler even endowed the arabesque with magic properties: ' It is as anti-plastic as it is possible to be, equally hostile both to reality and its representation – essentially a magical motif. Being itself noncorporeal, it de-corporealises the object which it enriches to an infinite degree' (112). In the morphology of Spengler's culture the arabesque belongs to the same species of means by which the artist's dream is freed from the weight of matter (its material) as Wagner's *unendliche Melodie* – or, at any rate, it stems from the same source: the nostalgia for an extra-terrestrial world, the desire of the soul which yearns to be one with infinity.

And yet, if we abandon this interpretation, which rightly or wrongly sees a metaphysical motive in the mere fact of employing an arabesque (whether in painting or *per analogiam* in music) and return to those sayings of Debussy which we have just quoted, we are obliged to admit that there is nothing to show that the composer of *Pelléas* was at all interested in metaphysics. What Debussy found so charming in the arabesque was primarily its abstract character, and especially its lack of definite symbolic values. What delighted him was the fact that its attraction lies uniquely in its pure beauty, non-individualised and free from any psychic element. 'Through this conception of the role of ornamentation', explained Debussy, (though he added that what he meant by 'ornament' had nothing to do with the meaning that musical theory ascribes to the word) 'music acquires an unfailing, almost mechanical means of impressing the public . . . This does not mean that we have here something unnatural or artificial. It is, on the contrary, infinitely

more 'real' than the poor little human cries which opera tries to
imitate. Above all, music (through this conception) retains all her
nobility, and never condescends to satisfy that craving for sentimentality exhibited by people who are said to be "so fond of music";
in a loftier vein she forces them to respect and even to adore her . . .
I should add that this ornamental conception has now completely
disappeared' (113).

It is noteworthy that the 'Nabis' – or, more particularly, Maurice
Denis, were of the same opinion which, incidentally, was certainly
not shared by the Romantics, but nevertheless had much in common
with the ideas of Eduard Hanslick. In his insipid paintings Maurice
Denis had got no further than a vaguely classical traditionalism;
but in his writings had expressed ideas which already foreshadowed
the modern approach. None of his contemporaries had so clearly
distinguished between 'mystical and allegorical tendencies – that
is to say seeking expression in terms of the subject matter – and the
aims of the Symbolists who sought expression through the work of
art in itself. Here it is the form itself which is expressive, while the
Romantics proceeded by imitating nature. Art is above all a means
of expression, a creation, a creation of the mind in which nature
plays a secondary part'. We should not forget, he said, that a
picture is 'essentially a flat surface covered with colours assembled
in a certain order'. He completed this definition of a picture, which
was celebrated at that time, by adding that traditional perspective
ought to be replaced by a new conception of space where nothing
would prevent the eye from following the pattern of arabesques;
in this way painting would acquire that 'ornamental' character that
Albert Aurier was already demanding, and which was practised by
the Pont-Aven school, led by Gauguin.

This clearly meant opening the door to non-figurative painting
(as Bernard Dorival, from whom we have borrowed the quotations
from Maurice Denis had pointed out (114)) to which, after Gauguin,
Fauvism and Cubism would ultimately lead. But what interests us
here is the way in which these ideas coincide with what Debussy was
proclaiming when speaking of music. For him, too, as for Gauguin,
Mallarmé or Denis, the important thing was to give prominence to
the way in which a work of art expresses the personality of the artist,
the essence of reality, or the spirit of the times; indeed, Debussy
understood better than any of his contemporaries (before Stravinsky) that the traditional forms of expression, hackneyed and worn

out, were not capable of capturing the diversity of a world transformed, and had ceased to be a factor that would stimulate the
hearer's imagination to make any creative effort.

We shall revert to the arabesque, in its strictly musical conno-
tation, in the chapter devoted to Debussy's new ideas in the realm
of sound. We shall then understand better the significance accorded
to this concept by the composer. And yet it would be difficult not
to express at this point our astonishment that musicologists between
the two World Wars, when seeking the key to Debussy's work,
only noticed its complication (having only studied it from the
harmonic point of view), without discovering that this artist, while
rejecting ostentatiously the affectations of the Romantic school, was
in fact formulating, knowingly and systematically – his aesthetic
views confirm this – new methods of determining the structure of a
musical work, free from any *a priori* notions, which would deliver
music from the burden of traditional symbols. Debussy's arabesque
is rarely the product of a subjective lyricism, as was the case with
the Romantics; it is more often the product of massed sonorities,
moving horizontally, a polarising centre of movements making it
possible to grasp in a flash the meaning of the transformations
taking place; music of this kind unveils the subconscious substances
of which one dreams in the form of symbols, but does not imagine
in terms of concepts. 'Previous researches I had made in pure music
had aroused in me a hatred of the classical "development" whose
beauty is purely technical and can be of interest only to mandarins.
I wanted music to enjoy that liberty which she possesses perhaps to
a greater degree than any other art, not being confined to a more or
less exact reproduction of nature, but having access to the mysterious
correspondences of Nature and the imagination' (115).

Debussy kept an open eye on the changes which occurred in the
culture of his time. He did not accept everything that resulted
from developments in the arts. The spirit of the new age excited his
creative imagination, but on the other hand, its brutality alarmed
him. His attitude towards *The Rite of Spring* was one of admiration
mingled with fear. In any case, he understood perfectly that every
epoch has its own forms of art, and that it is obvious that – as he
said himself – 'the age of aeroplanes has a right to its own music'
(116). He also foresaw that as it became more widely diffused the
democratisation of culture would create, for its own ends, new
forms of art and that it would perhaps resuscitate old forms by

filling them with a new content. As if he foresaw the renascence of the oratorio and of ancient themes in music for the stage (Milhaud, Honegger) he wrote: 'Is it not in Euripides, Sophocles and Aeschylus that one finds those great movements of humanity, simple in outline but in their essence so tragic that they can be equally well understood by the least discriminate as well as by the least sophisticated souls?' (117).

His visionary foresight was well in advance of his times on that Sunday when Debussy listened to a band playing at an open-air concert in a park: 'I foresee the possibility of music written specially to be performed in the open air, constructed on broad lines, vocally and instrumentally audacious, floating freely in the air and soaring gaily over the tops of the trees. Certain harmonic progressions that might seem abnormal in the concert hall would certainly be appreciated at their real value in the open air. There would be a mysterious collaboration between the air, the fluttering of the leaves and the scent of the flowers and the music itself; the latter would unite all these elements in such perfect harmony that it would appear to be a part of each one of them . . . Finally, one would be able to verify once and for all whether music and poetry are the only arts which move in space . . . I may be mistaken, but it seems to me that there is enough in this idea for future generations to dream about' (118).

The realisation of this 'spatial music', outside the traditional concert-hall – an idea which we find already put in practice by the Venetians (their polychoral works), Mozart (*Serenata Notturna*, K.239), Berlioz and, more recently, Karlheinz Stockhausen (119) – Debussy left to his successors; he was aware that the time was not yet ripe for his idea to be taken seriously. He himself was content to practice that 'alchemy of sound' he often mentioned in his letters, knowing that, sooner or later, what he had achieved would be appreciated by creative spirits, and would revolutionise composers' ways of thinking. He was right when he said: 'I am working at things which will only be understood by our grandchildren in the twentieth century' (120). And indeed it is only the generation of Pierre Boulez which will benefit from the results of his 'alchemy'.

We have already observed that Debussy was in general hostile to the musical analysts. When René Lenormand presented him with his book on modern harmony (121) in which he often referred to examples taken from his works, Debussy did not hesitate to say to him: 'Think of the inexpert hands into which your study may fall, the only result of which will be to destroy those fine butterflies which have already suffered from being analysed' (122). He also used more serious arguments to convince his readers that his animosity in this connection was well-founded: 'When the god Pan assembled the seven pipes of his syrinx, at first he imitated only the long-drawn-out and melancholy note of the toad voicing his sorrows in the light of the moon. Later he turned to bird-song. It is probably from that moment that the birds enriched their repertory. These are her sacred origins of which music can well be proud and which enable her to maintain an element of mystery... In the name of all the gods let us try neither to deprive her of them, nor to seek to explain them' (123).

In seeking thus to preserve the mystery of music, was Debussy acting in the interests of the listener, or did he merely wish to preserve intact for the latter the charm of the surprise one experiences in plunging into the unknown? I do not think so. His experience of life had taught him that knowledge destroys an object which arouses our curiosity, deprives it of that special value it has for us, and turns it into something that detaches itself from, and becomes biologically foreign to us. But this does not apply to works of art. It would seem that Debussy sometimes forgot that intelligence alone is not enough, and that a work of art must be felt as well as understood. The force with which it acts on the imagination and awakes emotions is due to the fact that it is at the same time a particle of matter that can be apprehended, and an indescribable act of the human conscience, creating, thanks to this element of matter, a reality which, without this act of conscience, would not exist. Thus, a work of art is not only something that can be known, but also has an existential aspect.

Art, almost by definition, must conceal secrets which our intelligence cannot grasp. Otherwise there would be no difference between art and science – for which, according to Marcelin Berthelot (1900) the world holds no mystery. Alain attached the highest value to those works of Balzac which, while stimulating the reader's imagination, keep their secret for a very long time. Symbolical, ambiguous, unattainable, the great and the smaller masterpieces of Debussy were less likely than the novels of Balzac to lose their force after being subjected to a critical analysis; and yet neither time nor the hundreds of studies devoted to them have succeeded in detaching La Comédie humaine from the living body of culture.

THE MUSIC OF DEBUSSY:

Vocal works of the first period

THE vocal works of this period comprise some sixty songs – that is to say, more than two thirds of Debussy's total output in this field. Being for the most part unpublished or disseminated in private collections, they still await study. Georges Servières was the first to take an interest in them; after him Charles Koechlin collected quite a lot of material; and finally Léon Vallas and other biographers have attempted to describe them; but in fact no one up to now has undertaken a serious analysis of this very important and significant part of Debussy's *oeuvre*. It is true that in one of her first studies devoted to the great composer, Stefania Lobaczewska (1) examines in detail the harmony of certain unpublished songs, from the 'impressionist' point of view, while considering, in accordance with the generally accepted theory at that time (1929), Symbolism to be one of the manifestations of Impressionism; however, after analysing the music without reference to the poetical text, she rightly observes that nearly all Debussy's harmonic innovations appear for the first time in his vocal works composed for the most part on texts by French Symbolist poets – only to draw from this fact the paradoxical conclusion that this confirms Debussy's connection with the Impressionist movement.

We have tried to pay more attention than hitherto to Debussy's unpublished songs, but our studies have still not exhausted the subject; moreover, we have only undertaken this task in order to show the links which connected Debussy with Symbolism almost from the beginning of his artistic activities. These affinities are visible not only in his choice of poems, but also in the unusual way in which the texts are treated and in the purely musical invention which is superimposed on the canvas of the words thus enabling the composer to escape from the confines of purely functional music, with its worn-out symbolism, and opening up new perspectives for the music of the future. We may add that the evolution of Debussy's vocal output during this first period – something that no one seems to have noticed until now – appears to reflect precisely that of the Symbolist movement itself, from its birth on the slopes of Parnassus until its fulfilment in the unfinished works and the *Divagations* of Mallarmé, the plays of Maeterlinck, and the paintings of Redon, Gauguin, and Monet in his last period. Between 1876 and 1884 Debussy's imagination was exclusively under the influence of the Parnassians Théodore de Banville and Leconte de Lisle and their imitator Paul Bourget. Having a superficial acquaintance with the works of Verlaine and Mallarmé at the end of this period of his life, he became their ardent admirer during the years 1885–91, with a short interruption when he came under the spell of Baudelaire. Then followed Debussy's own poetic experiments and his absorption with Maeterlinck, Pierre Louÿs and Mallarmé, and finally his own maturity, which brought with it the consciousness of his own creative powers, open to all the voices of the universe.

In 1911 Debussy published a document which throws a significant light on the attitude of the composer to poetry: 'Musicians who understand nothing about poetry ought not to set it to music . . . Schumann never understood Heine – at least, that is my impression. One can speak of his genius, but he was incapable of understanding all Heinrich Heine's subtle irony. Take, for example, the *Dichterliebe* – here he has missed a lot . . . Henri de Régnier, who writes good classical poetry, cannot be set to music. And can one imagine music to the poetry of Racine or Corneille? Real poetry has its own rhythms. It is very difficult to follow closely or to "impose" rhythms, while maintaining the inspiration. Classical verse has a life of its own, an "internal dynamism" . . . Rhythmic prose is easier to set – one has more freedom in every direction. The musician ought to make his own rhythmic prose. Why not? What is to prevent him? Wagner did this; but Wagner's poems are like his music – not a good example to follow. His libretti are no better than any others. He thought they were better – and that is what matters. Let us leave the great poets alone' (2).

We have given this long quotation because, in our opinion, it sums up the youthful experience of the composer who, for several years, had been living in such close contact with poetry. Do the above quotations prove that Debussy later on was inclined to doubt the service which poetry was able to render to music? I believe rather that they bear witness to his faith in the all-powerfulness of music. He had drunk deeply from all the springs of contemporary poetry, but in the end had detached himself from such sources and found a sublimated form in music alone.

The first poet the young composer had loved was Théodore de Banville, no doubt because, of all the 'Parnassians', it was he who mingled melancholy and irony with the greatest subtlety, and who paid particular attention to the 'music' of his finely chiselled verses; hence, later on, his success with the Symbolists. The opinion he expressed in his *Traité de versification* might well be applied to the aesthetic of the Symbolists: 'Poetry is at one and the same time music, sculpture, painting and eloquence; it should charm the ear, enchant the mind, represent sounds, imitate colours, make objects visible and arouse in us the movements the poet wishes to inspire' (3).

The songs he wrote to words by Banville, about ten in number, are among Debussy's earliest compositions. Of those which have survived two especially merit attention: in the first, published in 1882, *Nuit d'étoiles* (the date 1876, added later by the composer himself, does not appear to be established) the first five chords of the accompaniment clearly foreshadow the theme of Mélisande. And since this is closely related to the main theme of *La Damoiselle élue* (1888) as well as to the opening of *De fleurs* in the *Proses lyriques* (1892–3), and since, in addition, the melodic design accompanying the words 'La sereine mélancholie . . .' are repeated later by Mélisande at the beginning of the third scene of the first act to the words: 'il fait sombre dans le jardin' (p. 47 in the score), it seems fair to state that the germ of Debussy's melodic style is to be found in *Nuit d'étoiles*.

The second of the Banville settings, *Pierrot*, (about 1882) already foreshadows that subtle humour which finds such brilliant expression in *Fantoches*, *Children's Corner* or *La Boîte à joujoux*. The first bars of *Au clair de la lune* serve as an accompaniment to the semi-humorous anecdote of the young man who, on leaving the theatre where he had been playing Harlequin, is walking along the boulevards, immersed in thought and indifferent to the advances of a street-walking Columbine; his virtuous disdain arouses the curiosity of 'la blanche lune aux cornes de taureau' who in the end recognises him, not as the romantic Gaspard de la Nuit, but a simple office boy, Jean Gaspard de Bureau. The subtlety of the harmonisation (with already parallel sevenths and an ingenious transformation of the theme of the accompaniment at the end) heralds the composer of *Colloque sentimental*.

The juvenile imagination of Debussy ventures into the regions of Mount Parnassus, cold and classical, but not devoid of charm; he finds inspiration in texts by Leconte de Lisle: *La fille aux cheveux de lin* (*c.* 1880) whose vernal grace will appear again, but in an entirely different form in the well-known piano *Prélude* bearing the same title (Book I. No. 8); in *Jane* (1882), the sweetness of whose melody (according to those who were able to hear it sung by Claire Croiza in 1938, since the manuscript has since disappeared) will recur again in *Green*, one of the six *Ariettes oubliées*.

More than by Spanish folk-lore, of which he became aware only in 1907, thanks to Felipe Pedrell's collection of popular songs, the young Debussy was attracted by the subtle irony with which Alfred de Musset portrayed both the people and the landscape in his *Contes d'Espagne et d'Italie*. It was this work that inspired him to write the music for the little satirical sketch *Madrid, Princesse des Espagnes*. Unfortunately the manuscript has been acquired by a private collector as well as the music for another piece by de Musset, *Ballade à la lune* which, it would appear, is more reminiscent of Gounod than of Lalo who had attempted to set the same poem to music. It was not until his *Sérénade interrompue* that Debussy succeeded in combining, like de Musset, the irony and 'Iberian' fascination in his music. At that time he could not do more than create a 'Spanish atmosphere' in the conventional romantic vein.

He succeeded in striking a more authentic Spanish note in the duet, to words by Théophile Gautier, *Chanson espagnole* (1882) thanks above all, it is true, to the rhythm of the Bolero, whose melodic design we shall meet with again twenty-five years later, and almost unaltered, in the second of the three *Chansons de Charles d'Orléans* for unaccompanied chorus (*Quand j'ay ouy le tabourin sonner*). What is particularly striking in this 'duo de voix identiques' is not so much the tessitura of the first voice, beyond the range of the normal soprano (as Charles Koechlin has pointed out), nor the succession of fifths in the accompaniment imitating the guitar – we find the same thing in *Mandoline* written about the same time – as the injunction imposed upon the singers to sing their highest notes *pianissimo* – a recommendation typical of Debussy, always anxious to play down any manifestation of romantic exaltation.

We come now to the ten settings of words by Paul Bourget, written under different conditions and for various reasons. Their artistic value is unequal. Only those whose attitude towards great creative artists is somewhat naive will be surprised to see these songs included among the works of a composer of such refined literary tastes. The quality of the text, however distinguished, is no guarantee of the quality of the music; and, inversely, many famous musical works have been based on mediocre texts. But apart from the friendship that in his last years at the Conservatoire linked Debussy with Paul Bourget, who was already a well-known poet and writer, it must not be forgotten that the kind of lyrical feeling that the author of *Le Disciple* cultivated in his youthful poems was typical of the sentimental atmosphere in vogue at that time, and that Debussy, tormented by his own sometimes unfortunate love affairs, was bound to be affected by it. Nearly all the poems of Bourget that Debussy set to music are concerned with the melancholy recollection of happier times. Most of them are only of minor importance, and would doubtless have disappeared had not the composer, normally so highly self-critical, not been obliged for financial reasons to agree to their publication. In any event, it is impossible to pass them over in silence, if only because some of these songs still appear in concert programmes.

Already in the first of them, *Beau soir* (about 1876) under a melodic line suggestive of Massenet, there are features which foreshadow *Pelléas*. The melodic line follows the text very closely, and its charm has none of the sentimentality in which the composer of *Manon* excelled; while, as regards the harmony, the budding composer shows himself to be far more audacious than his master. In the very first bars two different tonalities are heard side by side, and a chord of the ninth makes its appearance in bar 32 at the words: 'Car nous nous en allons'. The critics must have found it very difficult to analyse, in accordance with the established principles of functional harmony, the accompaniment to this song, composed ninety years ago.

The romance *Voici que le printemps,* composed between 1880–3, is in no way especially remarkable except for the succession of parallel chords which accompany the words 'et sur leurs petits pieds'. One may disagree with Léon Vallas who discerned in *Paysage sentimental,* dating from the same period, the influence of Borodine (4), or with Heinrich Strobel who thought it was modelled on Balakirev (5): it is nevertheless true that before becoming an original artist Debussy had undergone all sorts of influences: that of Russian music and the music of the Far-East; Wagner, etc. But what is extraordinary in his case, in his earliest as well as his latest works, is his acute sensitivity to the *sound* of words and to their connection with music. And even if pieces such as *Silence ineffable* (1883) or *Regret* (1884), which 'prolongs the hours in which he was loved', or again *La Romance d'Ariel* (1884) which attempts to evoke 'the music of the voice of Miranda "vibrating in his heart"', are negligible in comparison with Debussy's major works, they would nevertheless ensure a measure of fame for a minor composer. Take, for example, bars 1 – 6 of *Les Cloches* (1891): and notice the delicate and refined construction of this melody which, from the first bars to the last, is marked *piano* throughout as if the composer was afraid of disturbing by a louder tone or by a higher sound the memory of those *années de bonheur* evoked by the sound of distant bells.

There is a comparison to be made between Hugo Wolf and Debussy: on the one hand a discreet illustration which does not impose on the imagination any precise association of extra-musical ideas, since even the bells do not imitate 'real' bells but preserve the timbre of the piano; and on the other the heavy accompaniment, so characteristic of the 'symphonic' style of Hugo Wolf's *Lieder* (to mention only *Auf einer Wanderung* or *Im Frühling,* both dating from 1888 and composed on texts by E. Mörike; or, again, the *Spanische*

Liederbuch on poems by Heine and Geibl (1891) – and, above all, *Auf dem grünen Balkon* where, in order to increase the expressive force of the poem Wolf allots to the piano the whole weight of the action). In the vocal writing of even his earliest songs an abyss separates Debussy from the aesthetic concepts of a romanticism which had had its day.

Among the songs composed on less well-known texts, there are three which deserve special mention. They all date from roughly the same period (about 1890) and were published during Debussy's life in different years. *La Belle au bois dormant,* to words by Vincent Hyspa, which Vallas looked upon as a French counterpart of Borodin's *Blanche-Neige,* is almost a music-hall song on the popular tune of *Nous n'irons plus au bois* which Debussy was to make use of later in two works: *Jardins sous la pluie* and *Rondes de printemps*; *Les Angélus,* to words by G. Le Roy, is noteworthy for its skilful transposition of the sound of bells; and finally *Dans le jardin* on a text by Paul Gravelet, breathes an atmosphere of serenity in which everything seems softened and toned-down – an atmosphere created by the very simple expedient of a succession of chords of the seventh, with a pentatonic towards the end. In his vocal music Debussy achieved some very interesting results, perhaps the most remarkable in his entire *oeuvre,* when he had to cope with the poetry of Baudelaire, Verlaine or Mallarmé. It was to their texts that he turned most readily, perhaps because they offered no obstacles to his imagination and left him free to complete with his music the sense of the words which was never explicitly revealed. Was it not Debussy who said: 'Music can express what words are incapable of conveying'.

The extraordinary musicality of the poetry of a Verlaine or a Mallarmé stimulated his imagination prodigiously. How was it possible to set such poetry to music? What could one add to a *Chanson d'automne* where everything is music, and what reason could there be for trying to do so?

> Les sanglots longs
> Des violons
>   De l'automne
> Blessent mon coeur
> D'une langueur
>   Monotone.

Mallarmé's poems posed another kind of problem; in addition to their 'harmony', it was necessary not only to transpose their syntax and 'baroque' vocabulary in which the moment of 'making sense' is postponed almost to infinity, but also to exercise considerable ingenuity in order not to lose any of their 'music' or grammatical structure. Debussy was bold enough to tackle several of Mallarmé's poems, but only those which departed the least from traditional forms such as *Apparition, Placet futile, Soupir, Eventail de Mademoiselle Mallarmé*; it would seem that he was afraid of not being able to penetrate deeply enough the poet's most 'advanced' texts (*La vierge et le bel aujourd'hui, Surgi de la croupe et du bond, Une dentelle s'abolit*) (6), or of not being able to interpret them with sufficient clarity to enable his musical commentary to be on a par with their profundity. And yet even these less ambitious poems had a powerful influence on Debussy's imagination: each of them stimulated his passion for exploration and seemed to provide him with a new musical language, a new syntax or a new style. Examples of this influence can be seen in *Apparition* (1884), in *L'Après-midi d'un faune* (which, after several different projects had been abandoned, finally became, in 1894, the purely orchestral *Prélude*), and again in the *Trois poèmes de Mallarmé* (1913).

It is the first of these attempts that interests us at this juncture. The young composer (he was then twenty-two) may well have been attracted, in *Apparition*, by the atmosphere of the first quatrain, with its Pre-Raphaelite affinities:

> La lune s'attristait. Des séraphins en pleurs
> Rêvant, l'archet aux doigts, dans le calme des fleurs
> Vaporeuses, tiraient de mourantes violes
> De blancs sanglots glissant sur l'azur des corolles.

But as he listened to the poem read out loud, he must have had some doubts: was it possible to compose music which would match that of these verses, or, at least, would not introduce a dissonant note? He had to submit himself to the words and seek a musical equivalent, forgetting what he may have learnt at the Conservatoire, and obeying only his own intuition. Thus we shall find in this youthful song the contrast between an extended compass (nearly two octaves) of the human voice and a very limited one, resembling a recitative, as in the following example (7):

as well as an unusual system of chord construction: the functional relations being completely suspended, either as the result of the super-imposition of semitones or seconds over ordinary tonal relationships, or of unexpected and highly expressive modulations; or, again, owing to the introduction of non-functional chords, as in bars 4–8 of Ex. 3 where chords of F major, D minor, B flat major, connected only by notes common to each and the uniform rhythmic design of the upper note of the accompaniment, completely hides the overall tonality of E major. (*See Example overleaf.*)

That the experience acquired through confrontations of this nature with poetic material of the highest quality left its imprint on Debussy's mind, gave him an experience he was never to forget is apparent from a certain similarity between *Apparition* and *Le Balcon* (*Poèmes de Baudelaire*), which was written later, and also from the fact that the melodic phrase accompanying the words: '*dans le calme des fleurs vaporeuses*' was to be repeated, as well as its accompaniment, ten years later by Debussy (as Oswald de l'Estrade-Guerra has pointed out (8)) in the scene by the fountain in Act II of *Pelléas* where it accompanies the timid invitation addressed by Pelléas to Mélisande: 'Voulez-vous vous asseoir au bord du bassin de marbre?'

Debussy accepted, in principle, the absolute submission of music to a text, but only when the poem allowed free scope to his own

imagination. We shall find proof of this in a letter he wrote to
E. Vasnier in June 1885 from the Villa Medici in Rome, barely a year
and a half after he had written the music for *Apparition*. This also
shows that his attitude towards poetic texts, defined in 1911, had
been determined long before: 'I do not think I could ever entrust
my music to too correct a mould ... I am not speaking about
musical form, but merely from a literary point of view. I shall
always prefer a text in which, as it were, the action will be sub-
ordinated to a full and complete exposition of the emotions of the
inner self. It seems to me that, in this way, music can become more
human, in closer touch with life, and that we can thus enlarge and
refine our means of expression' (9).

At the time when these lines were written he was already the author of several songs to words by Verlaine which had convinced him that he had done well in choosing a poet who was neither as 'classical' as the Parnassians, nor possessed to the same degree as Mallarmé by the idea that the separation between poetry and music should be abolished. Verlaine did not perhaps inspire him to the same degree as Baudelaire or Mallarmé to try out new experiments, but did give him an opportunity of satisfying his need for lyricism which enabled him to produce in succession works of which the greatest composers of vocal music would not have been ashamed. Of the eighteen songs inspired by the poetry of Verlaine which are known to us, fifteen were written before 1891, and consequently in the period with which we are especially concerned at this stage.

With the exception of *Sérénade* (also sung by Claire Croiza in 1938 and thought highly of though now no longer extant) and *Pantomime,* suspended between major and minor, very similar to *Pierrot* (Banville) and *Fantoches* (Verlaine) though inferior in quality, we must count among the first of Debussy's vocal compositions the celebrated *Mandoline* as well as the songs written in 1881–2 which, after being slightly altered or touched up, form part of the first series of *Fêtes galantes* (1891: *En sourdine, Fantoches* and *Clair de lune*). Composed in 1881, *Mandoline* remained almost unchanged in the 1890 edition. Koechlin was right when he referred to it as 'this little masterpiece'. A combination of melodic invention, harmonic sensibility and an extraordinary rhythmic *verve* gives a slightly bitter flavour to the poem's humour, which tends to conceal the tenderness and melancholy that the poet must have felt at the recollection of this scene, which might have been conceived by Watteau, and which fades away like a dream in the final and apparently carefree vocalise. As in the *Chanson espagnole,* somewhat earlier, fifths were used to imitate the guitar; here, from the very first bars, they imitate the mandoline (10).

An example of at least one new way of conveying the real sound of the timbres can be seen below in the superimposition of the two fifths. The juxtaposition of five common chords: G major, G flat major, C major, C flat major, B flat major, without any modulations or transitions (11) is not so much a proof of skilful harmonic manipulation as of a way of thinking in terms of the new theories about sound which serve here to underline the profound meaning of the words. Later these methods will also be freely employed in purely instrumental music.

Whereas *Fantoches,* in which tonal unity is successfully replaced by a rigorous thematic structure, was hardly altered at all in its final version, *En sourdine* was considerably revised (the pentatonic nightingale's song at the beginning and the end will appear again in *Colloque sentimental*). Changes were made, too, in *Clair de lune,* but they are not essential and even if the few naiveties that Debussy decided to suppress had been kept, this song would have had an assured place in his vocal output. From a harmonic point of view, it is not remarkable for any particularly bold innovations. All the first part is both tonal and functional, and the chords, despite their tritonal relation, do not depart from the functional system; and this also applies to the successions of common chords or chords of the seventh and ninth which appear later on in the accompaniment. The very original melody soars above them, adapting its form to the phonetic modulations of the words, and sometimes adopting waltz rhythm. Its line, astonishingly concise and already very 'Debussyian', lends its character to this work in which one does not know which to admire most: the infallible choice of the means which the young composer employs to communicate its melancholy to the hearer, or the perfection of the allusive equivalents he invents to underline discreetly the poet's words (e.g. in the passage: 'Tout en chantant sur le mode mineur . . . Ils n'ont pas l'air de croire à leur bonheur').

There is not a great difference between the first version of the songs in the first collection of *Fêtes galantes* and the *Six ariettes oubliées* composed between 1886–8, each one of which is worthy of inclusion in an anthology of the finest French songs. All the texts are taken from Verlaine's *Romances sans paroles.* The last one, *Spleen,* is perhaps the least original, since its melody repeated seven times, reminds one, as Vallas has pointed out, of the *Epithalame* in Chabrier's *Gwendoline.* In the others the personality of Debussy is so apparent that there is no need to seek for any other influence. *C'est l'extase langoureuse* is noticeable for the complete unity between the text and the music. Its opening parallel fifths and octaves seem perfectly natural, and the chord of the ninth into which they close cannot sound like a discord because the key of E major is so carefully avoided and concealed that the ninth (on B) loses its 'dominant' character; moreover, throughout the whole song the (harmonic) functions are suspended.

In *Il pleure dans mon coeur* the monotonous accompaniment of semiquavers evokes irresistibly 'le bruit doux de la pluie' and combines with the melodic line in a contrapuntal texture in the key of G sharp minor. *L'Ombre des arbres dans la rivière embrumée* whose harmonies recall those of *Tristan,* plunges into a tonal obscurity from which we emerge only in the last bar. *Chevaux de bois* is a kind of agitated toccata consisting of repeated melodic and rhythmic figures with harmonies that change with every verse before returning to their point of departure, passing through the keys of E, C, E flat, D, G, E flat, F sharp and E. Debussy has taken the eighth couplet, the one that ensures the unity of the whole song (in the key of E) from a little-known version of the poem published for the first time in the collection *Sagesse* (12). Finally, *Green,* so full of charm, refutes the principal accusation of those who, unable to forgive Debussy for his disregard of accepted rules, blamed him for his lack of melodic invention. The freshness and spontaneity of his music once again proves the falsity of these ill-advised assertions.

The other three songs to words by Verlaine from the collection *Sagesse, Le son du cor s'afflige* (VI), *L'Echelonnement des haies* (VIII) and *La mer est plus belle que les cathédrales* (IX) were composed in 1891; here the characteristics of Debussy's vocal style – melody in which the special intonations of the words is respected, and a flowing and allusive accompaniment showing an extraordinary musical invention – attain a degree of formal perfection which proves that, from now on, the composer was ready to assume the most formidable tasks. The artist halted at this point – perhaps in order to take the fullest advantage of the experience he had acquired; for example, in the second song the piano part is a development of the theme of the *Tarantelle Styrienne* of 1890, with slight changes in the rhythm (*Danse* for piano); or, again, perhaps on account of his growing desire to go beyond the conventional musical system of his day: as, for example, in the first song, suspended between major and minor thanks to the use of the whole-tone scale, and already foreshadowing *Pelléas et Mélisande*, especially at the end, with its parallel chords of the seventh and the ninth.

Debussy only returned once to the poetry of the 'pauvre Lélian' (13) after thirteen years of great artistic adventures, as if to pay a last homage to the one who, of all the poets, aroused in him 'the strongest spiritual sensations'; but this time it was a different Debussy – no longer the young revolutionary, but a master, in complete command of his language and showing in the second series of *Fêtes galantes* that he knew how, in spite of the extreme economy of his means of expression, to remain sensitive to all the poetic refinements of the poet whom at one time he had admired above all others. Leaving aside *Colloque sentimental*, perhaps over-rated in comparison with the other two songs in this series, let us take a look at the two couplets of *Le Faune* woven, it would seem, over the ground-bass of the tambourine, above which is heard a flute-like melody, and above that again the recitative. At the precise moment when the latter reaches the words: 'Jusqu'à cette heure dont la fuite tournoie au son de tambourins', the gulf between the lowest and highest registers grows wider, thus introducing an impression of different 'levels' in a hitherto homogeneous structure and also the emancipation of the rhythmic element corresponding to the sense of the last verses of the poem.

Henri Gauthiers-Villars (Willy) said, with reference to Debussy, that he was the 'Verlaine of music, the equal of that other Verlaine, and one who also heard voices that no one before him had heard' (14). He hoped, no doubt, and rightly so, that by this comparison he would add to the fame of a composer who was still almost unknown to a large section of the public. Today we judge these two artists differently. Whatever the links which may have brought them together, and despite the composer's appreciation of the poet, Debussy seems much more of an innovator, in the avant-garde of his epoch, and quite uninfluenced by Wagner. As for Verlaine, he was much closer to the Romantic poets and the Parnassians.

It was no doubt the songs composed to the poetry of another great poet, Baudelaire, that marked a decisive stage in Debussy's *oeuvre*: was he going to follow Wagner, or develop in quite a different direction? In the *Cinq poèmes de Charles Baudelaire* which Gabriel Fauré described, perhaps too hastily, as 'a work of genius', the composer detaches himself from the Romantic past and from Wagner, and revives the function and character of ancient models. These songs were conceived under the influence of Baudelaire, himself an ardent Wagnerite, and also under that of Wagner himself during the period of 'pilgrimages' to Bayreuth. During the sixteen long months which separated the first song, *La mort des amants* (XII, 1887) from the last, *Le jet d'eau* (III, 1889), Debussy succeeded in freeing himself completely from the influence of Wagner, and putting in its place his own aesthetic and his own vocabulary.

A feature of *La mort des amants* is a romantic melodic line, fully extended and supported by a rich accompaniment. In *Le balcon,* which both Paul Valéry and T. S. Eliot consider Baudelaire's finest poem, the touch is perhaps slightly heavy, while the theme borrowed from *La Damoiselle élue,* composed at the same time, is accompanied by harmonies which recall Chausson. Notice, however, the curious transformation of the 'Tristan' motif (E – G) in the final sigh of the poet as he dreams of happier days (15):

Wagner would have reinforced it with an extended cadence; and the same text would have given him an opportunity to illustrate the poignant sorrow of remembrances: he would not have hesitated to tear open with dissonances his healed wounds. With Debussy, the parallel chords invest the theme with a static quality; everything happens as if he had paused for a moment to find the past intact:

'serments parfums, baisers infinis', without any suggestion of despair. The chord of the ninth itself sounds here like a quiet consonance.

Some 'Wagnerian fumes', and occasionally a whiff of the Russian school can be detected in *L'Harmonie du soir,* the least original song in this series and clearly the result of a recent visit to Bayreuth. In *Recueillement,* on the other hand, despite the 'Tristan' atmosphere created at the opening by an echo, it would seem, of the horns in the second act of Wagner's opera, one can already hear the mature Debussy, especially towards the end of the piece, in the alternations, so full of charm, between the discreetly allusive simple common chords and chords of the ninth (bars 56–8) which accompany the words: 'Et comme un long linçeul trainant à l'Orient'.

But it is only in *Le jet d'eau* that Debussy succeeds in freeing him-

self completely from outside influences; and it is here that one can best observe his changed attitude towards sonorities and the harmonic element. In the very first bars we are struck by the modal character of the melodic line at the end of certain sentences; these modal effects are based on the use of whole tones and a descending third. Even a broken chord has no harmonic character.

In the accompaniment, the isolated seconds create as it were a third level, independent of both the melody and the corresponding lower parts in the accompaniment. This interval of the second is evidently not there by chance; its function becomes clear in the succeeding lines of the poem, where the murmur of a fountain is said to reach the place where the lovers sit. In the following passage:

the apparently wholly traditional harmonic sequence – dominant to tonic – is super-imposed on a chord of the ninth, with the result that the sonority of the second stands out still more clearly, which is in keeping with the words. Here now are the concluding bars (94–7):

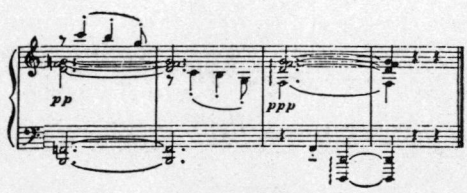

Their dynamic development is the opposite of Romantic rhetoric: the intensity of the sound, instead of increasing, descends from *pp* to *ppp*. Debussy himself liked this progressive disappearance of sonorities, of which numerous examples are to be found in his works.

Though marking a decisive stage in the crystallisation of Debussy's personal style and 'advanced' tendencies, *Le jet d'eau* does not mean that he had by now found himself completely. Although, as we have seen, three settings of poems by Verlaine (1891) can be considered as forerunners of masterpieces yet to come (the *String Quartet, L'Après-midi d'un Faune, Pelléas et Mélisande*), it must not be forgotten that it was in the same year (1893) that he finished the *Quartet* that Debussy completed his *Proses lyriques* set to words of his own and which cannot be considered an entirely homogeneous work. It is possible to admire the composer's poetic gifts, his taste and feeling for words, while at the same time noting his dependence on the fashions of the time which have lost much of their charm today. As for the music, we must admit it is of a composite nature. The finest of the four songs is no doubt *De grève*, a poem about the sea whose undulations are suggested at the outset by a non-functional accompaniment. Towards the end chords of the sixth make their appearance, and their gentle swinging motion evokes the 'cloches attardées des flottantes églises' in the text. The three other songs are not up to the same standard as this one: neither *De rêve*, with its three repeated themes (recalling the Wagnerian *Leitmotif*) supported by fluid harmonies; nor *De fleurs*, resembling the 'Wagnerian' settings of the *Poèmes de Baudelaire*, although the words 'l'ennui si désolement vert de la serre de douleur' are marvellously reflected in the music; nor, finally, *De soir* with the contrast of the gaiety of the initial theme 'La tour prends garde' and the sweetness of the prayer addressed to 'La Vierge or sur argent.'

If we are to speak about song-cycles rather than individual works, we would suggest that Debussy attained perfection and at the same time his full maturity in the three *Chansons de Bilitis* on texts by Pierre Louÿs composed in 1898 – that is to say, after the first version of *Pelléas et Mélisande* (1893–5). One finds here all the idiosyncrasies of his language and musical style: these were visible in previous works, but here they are combined with a skilful pastiche of frivolous Greek erotic poems which left greater freedom to the composer's imagination than rhymed poetry. This work is rightly considered to be the summit of Debussy's achievement in the field of vocal music.

Their spontaneity and freshness of invention, refinement and incomparable charm have ensured immortality for these songs which are a manifestation of a kind of beauty which could only have been conceived under the clear skies of France. *La Flûte de Pan* with its simple pentatonic melody which follows closely the sinuosities of the declamation, accompanied by sequences of chords constructed on a modal scale (Lydian mode), is a miracle of equilibrium and good taste. The peculiar French 'emotional restraint' has rarely found a more perfect musical expression, especially in the final phrase: 'Ma mère ne croira jamais . . .' uttered almost in a whisper and all on the same note: (Ed. Fromont, bars 24–30):

The use of different registers and the sequences of chords in the accompaniment cannot be explained in terms of functional harmony since they are resolved on a chord of the ninth with a major seventh.

Le Tombeau des Naiades is quite different in character: the harmonic basis of this fresco, which recalls a Javanese *gamelan*, consists of sequences of diatonic chords interspersed, here and there, with chords of the seventh and ninth; and it is on this foundation that the melody is consistently developed, based on a chromatic and on a whole-tone scale. The second of these three songs, *La Chevelure*, has an extraordinarily expressive intensity, comparable, no doubt, to that which we find in the celebrated opening scene of the third act of *Pelléas* – as if the composer had wanted to tackle the same problem in a different way. Here the recitative soars above a torrent of dissonant harmonies (tritonal relations) converging at the end in a diatonic chord.

In our brief analysis of Debussy's 'first period' vocal music, we have often made comparisons with *Pelléas et Mélisande*. This is because Debussy was to exploit all the experience he had gained in this domain when moving on to a more complex form – a music drama based on a play by Maeterlinck. More than seventy years have passed since the creation of this masterpiece of Debussy's, completed in principle in 1895* – the only additions to the final version, besides a few corrections and revisions, were the Interludes composed to fill in the time taken in shifting scenery. Throughout the years, the work has been the subject of so many analyses and commentaries that we shall confine ourselves to recalling certain features essential for our argument, or which bring us back to the problems so often raised in the present chapter.

What had attracted Debussy in Maeterlinck's play had been, as he himself admitted, 'an evocative language whose sensibility might find its counterpart in the music and orchestral décor' (16). But it was not only a question of language: the art of Maeterlinck corresponded exactly to the ideal drama which Debussy described in his conversations with Guiraud quoted above – a drama which would have characters 'whose history and dwelling place would belong to no specific time or place', and who 'would not discuss, but would just endure, whatever life or destiny offered them.' Debussy, in fact, rejected the traditional ways of differentiating characters and the rudimentary psychology of contrasting characters and situations – that sacrosanct rule of Opera which Wagner himself had never really succeeded in overcoming. But to make, as Wagner did, 'the symphonic development responsible for the dramatic action' (17) did

* [This is not quite correct as Debussy destroyed this first draft; it would be more accurate to say that the opera as we know it was begun in 1895. *Translator's note.*]

not interest Debussy; nor did the custom of presenting the *dramatis personae* so that the spectator can imagine them in real life and on the stage. His ambition went further: he wanted to create a dramatic work which would reveal to us the characters' inmost thoughts and embody the forces which determine man's destiny, not in outward events, but in the man himself. Maeterlinck's theatre corresponds to some extent to this desire, because the drama is played out on two different planes at the same time: one external, consisting of the words and gestures of the actors, and the other internal, where the real action takes place which conditions the action on the stage. The actors' words and actions are only important in so far as they reveal the existence of ineluctable laws. The heroes act like persons in a dream. They do not know where they come from or where they are going. They are like blind men, or men with no will of their own whose destiny is governed by cruel and invisible powers. It is these that are the chief characters in the drama.

This piece saw the rebirth, in a somewhat naive and schematic form, of the tragic view of life (a subject particularly dear to Debussy) which had been played down by 'scientism': here symbols and allusions play a predominant part, as does likewise the subconsciousness of the characters, their words, their sober gestures and their silences. Must we add that it was precisely these features that had attracted the composer, who thought that music had to 'express the inexpressible'. It had to be a drama of this kind to fire the imagination of the artist who wanted to free opera from the burden of worn-out formulae, and to 'de-Wagnerise' it by removing the Teutonic pathos and 'will to power'.

What means did Debussy employ to bring to life the pale shadows of the Maeterlinckian drama and persuade the onlooker to take an interest in their destiny? Apparently simple means that had mostly been employed before in his vocal music, proving his wide musical culture and refined taste. He makes a frequent use of recitative, which respects the inflections peculiar to the French language, but he does not become a slave to this formula. To grasp and transmit the hidden meaning of the words he turns recitative into an instrument of infinite flexibility, and does not hesitate to employ means already used by others, even by Wagner, while adapting them to his own personal style.

It has often been said — and still is today — that Debussy in *Pelléas* makes use of those *Leitmotifs* which he denounced so bitterly in the works of other composers. Such an assertion could only be made by someone totally incapable of understanding the gulf that separates the world of Wagner from that of Debussy. With the former the *Leitmotifs* have a dynamic character, their object being to cement the orchestral masses by giving them a thematic continuity, and also to underline the story. With the latter, on the other hand, the motifs (Maurice Emmanuel discovered thirteen in *Pelléas*) are static, and often fragmentary; they change according to the situation, the atmosphere of the moment and the state of mind of the principal characters. They have a different role to play, and are the result of a different way of treating the actual sounds. Vincent d'Indy had already noticed this difference, calling Debussy's motifs 'pivotal themes' whose function it was to disseminate clusters of harmonic rays. With what object? To avoid that kind of clarity which Wagner aimed at in his *Gesamtkunstwerk*, in order not to conceal under too transparent musical symbols the obscure and ambiguous significance of men, things and situations.

At the beginning of the first scene of the second act the flutes announce Pelléas (Ed. Fromont, p. 70 of the score):

but this motif will not appear again in exactly the same form, nor in a similar context, any more than will the motifs of Mélisande, Golaud, or the fountain in the garden; others only appear once. One of the variants of Golaud's motif is the same as that which accompanies the ring that Mélisande lets fall into the water: others inter-

(Reproduction authorised by Durand & Co., Paris)

mingle and change colour and consistency, sometimes suggesting reality, at others only the idea of reality. When the ring falls into the water, with the *glissando* accompanying its fall the tonal character of the music also fades away. Debussy does not rule out illustration altogether; if necessary he even resorts to traditional methods as, for example, at the beginning of the second scene of the third act (p. 187 of the score) where the lower registers of the orchestra convey the gloomy atmosphere of the castle's vaults. In such cases the composer sometimes makes use of new sonorities, as in the Interlude between the second and third scenes of the second act (p. 131 of the score) where the strings and drums imitate the sound of the wings of a flock of great birds in flight.

Debussy also makes use of what are purely sound-effects in the Interlude which follows the second scene of the third act (pp. 193–8 in the score): the passage where Pelléas, emerging with Golaud from the darkness of the vaults exclaims: 'Ah, je respire enfin!' over a chord of the ninth (p. 200 in the score). But this is not an example of either romantic illustration or of naturalistic onomatopoeia, to which Debussy only rarely has recourse.

What interested him much more than the mere experiencing of phenomena was to associate them with thoughts and feelings. Thus, for example, the theme in arabesque at the beginning of the second act does not imitate the sound of the fountain in the garden (it was the same in *Jet d'eau*); it suggests fluidity in general and a certain freshness; but in other circumstances it could suggest something quite different. It was by procedures of this kind, very simple in appearance, that Debussy gradually liberated music from the dense layers of traditional symbols, and thus restored to it its ambiguity.

He avoided romantic models, and the example of Wagner, especially when dealing with 'eternal subjects' such as Love or Death. The transports of love, sorrow and despair were, according to the time-honoured traditions of composition, a pretext for re-inforcing 'expression' by all possible means. Debussy was the first who dared to rebel against the pundits and to replace romantic emphasis (whether Germanic or Slav) by a characteristically French discretion, without thereby detracting from the expressive value of the music. In the first tableau of the third act (p. 170), the big scene between Pelléas and Mélisande leaning from the window of the tower is conducted throughout, in spite of its emotional tension, over a *pianissimo* orchestral accompaniment:

Wagner, to take only one example, would at this passage have driven the orchestra into a frenzy so that nobody could fail to grasp the nature of his hero's sentiments.

In the fountain scene (pp. 332–3 in the score) Debussy goes even further: at the moment when Pelléas and Mélisande confess their love the orchestra, which up till then had been playing *forte*, is suddenly silent, then re-appears, as if coming out of the shadows, *ppp*, to accompany Pelléas's impassioned recitative (for it is, characteristically, a recitative and not an aria):

(Reproduction authorised by Durand & Co., Paris)

(Reproduction authorised by Durand & Co., Paris)

Debussy's vocal music and the lyric drama of *Pelléas et Mélisande*, its crowning glory, mark the beginning of the process of renovating the language of music and its symbolism. Let us now consider this dual aspect of the great composer's *oeuvre*.

Innovations in Sound

The purely sonorous, or 'sonorial' values as we should say today, only began to play their part in the music of the eighteenth century; indeed, it was only then that instrumental forces were defined with any degree of precision. With Beethoven, the dynamic categories (from *fff* to *ppp*) and those of articulation (*legato, staccato*) varied, but the most important element was the thematic thought closely connected with the tonal and harmonic structure of the work, to which the instrumentation was entirely subordinate. One can find examples of a certain sensitivity to purely sonorous values in certain works by Berlioz and Liszt; but these are comparatively rare in the nineteenth century. In his study of Stravinsky, Boris de Schloezer justly observes that if it can be said of Berlioz that 'he harmonised with timbres', then it is equally true that Wagner 'orchestrated with harmonies' (18). Schloezer was doubtless thinking of Wagner's famous orchestral 'pedal' which Debussy compared to 'a kind of multicoloured mastic spread over almost the whole orchestra' in which he declared . . . that he was unable 'to distinguish the sound of the violins from that of the trombones' (19).

Debussy was, in fact, the first composer for whom the actual sound-image of a musical work was an essential element which he cultivated very carefully. In his letters and articles, at any rate after 1894 (cf. the letters to Eugene Ysaÿe and Henri Lerolle) he frequently discusses the question of 'sound-placing' and the efforts he was making to extend the range of sound manipulation beyond the traditional horizons by which the musician's imagination had hitherto been limited. In a letter of 1915 addressed to Bernardino Molinari there is a passage which ought long ago to have led students of his works to revise their methods and to study Debussy's music in its purely sonorous aspects: 'We are still at the stage of "harmonic progressions", and there are very few musicians who are satisfied with *beauty of sound alone*' (20).

This sentence alone is ample justification for our having devoted a whole chapter to Debussy's concern with the technique of sonorities.

It is in this field no doubt that he brought about the most far-reaching revolution: he laid the foundations of a whole new way of thinking with regard to musical composition. After Debussy, except in purely abstract terms, it is no longer possible to study tonal and harmonic problems without taking into account their structural aspects.

When discussing the actual sound of a musical composition, two things have to be taken into consideration: the source of the sound — i.e. the means employed in its performance, and the way in which the composer treats his sound material. We know that Debussy made use of traditional instruments. It could be said that, generally speaking, he tended to reduce the size of his orchestra. He put an end to the predominance of the brass; used mostly muted horns and trumpets, gave priority to the woodwind; made free use of harp, celesta and gongs; frequently entrusted important parts to *pizzicati* strings; and where necessary (as in *Printemps* and *Sirènes*) treated human voices as instruments. Economy of means was his motto. He avoided doubling different *timbres*; discreetly underlined the individuality of instrumental groups; divested the quartet of any 'choral' influences by a frequent use of *divisi*. In *Pelléas et Mélisande* and *La Mer* the strings are often divided into from twelve to fifteen different parts. Victor Ségalen has recorded a very significant statement by Debussy on this subject: 'Musicians', he wrote, 'no longer know how to decompose sound — to give it in all its purity. In *Pelléas* the sixth violin is just as important as the first. I try to employ each *timbre* in its purest form. . . . We have been too clever in mixing our *timbres*, and Wagner went very far in this direction, doubling and tripling most of his instruments. Worst of all is Richard Strauss who has made a mess of everything, combining the trombone with the flute. . . . I try, on the contrary, to preserve the purity of each *timbre* and to put it in its proper place. Strauss's orchestra . . . is a cocktail orchestra' (21).

In order to exploit to the full all the potentialities of an instrument Debussy rejected the myth of 'natural' registers. In one of his letters to André Caplet it will be remembered, he protested against Pierre Lalo [music critic of *Le Temps* – Translator's note] for having accused him of never employing the instruments of the orchestra 'in their natural timbres' (22). He was also familiar with the problem of the 'stereophonic propagation' of sound and the organisation of acoustic space. As early as 1894 he described how he had planned, for the death scene of Mélisande, to have 'a group of instruments on the stage so as to create, as it were, an impression of death in sound' ('pour avoir en quelque sorte une mort de toute sonorité') (23). Several years later, in an interview with Victor Ségalen, he was to speak of a general reform of the traditional disposition of the instruments of the orchestra on the platform: 'The strings should form, not a barrier, but a circle round the other instruments. The woodwind should be dispersed: the bassoons with the 'cellos, the oboes and clarinets with the violins so that their entries should not produce a 'package' effect ('pour que leur intervention soit autre chose que la chute d'un paquet') (24).

These various methods of treating sound with the aid of dynamics and articulation are the consequence of Debussy's tendency to enlarge the scale of sound-values. Whereas with the Romantics the volume of sound is almost bound to be in direct proportion to its density, with Debussy it is often just the opposite: a considerable volume combined with a relatively restricted intensity. He rarely has recourse to the dynamic effects resulting from an alteration in the original volume of sound, and shows a marked preference for *pianissimos* and *pianos*. Eimert has calculated that in *Jeux* 557 bars out of 709 remain within those limits (25). His other works show a similar percentage (80 per cent). It can therefore fairly be said that Debussy 'reduced the dynamics of music'.

On the other hand, the question of articulation was an important one for him. A glance at any one of his compositions is enough to show the richness of the means of articulation he employs to give the desired form to his musical idea. In *Ibéria*, for example, one finds a constant alternation between *arco* and *pizzicato* in the divided strings as well as various kinds of *tremolo* ('on the fingerboard and on the bridge'), *glissando* chords in the violins and percussion effects obtained by the *pizzicato* of the strings imitating the guitar. In *Rondes de printemps* harmonics on the 'cellos occur in the first bars (*See opposite page*).

By greatly enriching the instrumental structure of a work all these methods help to create its own special sound characteristics.

The rationalisation of time in Debussy's music is a feature that merits special attention. It is no longer necessary to prove that the temporal organisation of a work is of the greatest importance from the point of view of sound. And yet, by admitting *a priori* a fixed order, functional harmony gave little opportunity of arriving at a real understanding of the essential part played by the time factor.

It is only since the most recent developments in music that it has been possible to appreciate the important part played by *tempo*, or 'movement' in determining how a work will 'sound'. And since it is the relations between duration and intensity which determine the *tempo* of a work, our conception of the role played by rhythm, metre and 'agogia' has fundamentally changed. In the past, when analysing a musical work no attention was paid to the actual duration of a sound. And yet it is this factor that determines its selectivity or, on the other hand, its blending with other sounds. The harmonic significance of chords is lost in a quick tempo where they can be transformed either into dynamic values, or into what today we should call 'bands of sonority'. The same succession of sounds creates different values if there is a change in the agogic conception.

Debussy employed a great variety of methods. He introduced agogic and rhythmic relationships; sometimes he favoured an autonomous perception of sounds in succession – as for example in the Tenth *Prélude* (Book I):

sometimes, again, their integration, as in the Third *Prélude* (Book I):

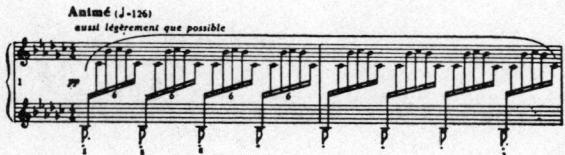

Selective sonorities determine the course of the melodic line which they can divide up into separate 'motifs', as at the beginning of *Rondes de printemps*, or even into isolated notes, as in the Twelfth *Prélude* (Book I):

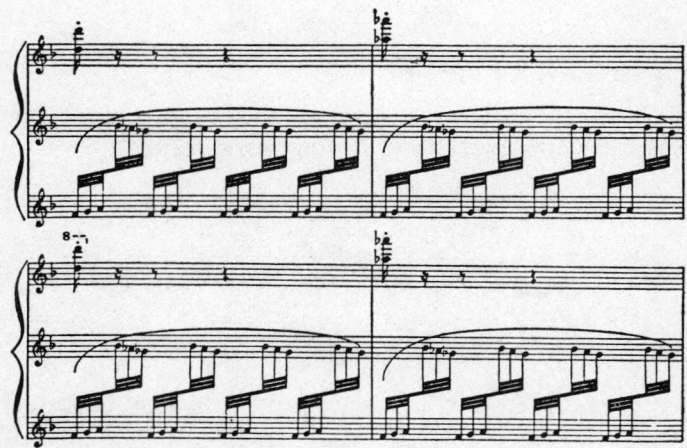

The Eleventh *Prélude* (Book II) enables us to see how the combined action of agogia and short bars can lead to a fusion of sonorities (bars 1–10):

The exploitation of minor seconds is, moreover, the characteristic feature of this polytonal *Prélude*. An effect of resonance becoming vibration can be seen in the Fifth *Prélude* (Book I):

At the opposite extreme we find in the Seventh *Prélude* (Book I) a very rapid tempo leading to a fusion of sonorities:

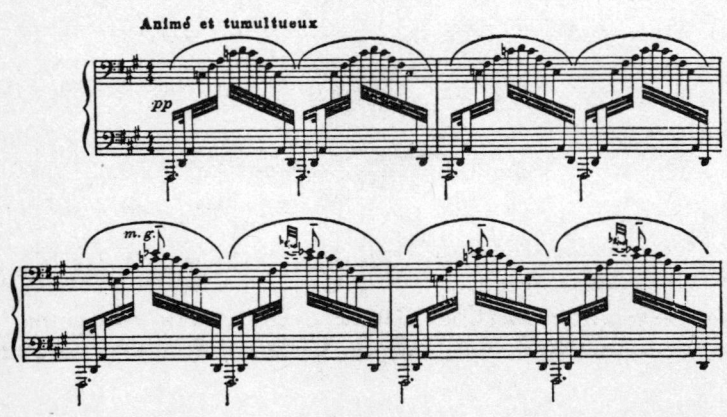

Since the Renaissance European music has cultivated monochronomy and an invariable unity of tempo regardless of the principle governing the division and nature of the metre. The first departure from this practice was the association of the duolet and the triolet. We frequently find examples of polyrhythm in Debussy (e.g. the Sixth *Prélude*), and it can bē stated categorically that, had it not been for the liberty of rhythm Debussy cultivated, the innovations of Stravinsky in this field would not have been conceivable.

The cultivation of polychromy is noticeable in Debussy more than in any of his predecessors; and it is noteworthy that the diversity is less the result of the 'great' than of the 'small' divisions, especially when combined with agogia. A change of tempo assumes the importance of an accent. Micro-structures frequently assume, as for example in *Jeux*, in the violin part the character of 'sound bands'. One bar of notes of brief duration (12/16) in the Fifth *Prélude* (Book I) may be considered as an example of precision in the extinction of sonorities, but Debussy more often uses them to stress the relativity of time relations, e.g. in *Jeux*, p. 21, where we find juxtaposed bars in double, triple, quadruple and quintuple time (which occur also at the beginning of *La Mer*). This is not the only example to be found in *Jeux*. One of the most significant will be found on p. 112 (see page 144) where the variability of time values is extreme, and where, in the clarinet parts for example, we find already in a rudimentary form those 'added values' (note the dotted semiquavers) which Olivier Messiaen was later to exploit in his own fashion. In fact, the significance of these values is primarily auditive, since they tend to efface the rhythmic impulses and produce a fusion of sonorities.

We have described above how the selective timbres determined the movement of the melodic line. They can also lead to the disintegration of the linear element, and create horizontal structures that cannot be included in the category of melodic phenomena in the traditional sense of the term. Evidently we find in Debussy different types of horizontal structures, the broad, traditional melody, as for example in the first seven bars of the Eighth *Prélude* (Book I) as well as rotative melodic structures, especially in works with expressive or dance rhythms. But Debussy generally preferred short phrases,

(Reproduction authorised by Durand & Co., Paris)

144

more suitable for selection. In the Seventh *Prélude* (Book II)

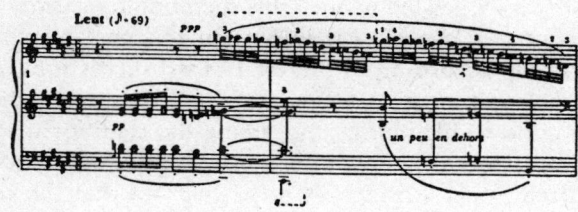

the themes cannot be described as melodic. They are autonomous sound complexes having, as in the case of the isolated sounds in the Fourth *Prélude* (Book II) (bars 8–10)

a purely sonorous significance. The Twelfth *Prélude* (Book II, which is full of such purely sound values) shows how a figurative and ornamental melody can, thanks to a rapid *tempo*, transform a horizontal structure into a vertical one (bars 25–26):

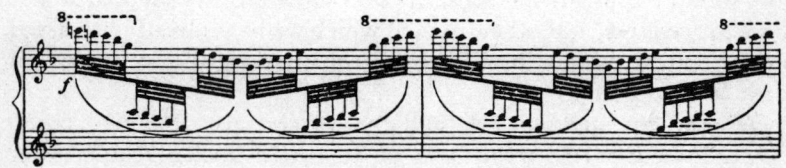

The Eleventh *Prélude* (Book II) affords a striking example of thirds being treated as sound elements (bars 1–10: see Example at top of p. 142).

We are accustomed to a linear interpretation of harmony. It is this thematic way of thinking, from which Schoenberg was never able to free himself, which has led us into this methodological rut. Because the actual sound of chords was important to him, and not merely their relationship according to pre-established successions, Debussy actually separated melody from harmony. The parallel chords, so frequently found in his music, undermine the traditional principles of treating the different 'voices'. The notion of the 'arabesque' which recurs so often in his writings, is in itself proof that the composer was thinking along new lines. The arabesque, as he understood it, is an undulating melodic line, independent of any notion of the development of themes or 'motifs'.

Françoise Gervais (26) points out that certain chord parallelisms (e.g. at the beginning of *La Cour des lys* in *Le Martyre de Saint Sébastien*) can be considered as a kind of 'chord melodies' (Schoenberg's *Klangfarbenmelodie*), and various other sound clusters which cannot be analysed harmonically, as centres of a convergence of harmonic lines. It would seem, nevertheless, that this conception, though interesting, has led its author to stray too far from the actual sound values of this music, in which the distinction between the notions of homophony and polyphony often becomes meaningless since even the polyphonic structures often have only a purely 'sonorous' character. Debussy's use of parallel chords is the result of thinking in terms of sound categories. In the Twelfth *Prélude* already cited, the chord sequences have no functional character at all. A rapid design creates associations of sounds for which one could seek in vain any justification in the rules of traditional harmony. The same applies to the *glissando* chords so often found in Debussy's music (e.g. in *Ibéria*, pp. 56–7 of the score). What are they in reality but 'sound bands' in the sense in which the term is used today? In these procedures, and others as well which we have already discussed, one is fully justified in discerning the first signs foreshadowing 'post-Webernism'.

Debussy changed the role and the significance of the harmonic factor. Functional harmony was based on an unchangeable order, whereas with Debussy chords and aggregations are in the nature of polyvalent structures. Andreas Liess had already pointed out that Debussy had replaced cadences and modulations by sequences as constructive elements (27). For, in fact, the series of non-component sounds which, in traditional harmony, were considered as non-

functional elements were seen by Debussy as the equivalent of formal
integration. Almost everything which in functional harmony was
rated as a manifestation of the forces of inertia – static in character,
or at any rate looked upon as an element retarding or arresting the
movement of the sound-mass as a whole – had by now become a new
fashion in musical thinking. Hence, it is only by obstinately con-
tinuing to consider Debussy's work from a purely functional point
of view that it has been possible to continue to describe it as
'impressionist', or to speak of it in terms of that 'colour' and
'*höchste Passivität*' on which it was supposed to be based and which
were its *raison d'être*. Any element which could not be classified as
'harmonic' was considered to be a manifestation of 'colour'; the
selective elements 'coloured' the melodic line. It had not been
realised that not every chord necessarily has a harmonic significance.
Any analysis of Debussy's music that fails to take into account its
purely 'sonorous' values can only be partial, incomplete and misleading.

Not so long ago the notion of verticalism was always associated
with harmony; and yet these two conceptions are not identical since,
according to the sound-material employed, vertical structures will
always be homogeneous and compact, and will either dissolve into a
single sonorous stratum or, on the contrary, will be heterogeneous
or 'polygeneous', and it will then be possible to distinguish two or
three strata (purely sonorous, and having nothing in common with
melodic lines). The horizontal structures will not necessarily present
a melodic design, and the vertical ones may be decomposed or
divided into separate sonorous levels, while their harmonic links

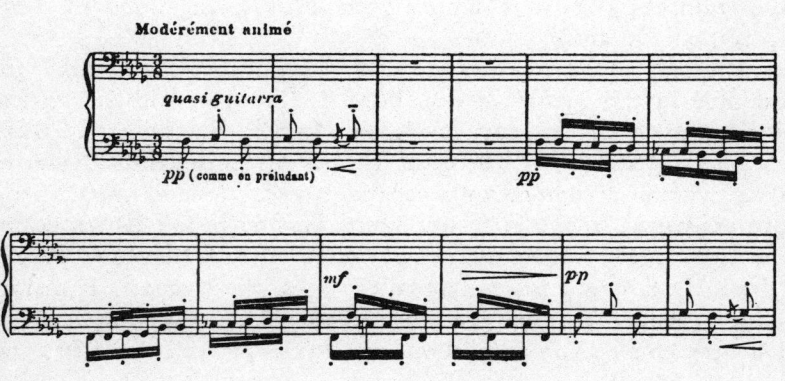

may be weakened, or even disappear, when subjected either to agogic elements, or elements of articulation, or else to different instrumental values (association of different registers).

The fact that a structure may be either monophonic or polyphonic does not in any way ensure its homogeneity. These are two quite distinct categories. A monophonic structure may be richer in 'sound' than a polyphonic structure, as can be seen in the Ninth *Prélude* (Book I). (See example at foot of previous page).

The essential feature of polyphonic structure is that, as it were, it neglects harmony. This can be seen when there is no integration of different sonorous strata, e.g. in *Gigues*:

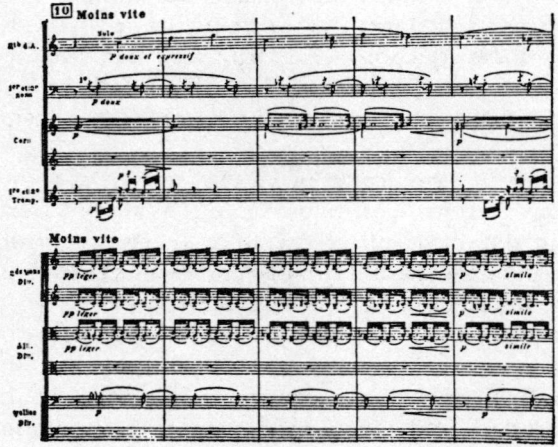

Here the strings form one stratum, the horns and oboes another, and the trumpets a third; a similar example is to be found in *Ibéria* (p. 54, ed. Durand).

Heterogeneous structures are also found in the piano works: for example in the Tenth *Prélude* (Book I) (Ex. 16), with its vertical structures on two distinct levels, or again in the Seventh *Prélude* (Book II) (bars 34–5), where the chords of the seventh, owing to their dynamic accents, form a separate 'voice'. (See example at top of next page.) In the First and Third *Préludes* (Book II) structures on two levels frequently occur, while in the Eleventh *Prélude* (Book II), despite a few polytonal passages, the structure is mainly homogeneous. In the Eighth *Prélude* (Book I) already cited, Debussy employs, in addition to traditional vertical structures and

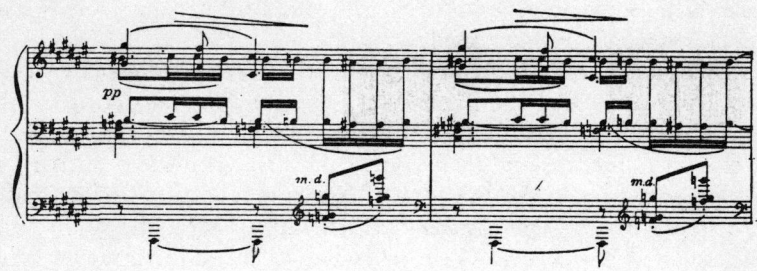

some interpenetrating polytonal fragments, vertical structures on two different levels. In other words, he introduces, when necessary, new forms into his harmonic writing. This *Prélude* is characteristic of the dialectic of Debussy's harmonic and sound-orientated thinking which is noticeable in the majority of his works, even the earliest in date. We have endeavoured to make this clear in the chapter devoted to his vocal music.

It must not be assumed from the foregoing that the importance he attached to 'sonorial' thinking makes it unnecessary to study the harmonic and melodic aspects of Debussy's music. We have dealt at some length with this purely sonorous aspect of his music which until now has never been taken into serious consideration, in order to show, perhaps in too summary a form, that it was Debussy's technique in the handling of pure sound that has been at the root of all the most up-to-date ideas and experiments in the music of our time.

Symbolic Elements

In order to avoid the worn-out *clichés* of Symbolism in sound, Debussy employed the cunning of Ulysses. He avoided the stumbling-block of functional harmony, and approached with caution the conception of music as pure sound. In this way he succeeded in bridging the gulf separating two epochs without experiencing that feeling of isolation which was to be the lot of his successors – Webern or Varèse – who, encouraged by his example, acted less prudently. Using much the same technique as Mallarmé, the composer of the *Prélude à l'après-midi d'un faune* refers us now to the 'sense' (which can be interpreted according to the code of functional harmony), now to the 'sound' (sound values); he creates in this way a symbolic ensemble, a 'total work', ambiguous, incantatory and 'evocative of the hidden idea'.

If he had accorded more importance to 'affective values', he would only have been, like the Romantics, yet another 'translator' of the human soul. But because he shunned the *appassionato* approach and Narcissism – because he turned his back to Hérodiade's mirror and was prepared to accept the idea of 'depersonalisation', he was able to discover those *correspondances* which link us with the world, and so disturbed Baudelaire. Gaston Bachelard distinguishes two types of imagination: formal and material. Debussy was certainly endowed with the latter – that is to say, the type which does not seek for form in picturesque and changeable external objects, nor yet through introspection, but which penetrates to the heart of things, at the point where 'form is enveloped in substance, where form is inert.' 'Material imagination', says Bachelard, 'dramatises the world in depth. It finds at the innermost heart of substances all the symbols of the intimate secrets of human life' (28). In order to arouse the atavistic *correspondances* which slumber in man – and to restore his union with the creatures and objects in Nature, Debussy, unlike Wagner, has no need for semantic substitutes. All he needs is to speak directly through bird-song, the sound of the sea, the rocking of a boat by the waves, the movement of clouds in the sky, or drifting mists, to lead our thoughts to the origin of things and cause them to dwell on the ultimate questions in life. His music does not answer any questions, create any myths, or suggest any solutions, but for that very reason acts all the more forcefully on our minds, and forces us to follow in its wake.

This does not mean that his music is lacking in traditional symbols; but their role is a comparatively modest one, and the way in which he makes use of them generally bears little resemblance to traditional models. For example, the distant sound of horns, a favourite Romantic cliché which the Symbolists also adopted, often appears not only in *Recueillement* (*Poèmes de Baudelaire*), but also on several occasions in *Pelléas et Mélisande* (notably in the first scene of Act I; in the Interlude that follows the second scene; and in the third scene of Act II); in *La Mer* (Part III, Nos. 52–53); and in the last four bars of the Fourth *Prélude* (Book I) where the score is marked: '*Comme une lointaine sonnerie de cors*'.

The flute was generally used to convey an atmosphere of bucolic serenity; with Debussy its evocative, delicately nuanced tones express melancholy and anxiety – as in *L'Après-midi d'un faune*, *Syrinx*, the *Sonata for flute, viola and harp* – and even in some piano writing, e.g. in the first *Chanson de Bilitis*, or the opening bars of *Le Faune*, the second series of *Fêtes galantes*, or the first *Epigraphe antique*.

The sound of bells must have exercised a great charm on the composer, who often makes use of their effect. Bells announce the twilight and approaching night; and Debussy maintains this symbolic and Christian association in his songs: *Les cloches* (Paul Bourget); *Chevaux de bois* (Verlaine) where he introduces into the poet's text the onomatopoeic effect 'din-din-don'; in *Les Angélus* (G. Le Roy), where the regular repetition of a major second at the beginning and the end evokes the sound of bells; and finally in *De grève* (*Proses lyriques*). *Cloches à travers les feuilles* (*Images*, second series) stems from the same Symbolist tradition, while the muffled sound of the bells of the buried cathedral of the town of Ys (Tenth *Prélude*, Book I) which can be heard from the bottom of the sea at all hours of the day, invites us to reflect on the vanity of worldly things.

But as often as not Debussy paid no attention to symbolic suggestions when deciding in what form his works would be performed or the way in which their sound-material would be organised. Thus the key of F sharp major, traditionally considered to be a warm, golden tonality, often inspired him to create a nocturnal atmosphere, as for example, at the end of *De rève* or in the last scene of the first act of *Pelléas* – or, again in *Pelléas*, in the Interlude which follows the first scene of the third act, and also at the end of the 'Battlefield' episode in *La boîte aux joujoux*.

His rejection of the Romantics' aesthetic and of the frenzies of Expressionism was no doubt never made to his contemporaries so overwhelmingly apparent as in *Pelléas et Mélisande* – a work which, compared to the floods of passion let loose in the operas of Wagner or Strauss, must have seemed a haven of calm and introspection. And, in fact, in his very first sketches Debussy was methodically putting into effect his aesthetic theories. 'I am searching now', he wrote to Chausson in October 1893, 'for a little chemical formula of more personal utterances, and I have tried to be both Pelléas and Mélisande; I have been seeking music behind all the veils with which she is surrounded as a protection against even her most ardent devotees . . . I have made use, quite spontaneously, of a medium which I think has rarely been used, that of *silence*, as an expressive element which is perhaps the only way in which the emotion of a phrase can be conveyed' (29). Scarcely two years later, when he had finished his opera, he wrote to Pierre Louÿs: 'Silence is a fine thing and God knows that the empty bars in *Pelléas* are evidence of my love for that kind of emotion' (30). He also speaks of the 'expression of silences' with which his works are permeated, in letters to Eugène Ysaÿe and Henri Lerolle (31).

In fact, 'silence' is not only a feature of *Pelléas*. Almost all Debussy's music emerges from silence, fades away at times, and then relapses once more into silence; the composer seems to be listening to the mysteries of life, of death and of what lies beyond our sensory capacities. Consider how many expressions he employs to indicate the different ways in which music can be extinguished: 'en s'effaçant' (*Brouillards*); 'en s'éloignant' (*La sérénade interrompue*); 'en se perdant' (end of *Mandoline, Apparition, De rêve, Colloque sentimental, Sirènes*); 'perdendosi' (*Le Faune, La Fille aux cheveux de lin, Pour un tombeau sans nom, Ibéria*, I p. 53, *Boîte à joujoux*, p. 24, *Le Laurier blessé, Martyre de Saint Sébastien*, p. 75, *Jeux*, p. 114); '*en affaiblissant*' (*Pelléas*, II. p. 149); 'estinto' (*Etude pour les quartes*); 'à peine' (*Etude pour les agréments*, and *pour les notes répétées, Eventail*); '*pp* doux et lointain' (*Ibéria*, II p. 79); 'aussi *pp* que possible' (end of *String Quartet, Pelléas*, end of Act V. p. 405); 'presque plus rien' (*Le Faune, Colloque sentimental*). *Nuages* ends with a *pppp* on the strings; in other words, the music dematerialises. In the same way the far-off bells in *De grève*, or the waves at the end of *Reflets dans l'eau* are faded out (32).

After the deafening tirades of Wagner and Strauss, Debussy's music seems scarcely audible, so softly does it fall upon our ears. *Les Ingénus* (*Fêtes galantes II*), *Nuages* (*Nocturnes*), *Les feés sont d'exquises danseuses, La terrasse des audiences, Le vent dans la plaine* are, as has been said, 'pianissimo poems' – a kind of sub-music. 'Et la nuit seule entendit leurs paroles', the final words of *Colloque sentimental*, 'could well be', as Jankélévitch has observed, 'the conclusion of *Pelléas et Mélisande* which relates in five acts the extenuation, or progressive rarefaction of existence – in other words, the apparition of Zero.' Debussy seizes the last breath of life at the very brink of what separates Being from Non-Being. His silences and pauses seem sometimes to come as if from 'the other side'.

The poetry of the agony of beings and things (Baudelaire,

Laforgue, Samain) must have made a profound impression on the young Debussy, for its influence can be observed at every stage in his music. The melancholy of the gradual fading and final disappearance of twilight, of extinction – whether of fire or of life – of the day's slow progress towards death when the sun descends from its zenith – these are the themes which haunt him and instil with their poetry the descending arabesques in *Brouillards, Feuilles mortes* and *Soupir* (*Poèmes de Mallarmé*). In *Le son du cor s'afflige* (Verlaine) 'the snow falls as if in long strips of shredded gauze', passing through six different successive tonalities: C, B flat, A flat, G flat, E, and D. In *Jet d'eau*, following Baudelaire's intention, Debussy places the accent, not on the upward jet of the water, but on its fall; the final words: 'falls like a shower of large tears' are accompanied by three descending arpeggios illuminated in succession by a G sharp minor, an F sharp major and an E flat major before being fused in a colourless C major, the note of Non-Being. Here we have, as Jankélévitch points out, in the words of Mallarmé: 'the tawny agony of October, pale and pure who sees reflected in the great fountains her infinite languor.'

Even when he takes his inspiration from Nature, Debussy never attempts to imitate her. He transposes her various elements for the pure joy of hearing them in music. It is not the picture that interests him but the perception – not the flower itself but its blossoming. As André Michel has so pertinently remarked, he lends his heart to things, and listens to it beating in their hearts (33). Why would he have translated into sounds the visual impressions which painting, whose function it is, conveys so well? Was it not Debussy who refused to recognise Berlioz as a musician because he 'gave the illusion of music with procedures borrowed from literature and painting' (34)?

The illusion of 'instantaneousness' that Monet sought to achieve: to render the changes that affect the surface of things at different hours of the day, was quite foreign to Debussy. Nature plays only a secondary role in his music; it is only a pretext, a canvas on which the artist weaves his dream. The titles he gave his music cannot mislead the listener. It is the spirit of the times which generally suggested them to him – but, it should be noted, only after the music had been composed. For example the celebrated titles in the 24 *Préludes* for piano are not placed at the beginning of these little masterpieces (intended, according to the composer, to be performed in an intimate circle rather than in a concert-hall) but at the end of each piece. They are generally speaking more poetical than picturesque and, contrary to what might appear to be the case, are calculated to conceal rather than express the real intentions of the composer. Moreover, what concrete images could suggest music garnished with titles such as: *Les fées sont d'exquises danseuses*; *Hommage à S. Pickwick Esq.*; *Les sons et les parfums tournent*; *Des pas sur la neige*; *la Sérénade interrompue*; or *La cathédrale engloutie*? The titles indicate the sources of inspiration; the original stimulus which inspired the composer; a representation of Nature; a poem; an ancient legend; a character in literature and so on; but the listener is free to place his own interpretation on the hidden meanings of the work.

What, for example, did Debussy want to express in *Des pas sur la neige*? Was it his intention merely to depict a wintry landscape? If we submit ourselves to the suggestive power of this music it will become clear that for him it was a matter of far greater importance – perhaps he was trying to describe the immense sense of loss caused by the disappearance of someone dear to him, or perhaps only the feelings inspired by solitude in general? This has often been claimed – especially by those who defend the theory of Debussy's Impressionism, because this seems to reinforce their argument that the composer of *Pelléas* was especially successful in evoking conditions of immobility and stagnation. They cite in support of their argument first of all, of course, *Des pas sur la neige, Canope, Brouillards, Le son du cor s'afflige* and *En sourdine*. Other examples evoked were the *ostinato* in *Vent dans la plaine*, or the *Epigraphe* 'Pour remercier la pluie du matin', the apparent movement and the 'turning round on itself' of *Mouvement*, and the incantatory repetitions of *Jardins sous la pluie* or *Masques*. What they do not notice is that all these procedures point to another and fundamentally different method of organising sound in both its formal and material aspects; to explain this music in terms of the methods and categories of a style hitherto accepted could only lead to dangerous generalisations. Debussy's detestation of 'developments', the ascetic sobriety of his melodic invention (which was the result of his opposition to Romanticism) were looked upon as a form of sensual naturalism (and indeed this was what Impressionism in music stood for at that time), whereas in reality his musical thought was totally opposed to any form of illustration, anecdote, or programme-music, as well as to any kind of subservience to Nature.

If Debussy occasionally picks up the painter's brush, it is only to paint immaterial bodies, without substance. True, there is nothing to prevent us from interpreting the processions of fifths and thirds in the second *Ballade de François Villon*, or in *Et la lune descend sur le temple qui fut*, or again in Part Three of *La Mer* (No. 53, p. 133) as a 'calm and white procession which glides across the night sky and alternately shrinks and expands'; but the important thing is that this image carries us into another dimension. When, at the end of the first act of *Pelléas* we hear the *tremolo* of the muted violins and, off-stage, the chorus singing '*à bouche fermée*', we cannot help feeling ourselves filled with a nostalgia for another world – a nostalgia that Debussy's music so often evokes, and especially in this scene in which, from the start, it underlines the strange anxiety of Mélisande.

'If', says Jankélévitch, 'Debussy's music is ... like a miniature cosmogony, a recapitulation of the history of the world, *Pelléas et Mélisande* is also a *résumé* of that *résumé*' (35). 'No music', I quote again from the same author, 'has ever been able to capture in full flight, as Debussy's can, an elusive correspondence or to intercept telepathic or sympathetic messages, listen-in to souls communicating with one another in the ether, and even to convey the equivocal sensation of what is at the same time here and there, near and far, Being and Non-Being. What we hear are the almost imperceptible quiverings of a melody, certainly not a "theme", elliptic reminiscences, fugitive as a thought ... The "theme" of Golaud, often reduced to a simple rhythmic figure in the bass, sometimes even to a single note repeated several times – the theme of Golaud, with its characteristic triplet and its dotted quaver evocative of far-off gallops on horseback ... wherever it appears it seems to be the harbinger of anguish and distress ... At times this anguish increases to the pitch of panic, as in the symmetrical crises reaching fever-point which occur at the end of Acts III and IV: the terror of little Yniold and Mélisande's wild flight into the night; here and there the wind of delirium bends the notes into a breathless pursuit, just as it chases the clouds and the cornfields and the whole countryside in the last paintings of van Gogh' (36).

Monet's seascapes are never terrifying. We share in the contemplation of the painter, who is himself in a pantheistic harmony with Nature. But in Debussy's *La Mer* everything seems to be happening – as with Turner – on a cosmic scale. In the last movement of this polyrhythmic symphony, *Le Dialogue du vent et de la mer*, the sinister noise of the hurricane seems to portend death and destruction; the same impression is conveyed by the Seventh *Prélude* (Book I.): *Ce qu'a vu le vent de l'Ouest*.

And yet, to see in Debussy the Edgar Allan Poe of music, the bard of the Sea of Darkness, would be a too hasty judgement. Scarcely two years before his death, when he was already a very sick man, he said in a letter that only the sea could cure him – 'la mer, notre mère à tous' (37). In her psychoanalytic study of Poe, Marie Bonaparte says that the sea is for all men one of the greatest and most persistent symbols of maternity (38). It is true Debussy sometimes mitigates the painful feeling of absolute solitude in the face of death by evoking the nostalgia of *'l'horizon chimérique'* which pervades him when he thinks of the immensity of the sea. It is this that he seems to be expressing in the third *Nocturne* (*Sirènes*): the ocean as a symbol of the primordial mother-figure to whom man returns at the end of his earthly life, and who sometimes, in the moonlight, summons with the voice of her sirens her prodigal children scattered all over the world.

Poe always fascinated Debussy, with his poetry based on terror and suffering. Since Baudelaire's and Mallarmé's translations, few artists of the Symbolist generation had been able to resist the 'frisson métaphysique' aroused by the wild visions of the author of *Ligeia* and *Ulalume*. Had it not been for Debussy's premature death, the drama of musical Expressionism would have been born, not in Germany, but in France. This Expressionism would have had nothing in common with the romantic *furor teutonicus* or with the Expressionism of the Viennese school. It would not have repudiated art as the ruling spirit of the elements, the emotions and the senses.

There is nothing more moving than to follow in Debussy's correspondence the gradual ripening of the idea of an opera in one act based on *The Fall of the House of Usher*. This is not the place to stray from our main subject in order to recount in detail the dramatic circumstances under which this work was conceived. We will confine ourselves to quoting fragments from the letters dealing with this work. 'There are times', he wrote in 1908, 'when I lose contact with my surroundings: and if Roderick Usher's sister were to come into my room I should not be all that surprised' (39). And two years later he was to write: 'It is indeed at such times that I am most likely to be able to satisfy *my taste for the inexpressible* [Author's italics]. If I succeed in bringing off, as I would like to do, *this progression in anguish* which is how I conceive the *Fall of the House of Usher,* I believe that I shall have served music well' (40). In 1911 he complained to a friend: 'I don't seem able to finish the two little plays by Poe (the second was to be *Le diable dans le beffroi*), the whole thing has become a complete bore. For every bar which seems more or less "free", there are twenty stifled under the weight of a single tradition whose spineless and hypocritical influence I am forced, in spite of all my efforts, to recognise. Note that it is quite unimportant that this tradition should, in fact, be my own . . . It's disappointing all the same because it means discovering oneself under various disguises' (41). Finally, in 1916, he remarked bitterly: 'One must profit from a few rewarding minutes to make up for wasted hours. I was just going to put the finishing touches – or something like that – to *The Fall of the House of Usher* when illness extinguished all my hopes' (42).

These quotations – especially the first – give some idea of the intensity of the composer's experiences and his constant need to renew himself. Scarcely a year and a half after finishing *Pelléas* he wrote: 'As for those people who are kind enough to hope that I shall never escape from *Pelléas*, they must be pretty blind. Don't they know that if that were to happen I should lose no time in starting to grow pineapples in my bedroom, as I happen to believe that there is nothing so boring as to continue imitating one's self' (43). What makes Debussy's work such an exceptional phenomenon in the history of music, and what creative musicians of today find so fascinating, is precisely his 'open' attitude – his contempt for formulae, his rejection of rigidity or automatism of any kind in connection with his own affective and intellectual reactions.

So as not to break all ties with tradition, and in order to keep in contact with his hearers, Debussy tried to remain within the boundaries of tonality and functional harmony; but he extended them to extreme lengths, and through the medium of pure sound, freed from any representational function, he prepared the way for the new musical thinking of today. Notice in his works the progressive invasion of seconds, intervals which are, after all, the negation of harmony. Having, to begin with, served to heighten the colour of the harmonic texture, after *Le Jet d'eau* they are used more and more frequently as integrating elements in the manipulation of sounds (*Jardins sous la pluie; Jeux de vagues* from *La Mer; Parfums de la nuit* from *Ibéria;* the final pages of *Gigues; Feux d'artifice; Champ de bataille;*

La Boîte à joujoux; Khamma; Martyre de Saint Sébastien) to become, in the end, independent entities of aggressive sound (*Jeux; Etude pour les degrés chromatiques* and *Etude pour les notes répétées; Eventail* and *Soupir* from *Trois poèmes de Mallarmé; En blanc et noir*). Jankélévitch sees in late Debussy 'increasingly harsh harmonies: the writing is complicated and perversely distorted, and becomes as corrosive as acid' (44).

The dissonant chords have by now ceased to be a transition between two tonalities; they no longer prepare a resolution – they dispense with it altogether, and claim equality – with the result that all the laws of gravitation and interdependence are flouted: everything is called into question again and takes on an ambiguous, polyvalent character, while the parallel chords clearly mark a new stage in the evolution of 'thinking in sound'. Trusting his own instinct, Debussy broke the traditional rules, instituted a new musical language and a new kind of Symbolism; he allowed his hearer's imagination free play, enabling it to explore a vaster realm, liberated from the narrow bondage of the traditional system. The public was deceived by the critics and musicologists who offered it a superficial analogy with Impressionist painting. Debussy makes us realise what the Romantics tried to make us forget: real music does not make its appeal to what is individual in man, but to what he has in common with his fellow-men, which is something much deeper. In concluding his fine study of Debussy, Jankélévitch is right when he says: 'There is no music in the world . . . that speaks more profoundly to a man of his mystery, which so disturbs his inner being, or which stirs his imagination more profoundly . . . He speaks to us only of the simplest and most important things, essential for mankind: of death and love, sorrow and destiny; a great white cloud in the sky during those long summer afternoons when the siesta is so welcome; or the west wind that causes the leaves to sigh, and speaks to man of his future. We can never replace Claude the Unique' (45).

6

DEBUSSY AND THE MUSIC OF THE TWENTIETH CENTURY

ATTEMPTS have been made to define Debussy's music with the help of all sorts of labels: Impressionism, Naturism, even Neo-classicism; but none of these magic formulae have succeeded in opening the doors of his kingdom, or understanding its essential nature. His *oeuvre* defies the classifications and scholastic definitions which its creator had so often denounced. 'All his life was a quest for everything that defies analysis' says Pierre Boulez, (1) 'and for a development which, by its very nature, incorporates the surprises that arise from our imagination. He distrusts architecture, in the old-fashioned sense of the term, and prefers structures that mingle rigour and freedom of choice. That is why, with him, those words, those keys with which we are saturated in our schools and academies have no meaning or purpose: the habitual mental categories of a worn-out tradition could never be applied to his works, even if we tried to adjust them by twisting them here and there.' We have no intention of ignoring this lucid and convincing judgement, nor of substituting a better label for a worse one, putting Symbolism in the place of Impressionism. While admitting there are good grounds for such a procedure, let us say that the only result would be to replace a great mistake by a lesser one, without escaping from the labyrinth of erroneous generalisations.

Impressionism has restored to the plastic arts their true nature by reminding them that they sprang from the need to express the experiences of visual sensibility; the term corresponds exactly to the movement's aesthetic principles. Would such a tendency, with similar principles (but not the same) have served any purpose in music? Certainly, if we admit that it would be based on auditive impressions. The fashion of thinking in terms of sound which, with Debussy, is beginning to have a decisive influence on the formation of a musical work, has no doubt favoured the invasion of music, that we see today, by auditive impressions coming from the outer world – or even in the form of purely acoustic happenings. We find here a confirmation of the progress achieved by 'bruitism', which introduced into music all kinds of sound effects hitherto excluded from its domain. Impressionism, we know, tended to transpose into art impressions received in their crude state before they had been organised by intelligence. Now, if we can to a certain extent consider the tendencies of 'bruitism' as a form of musical 'impressionism', the term is totally inappropriate when applied to the music of Debussy, in which auditive impressions, even if they occasionally appear (as we have been careful to point out) are never an essential part of the work. As to the transposition into music of visual impressions – an accusation which has been unjustly applied to the works of the purest musician who has ever existed since Mozart – we have already dealt with this question at sufficient length to make further comment unnecessary.

Since we reject the term 'Impressionism' as false or inadequate, at any rate so far as the music of Debussy is concerned, why not accept that of 'Symbolism'? There are many good reasons for not doing so, the chief of which is the fact that while the Symbolist movement, which had made its appearance in literature with Baudelaire, and had reached its climax in the years 1884–91, had exercised a profound influence on all branches of the arts, including music (and especially Debussy's), it was in literature that it had played a decisive role. By attaching almost as much importance to the sound of words as to their meaning, and in seeking unconventional relationships in their manipulation of language, the French Symbolists had restored to the art of words its true function, just as the Impressionists had done for painting. They called attention at the same time to the structural peculiarity of all truly artistic forms of communicating, namely its essential ambiguity. Now it happens that music, which, in principle, contains no elements required to fulfil a semantic function, is, almost by definition, ambiguous (evidently within the limits of a specific sphere of culture); and even the combined efforts of Wagner and the Romantics had never succeeded in eliminating entirely the role of the imagination. And so, although Debussy had considerably enlarged the field in which imagination can be exercised, it cannot be said that in this he was unique; his inspiration came, rather, from nature, since we have just admitted that music is 'by definition' Symbolist. Symbolism is no more peculiar to

Debussy's works than it is to the other arts, all of which aimed at imitating music and creating only 'symbolic works'. We can, however, ignore this aspect of the problem; such a transposition of terms and concepts from one domain to another is not without precedent. But the principal reason for rejecting the category of 'Symbolism' is that this term is not an adequate definition of Debussy's music.

We believe that we must respect his refusal to accept any 'label': indeed, in our opinion it would be impossible to find one that could be applied to him. He had been in contact with all sorts of artistic movements: Naturalism, Impressionism, Pre-Raphaelitism, Divisionism, Symbolism, Synthetism, Fauvism, Expressionism. With the exception of Cubism, whose birth and development he had witnessed without enthusiasm, he had learned something from all these movements, and had sometimes been profoundly influenced by them (in the case of Symbolism, for example); but he never sacrificed to any of them his own artistic personality, which had been crystallised at an early age, even though it took him some time to reach full maturity.

Despite his interest in literature, Debussy was too much of a musician to accept a 'pictorial' or 'literary' explanation of his work. He had several times expressed his opinions on this subject, opinions which were very similar to those of Whistler when, in *Ten O'Clock,* he reproached Ruskin for having treated painting merely as a 'means' by his literary way of interpreting pictures; the poetry of pure painting and the idea by which the artist was inspired – in other words, everything that distinguished his work from all others, cannot be dealt with in this way.

In his quest for a new form of Symbolism, Debussy freed music from the semantic approach, even before he began to think in terms of pure sound. His instinct as a musician obliged him to fly in the face of public opinion, bemused as it was by the magic of Wagner, and to find original solutions in that eternal dialogue with the world which the artist carried on in his works. His sense of equilibrium told him that he would have to restrain his excessive desire for expression, and keep under control his imagination, excessive sensibility and feverish sensuality. There is no better example of his reticence and distaste for emphasis and exaggeration in art than his revolt against the verbal debaucheries of d'Annunzio, or the excessively Byzantine scenery of Bakst in *Le Martyre de Saint Sébastien*. I would like to quote in this context the opinion he expressed on a certain volume of poems by Swinburne, a poet, incidentally, for whom he had a great admiration: 'This man is probably an admirable poet. But don't you think that his craze for imagery is so excessive that it makes him forget what he is talking about? I am well aware that in the realm of poetry madmen are kings. But all the same . . . ' (2).

In his music Debussy is most skilful in maintaining an equilibrium between Nature and Man, without ever granting supremacy to one side or the other, with the result that his creations are rarely marred by furious explosions of the forces of Nature, or by sudden upsurges of violent passion, whether the music is pursuing a solitary path of its own, or interpreting the words of a poem. Debussy does not try to be 'deep', and admits nothing *a priori*; he trusts his own instinct entirely, and only conceives his works in the course of their creation. Hence the impression of spontaneity created by his music, as if he were spinning it freely as he goes along. But is he spinning it? or does he not rather order it to remain static? He does both: every method is right for him so long as it suggests that he is dealing with the 'inexpressible'. The essential basis of his aesthetic is the same as that which underlies Mallarmé's poetry. Both being equally remote from 'Wagnerism', what they both sought was 'the essence of things', the naked truth undistorted by banal spatial categories or pompous rhetoric. But whereas Mallarmé's *oeuvre* is nothing now but an astonishing remnant saved from the wreckage, that of Debussy is very much alive, bringing joy to both our hearts and our minds. 'Total' in every sense of the word, it speaks to the whole man – not to his senses, alone, or exclusively to his sentiments or to his reason. Although he inveighed against Wagner, any extremist attitudes in criticism were foreign to Debussy's nature. And although he was opposed to subjectivism, even going so far sometimes as to sing the praises of de-personalisation, he never denied to music complete freedom of expression, as Stravinsky did, because he knew intuitively (or was it perhaps the 'Frenchness' of his genius that guided him?) that extremes always end by meeting so that, as Stravinsky said, 'the empty eyes of his music are sometimes more expressive than expression' (3).

Debussy was not joking when he said that he tried hard to forget everything he had learned. He was violently opposed to any form of academicism, and his art is an example of perpetual renewal. In the history of music Debussy opened a new chapter. Almost all the new tendencies that have appeared in the twentieth century had their origin in his art, were directly inspired by it, or sprang up in opposition to it. When the decomposition of the harmonic system which he had accelerated was finally accomplished; and when the music that came after him had rid itself of its aggressively polemical character, musicians ceased to see in his work nothing but negation. It has been said with reason that he revolutionised orchestral and pianistic techniques; but it has not been sufficiently emphasized that, thanks to his exceptional musical sensibility, he was the first to attach to isolated sounds, or groups of sounds the same importance as to melody, rhythm and harmony. (It was, in fact, only after Debussy that musicians began to speak, not of chords, but of 'sound aggregations'). This was to have very important consequences which only became fully apparent in the very newest music under the influence of Webern.

We are not suggesting that Debussy never hesitated nor never contradicted himself. As Adorno has observed: 'No artist is capable by himself of abolishing the contradiction between uninhibited art and an inhibited society' (4). Debussy did away with the interdependence of melody and harmony, allowed melody to soar freely, and annihilated sacred rules without, however, falling into an anarchic chromaticism. By evolving a style that was partly harmonic and partly modal he contributed largely to the renaissance of modal music. By rejecting chords of the third, the *a priori* structural basis, he was aiming instinctively, by means of modal scales, the pentatonic and the heptatonic, at a synthesis of sonorous material and, naturally, he arrived at a harmony which was a-functional, atonal and a-thematic. The idea of *Klangfarbenmelodie* would never have been conceived by Schoenberg and Webern if Debussy's music had not suggested it to them. Thinking in terms of sound, which we find in Debussy for the first time, was to find in Webern its true exponent, whereas Schoenberg, who had been the first after Debussy to follow this road, in the third movement of his *Fünf Orchesterstücke,* Op. 16, and in the *crescendo* of light section of *Die glückliche Hand*, was to abandon it completely in his dodecaphonic compositions.

The desire to renovate the language of music, to purge it of all its stale rules and abstract rhetoric which destroyed any feeling for the true significance of sound, drove Debussy to seek for new methods and to study seriously the problems of syntax. It is for this reason that, in some of his works, one might be inclined to discern destructive elements, and in others constructive ideas. But the truth is that his thought, entirely free from prejudice or myths sometimes retreats only in order to advance still further next time. His almost metaphysical feeling for pure musical material, free from the dualism between ideas and matter, form and content, led him to the eternal sources of music, to its magic origins at a time when sound, freed from the influence of preconceived ideas, was for man the instrument which helped him to dominate the forces of Nature.

Like the god Pan, who so often recurs in his works, Debussy had left the retinue of Dionysus to return to his own country. Enthroned on the dividing line between two epochs, he sang of his love for the earth and his nostalgia for heaven.

NOTES

INTRODUCTION

1 Roman Ingarden: *L'oeuvre musicale et le problème de son identité* (in Polish); (Etudes d'esthétique, Warsaw, 1958, vol. II, pp. 292–3).

2 See his study of eroticism in music, *Enten-Eller*, Copenhagen, 1842.

Chapter 1
IMPRESSIONISM IN NINETEENTH-CENTURY PAINTING

1 See Courthion et Cailler: *Manet raconté par lui-même et par ses amis*, Geneva, 1945.

2 Eugène Delacroix, *Journal*, 1822–62, Paris, 1932, vol. III, p. 18.

3 See Bernard Dorival: *Les étapes de la peinture française contemporaine*, vol. I.; *De l'impressionisme au fauvisme*, Paris, 1948, p. 226.

4 See Lionello Venturi: *Qu'est-ce que l'impressionisme*, Labyrinth, no. 11, Geneva 1945.

5 Quoted by J. Leymarie in *L'Impressionisme*, Geneva, 1955, vol. II, p. 115.

6 Cf. Gaston Bachelard: *L'Eau et les rêves; Essai sur l'imagination de la matière*, Paris, 1942, p. 203.

7 Marcel Proust: *A l'ombre des jeunes filles en fleurs*; Ed. Pléiade, Paris, 1964, pp. 836, 839, 840, 901.

8 Pierre Francastel: *Peinture et société. Naissance et destruction d'un espace plastique. De la Renaissance au cubisme;* Lyon, 1951, p. 171.

9 Marcel Proust, *op. cit.*, p. 902.

10 Maurice Merleau-Ponty: *Phénoménologie de la perception*, Paris, 1945, pp. 465–7.

Chapter 2
THE MEANING OF 'IMPRESSIONISM' IN MUSICOLOGY

1 See Report by the Permanent Secretary of the *Académie des beaux-arts*, 1887, in *Les Arts français*, no. 16, 1918, p. 92.

2 See Emile Vuillermoz: 'L'Oeuvre symphonique de Debussy', *Musica Album*, Paris, undated.

3 Quoted by Léon Vallas: *Claude Debussy*, Paris, 1958, pp. 175–7.

4 Among others: *La Corrélation des sons et des couleurs en art* (1897), and *L'Orchestration des couleurs* (1903).

5 Léon Vallas: *op. cit.*

6 In a letter to A. Vallette, Tahiti, July 1896, in *Mercure de France*, no. 999–1000, December 1946, pp. 220–2.

7 Cf. Camille Mauclair: 'La peinture musicienne et la fusion des arts', *Revue bleue*, 6 September 1902.

8 Letter to A. Serieyx; see Léon Vallas, *op. cit.*

9 Emile Vuillermoz: *Claude Debussy*, Geneva, 1957, p. 94.

10 Vincent d'Indy: *Cours de composition musicale*, Paris, 1933, vol. III. It should be added, that the relations between Debussy and d'Indy, though outwardly reflecting a mutual esteem, in reality masked a profound antipathy which was due to the fact that their respective aesthetic theories were totally incompatible. It is not from Debussy's 'polite' references to d'Indy that we shall learn what his real opinion was, but from the evidence supplied by René Peter, Ch. Koechlin and E. Vuillermoz.

11 René Lenormand: *Etude sur l'harmonie moderne*, Paris, 1913 (*Monde musical* XXIV).

12 Claude Debussy: 'Du goût', *Revue musicale S.I.M.*, February 1913.

13 Richard Hamann: *Der Impressionismus in Leben und Kunst*, Cologne, 1907, p. 64.

14 Werner Weisbach: *Impressionismus: ein Problem der Malerei in der Antike und Neuzeit*, Berlin, 1910–11, 2 vol.

15 E. Koehler: *E. und J. de Goncourt, die Begründer des Impressionismus*, Leipzig, 1911.

16 G. Loesch: *Die impressionistiche Syntax der Goncourt*, Erlangen, 1919.

17 Oswald Spengler: *Le Déclin de l'Occident*, Paris, 1910, trans. M. Tazerout.

18 Ernst Kurth: *Romantische Harmonik und ihre Krise in Wagner's 'Tristan'*, Berne-Leipzig, 1920.

19 See C.-F. Caillard et J. de Berys: *Le Cas Debussy*, Paris, 1910, pp. 84–7.

20 L. Fabian: *Claude Debussy und sein Werk*, Munich, 1923, p. 26.

21 W. Harburger: *Form und Ausdrucksmittel in der Musik*, Stuttgart, 1926, p. 127.

22 Werner Danckert: 'Liszt als Vorlaufer des musikalischen Impressionismus', *Die Musik*, 1929, p. 341.

23 Arnold Schoenberg: 'Composition with Twelve Tones', *Style and Idea*, New York, 1950, p. 104.

24 Hans Mersmann: *Angewandte Musikästhetik*, Berlin, 1926.

25 Emile Vuillermoz: *Claude Debussy*, pp. 33, 34, 37, 39.

26 *Op. cit.*, p. 120.

Chapter 3

THE SYMBOL IN ART

1 Ernest Cassirer: 'Das Symbolproblem und seine Stellung im System der Philosophie', *Zeitschrift für Aesthetik*, 1927, vol. XXI.

2 *Cinquième Congrès de l'Association internationale des Etudes Françaises*, Collège de France, September 1953.

3 Marcel Raymond: *De Baudelaire au surréalisme*, Paris, 1940, p. 58.

4 Saint-Antoine: 'Qu'est-ce que le symbolisme?', *L'Ermitage*, Paris, June 1894.

5 Wolfgang Goethe: *Spräche in Prosa. Maximen und Reflexionen*, nos. 742, 743.

6 Henri Bergson: *Le Rire*, Paris, 1958, p. 119.

7 Ernst von Sydow: *Form und Symbol*, Potsdam, 1929, p. 28.

8 J. Baruzi: *Saint Jean de la Croix et le problème de l'expérience mystique*, Paris, 1924.

9 Maurice Blanchot: 'Le secret du Golem', *N.R.F.*, no. 29, 1955, pp. 871–2.

10 Maurice Merleau-Ponty: *Phénoménologie de la perception*, Paris, 1945, p. 229.

11 T. S. Eliot: *Essais choisis*, Paris, 1950, pp. 168–9.

12 Guglielmo Ferrero: *Les lois psychologiques du Symbolisme*, Paris, 1894, p. 26.

13 Emeric Fiser: *La théorie du symbole littéraire et Marcel Proust*, Paris, 1941, pp. 43-9.

14 Stanislav Ossowski: *U podstaw estetyki* (Principles of aesthetics), Warsaw, 1958, p. 180.

15 Raymond Bayer: *Traité d'Esthétique*, Paris, 1956, p. 45.

16 Johan Huizinga: *Le Déclin du Moyen Age*, Paris, 1967, p. 213.

17 Cited by Wladyslav Tatarkiewicz, *Histoire de l'esthétique. I: L'Esthétique du Moyen Age*, Paris, 1967, p. 213. Trans. J. Bastin.

18 Etienne Gilson: *La Philosophie au Moyen Age*, Paris, 1944, p. 440.

19 Johan Huizinga, *op. cit.*, p. 218.

20 Cf. J. Seznec: *La Survivance des dieux antiques*, London, 1940.

21 Marcel Raymond: *op. cit.*, p. 12.

22 James L. Austin: *L'Univers poétique de Baudelaire. Symbolisme et Symbolique*, Paris, 1956, pp. 143-4.

23 Charles Baudelaire: *Salon de 1859; Oeuvres complètes*, Pléiade, Paris, 1956, p. 773.

24 *Ibid.*, p. 779.

25 *Ibid*: p. 1091, *Victor Hugo*.

26 *Ibid*: p. 1035: *Théophile Gautier*.

27 *Ibid*: p. 927, *L'Art philosophique*.

28 Edgar A. Poe: *Philosophy of composition. The Poems of E. A. Poe*, London-New York, 1900.

29 Alfred Cassagne: *La théorie de l'art pour l'art en France chez les derniers romantiques et les premiers réalistes*, Paris, 1906.

30 Stéphane Mallarmé: *Oeuvres complètes*, *La Pléiade*, Paris, 1945, pp. 866-7. A reply to Jules Huret's study on the evolution of literature.

31 *Op. cit.*, p. 400: *Variations sur un sujet*.

32 *Op. cit.*, p. 869: *Enquête de Jules Huret*.

33 Letter to Henri Cazalis, in Henri Mondor: *Vie de Mallarmé*, Paris, 1946, p. 145.

34 Stéphane Mallarmé, *op. cit.*, p. 858: Avant-dire au *Traité du verbe* by René Ghil.

35 *Variations sur un sujet*, p. 389.

36 Georges Cattaui: 'Notes', *Fontaine*, March 1942, p. 72.

37 Thrasybulos Georgiades: *Musik und Rythmus bei den Griechen. Zum Ursprung der abendländischen Musik*, Hamburg, 1958.

38 Stéphane Mallarmé: *op. cit.*, p. 366, *Variations sur un sujet*.

39 The allusion here is to Mallarmé's *Livre* – his life's work destined to remain unfinished. Cf. Jacques Schérer: *Le 'Livre' de Mallarmé: premières recherches sur les documents*, Paris, 1957.

40 Paul Claudel: 'La catastrophe d'Igitur', *N.R.F.*, November 1926.

41 Albert Thibaudet: *La poésie de Stéphane Mallarmé*, Paris, 1912, p. 66.

42 Jacques Rivière: *Correspondance avec Alain Fournier*, Paris, 1926, vol. II, letter of 11. July 1906.

43 Paul Valéry: *Variété*, Paris, 1924, p. 97.

44 Edouard Schuré: *Histoire du drame musical*, Paris, 1882, vol. I., p. 153.

45 Eugène Delacroix: *Oeuvres littéraires*, Paris, 1923, vol. I., p. 153.

46 Cf. Jean de Rotonchamp: *Paul Gauguin*, Paris, 1906, p. 214.

47 W. S. Johnson: 'Browning's Music', *The Journal of Aesthetics*, Winter 1963, pp. 203-7.

48 Edgar A. Poe: *Philosophy of composition*.

49 Cited by Guy Michaud: *Message poétique du symbolisme*, II: *La Révolution poétique*, Paris, 1954, p. 139.

50 Stéphane Mallarmé: *Variations sur un sujet*, p. 368 and 381.

51 Odilon Redon: *A soi-même. Journal 1867–1915. Notes sur la vie, l'art et les artistes*, Paris, 1922, p. 28.

52 M. Malingue: *Lettres de Gauguin à sa femme et à ses amis*, Paris, 1949, Letter, no. 170.

53 *Op. cit.*, p. 288.

54 Cited by A. Humbert in *Les Nabis et leur époque*, 1888–1900, Geneva, 1954, p. 15.

55 Joachim Gasquet: *Cézanne*, Paris, 1921. Debussy speaks of 'mysterious correspondences between Nature and the Imagination' – which comes to the same thing, though expressed in Baudelairian terms.

56 Marcel Raymond: *De Baudelaire au surréalisme op. cit.* Introduction de la deuxième édition.

57 Maurice Denis: *Catalogue de l'exposition consacrée à Henri Cross*, 1910.

58 Charles Morice: *La littérature de tout à l'heure*, Paris, 1889, p. 175 and 60.

59 Cf. M. Dufrenne: *Phénoménologie de l'expérience esthétique*, Paris, 1953, p. 315.

60 Friedrich Hegel: *Esthétique,* Paris, 1944, vol. III, p. 298. Trans. S. Jankélévitch.

61 V. Jankélévitch: *La musique et l'ineffable,* Paris, 1961, p. 41.

62 Rainer Maria Rilke: *Auguste Rodin,* Cracow, 1963, p. 119.

63 Jean-Claude Piguet: *De l'esthétique à la métaphysique,* The Hague, 1959, p. 105.

64 Robert Francès: *La perception musicale,* Paris, 1958.

65 Arnold Schering: *Das Symbol in der Musik,* Leipzig, 1941, p. 130.

66 Wladyslav Tatarkiewicz: *Historia estetyki, op. cit.,* pp. 100 and 105.

67 Saint Augustine: in a note on Psalm CLXIX, *ibid,* p. 90.

68 D'Alembert: *Discours préliminaire de l'Encyclopédie* (1751).

69 Jean-Jacques Rousseau: *Musique Imitation* in *Dictionnaire de musique*, London, 1766.

70 Georges de Froide-Court: *Correspondance générale de Grétry*, Brussels, 1962.

71 The popularity of 'programme music' is further proof of this, and also the growing inclination of composers to write commentaries explaining what they were trying to express.

72 Karol Szymanowski: *Romanticism in music, Draga,* Nos. 1–2, 1929.

73 Friedrich Nietzsche: *Human all too human,* (Warsaw, 1908).

74 Théophile Gautier: editorial in *L'Artiste* of 14 December 1856. Eduard Hanslick's *Vom musikalischen Schönen* had appeared in 1854.

75 Camille Saint-Saëns: *Harmonie et Mélodie*, Paris, 1890, 4th edition, p. 10 and 12.

76 *Revue Bleue*, 2 April 1904, Enquiry by Paul Landormy into the present situation of French music.

77 *Correspondance inédite de Claude Debussy et d'Ernest Chausson* in *La Revue musicale*, 1 December 1925. Letter to Ernest Chausson of 6 September 1893.

78 E.g. in post-war literature on the subject by Gisèle Brelet, Robert Francès and above all Vladimir Jankélévitch.

79 Paul Valéry: *Lettres à quelques-uns*, p. 205. Letter to Timmermans of 19 December 1932.

80 Jean-Claude Piguet, in his *De l'Esthétique à la métaphysique* makes the same point in speaking of Bergsonism. He even sees in this type of epistemological attitude a characteristic feature of our time.

81 Maurice Blanchot: *Le problème de Wittgenstein*, *N.R.F.*, no. 131, November 1963, pp. 866–75. Maurice Blanchot sees in Flaubert the precursor of Wittgenstein's thesis, or at any rate, of the problem it raises.

82 Kurt Westphal: *Die moderne Musik* Berlin-Leipzig, 1928, p. 49.

83 Werner Danckert: *Claude Debussy*, Berlin, 1950, p. 158.

84 Jan Bialostocki: *Le Baroque: style, époque, attitude*, in *L'Information d'histoire de l'art*, January–February 1962, strongly stresses this point.

85 See *Le Processus historique dans la littérature et dans l'art*, Warsaw, 1967.

86 Cf. Hans Albrecht: *Impressionismus*, in *Musik in Geschichte und Gegenwart*, Kassel, 1957, vol. XXX, VI, pp. 1046–90.

87 Stefania Lobaczewska: *O stylu w muzyce* (Style in music), *Studia Muzykologiczne* no. IV, 1955, p. 53.

88 Stefania Lobaczewska in a criticism of a work by Otto Wartisch: *Studien zur Harmonik des musikalischen Impressionismus*, *Kwartalnik Muzyczny*, nos. 6–7, 1930, p. 248.

89 In a critical article on Hans Mersmann, *Die moderne Musik*, *Kwartalnik Muzyczny*, nos. 6–7, 1920, p. 248.

90 This new method of musical analysis, introduced by J. M. Chominski, was concerned primarily with the technique of pure sound, the actual *timbre* of a work. The questions it dealt with were these: the technology of *timbre*; the rationalisation of tempo; the formation of horizontal and vertical structures; the transmutation of elements; problems of form etc. We shall later be employing the term 'sound-values' to signify pure sound-qualities, independently of melody and harmony in their traditional sense – values resulting from the choice of instrumentation and a particular way of treating sounds with the help of rhythm, dynamics, agogic accents and articulation. See Jozef Chominski: 'Some aspects of the technique of composition in the twentieth century' (*Z zagadnien techniki kompozytorskiej XX wieku*), in *Muzyka*, no. 2, 1957; 'Sound-colour in the works of Skriabin', *Muzyka*, no. 2, 1959; 'The principal problems of sound-technique in the music of Liszt', *Muzyka*, no. 4, 1961; 'Sound-techniques as a subject for instruction', *Muzyka*, no. 3, 1961.

91 Stefania Lobaczewska: 'The agogic accent as an element in historical style', *Mzyuka*, no. 3, 1962, p. 60.

92 Louis Laloy: 'The music of the future', *Mercure de France*, 1 December 1908. Laloy had, among other things, foreseen the coming of electronic music. The theses put forward in this article, today unjustly forgotten, were certainly known to Debussy, and must have been discussed with him, united as he was by close ties of friendship with Laloy.

93 Cf. Louis Laloy: *Claude Debussy et le Debussysme* in *La Revue musicale*, *S.I.M.*, VIII–IX, 1910.

94 Louis Laloy: 'La nouvelle manière de Claude Debussy', *Grande Revue*, 10 February 1908.

95 Daniel Chennevière: *Claude Debussy*, Paris, 1913, p. 28.

96 Ferruccio Busoni: *Entwurf einer neuen Aesthetik der Tonkunst*, Trieste, 1907.

97 Ladislas Fabian: *Claude Debussy und sein Werk mit gesonderer Rücksicht auf den musikalischen Impressionismus*, Munich, 1923.

98 Andreas Liess: 'Harmony in the works of Claude Debussy' in *La Revue Musicale*, January 1931, pp. 45–6.

99 Andreas Liess: *Claude Debussy*, Leipzig-Strasbourg, 1936, pp. 339, 316.

100 Wassily Kandinsky: *Du spirituel dans l'art*, Paris, 1954, pp. 339, 316.

101 Arthur Symons: 'Claude Debussy', *Saturday Review*, 8 February 1908.

102 M. T. E. Clark: *A modern French composer: Claude Debussy*; Lecture at Newcastle upon Tyne, 1908.

103 René Peter: *Claude Debussy*, Paris, 1944, p. 119.

Chapter 4

DEBUSSY AND SYMBOLISM

1 Félix Fénéon: 'Les Impressionistes en 1886' in *La Vogue*, 1886. Article published on the occasion of the eighth (and last) Impressionist Exhibition.

2 Isabelle de Wyzewa: 'Essai sur l'interprétation esthétique de Wagner en France', *La Revue Wagnérienne*, Paris, 1934, p. 75.

3 Oscar Wilde: *The Picture of Dorian Gray*.

4 *Le Décadent*, 10 April 1886.

5 Jules Laforgue: 'Critique d'art. L'Impressionisme', in *Mélanges posthumes*, Paris, 1903, pp. 133–7.

6 As early as 1896 Gauguin was demanding the dismissal of Camille Mauclair from the editorial board of the *Mercure*. See 'Letter to Alfred Vallette', *Mercure de France*, nos. 999–1000, 1946.

7 P. Burne-Jones: 'The Experiment of Impressionism', *Nineteenth Century and After*, March 1905.

8 The *Manifeste* was signed by Paul Bonnetain, Joseph-Henri Rosny, Lucien Descaves, Paul Margueritte and Gustave Guiches.

9 Joris-Karl Huysmans: *Là-bas*, Paris, 1891, pp. 1 and 3.

10 See *Echo de Paris*, 15 June 1891, in reply to questionnaire drawn up by Jules Huret.

11 Melchoir de Vogüé: *Le roman Russe*, Paris, 1886.

12 Jean Moréas: *Le Symbolisme*, in *Le Figaro Littéraire*, 18 September 1886.

13 Arthur Rimbaud: 'Une saison en enfer', *Oeuvres complètes*, coll. Pléiade, Paris 1954.

14 Paul Valéry: *Variété II*, Paris, 1929, p. 155.

15 Letter to H. Cazalis, October 1864. Quoted by Henri Mondor in his *Vie de Mallarmé*, Paris, 1946, pp. 144–5.

16 Henri Bergson: *Essai sur les données immédiates de la conscience*, Paris, 1889, p. 98.

17 Marcel Proust: *A la recherche du temps perdu*, coll. *Pléiade*, Paris, 1964, vol. 1, pp. 835–8.

18 Bernard Dorival: *Les étapes de la peinture française*, Paris, 1948, vol. 1, pp. 70–76.

19 Albert Aurier: 'Le Symbolisme en peinture', *Mercure de France*, March 1891.

20 Henri Bergson: 'Introduction à la métaphysique', *Revue de métaphysique et de morale*, vol. 1, 1903.

21 Henri-Frédéric Amiel: *Fragments d'un journal intime*, Geneva, 1911, vol, 1, p. 166.

22 Jules Laforgue: *Mélanges posthumes*, p. 181.

23 Hugo von Hofmannsthal: *Prosa I. Englischer Stil*, p. 301.

24 Jacques Rivière: *Corréspondance avec Alain-Fournier*, Paris, 1926, vol. 1, p. 72.

25 See Albert Aurier: *Oeuvres posthumes. Les peintres Symbolistes*, Paris, 1893, p. 293.

26 Ferdinand Brunetière. 'Après une visite au Vatican', *Revue des deux mondes*, 1895.

27 Paul Valéry: *Lettres à quelques-uns*, Paris, 1952, pp. 46–7. Letter to Mallarmé of 18 April 1891.

28 *L'Echo de Paris*, June 1891; Charles Lalo counted Charles Henry as one of the 'modern Pythagoreans'. In *Les Cahiers de l'Ecole* of January–February 1930 Valéry spoke of him in the most sympathetic terms. Charles Henry had a brilliant mind and was the friend, among others, of Jules Laforgue, Gustave Kahn, and also of Seurat and Signac whose 'divisionist' theories were strongly influenced by Henry's ideas.

29 Paul Gauguin: *Racontars d'un rapin*. Quoted by Jean de Rotonchamp: *Paul Gauguin*, Paris, 1925, p. 241.

30 Arthur Schopenhauer: *Parerga und Paralipomena*, 1851.

31 Hippolyte Taine: *Philosophie de l'art*, Paris, 1881, 3rd ed., vol. I, p. 115.

32 *Journal des Goncourt*, Paris, 1888–96, vol. III, p. 110; vol. VI, p. 70; vol. II, p. 12.

33 Catulle Mendès: 'Le jeune Prix de Rome et le vieux Wagnériste', *La Revue Musicale*, 8 June 1885.

34 Théodore de Wyzewa: *Nos maîtres. Etudes et portraits littéraires*, Paris, 1895.

35 Edouard Dujardin. 'La Revue Wagnérienne', in *La Revue Musicale*, 8 June 1885.

36 Léon Daudet: *Souvenirs des milieux littéraires, politiques, artistiques et médicaux*, Paris, 1920, p. 278.

37 Cf. *Divagation*. 'Richard Wagner; rêverie d'un poète Français'; *La Revue Wagnérienne*, 8 August 1885.

38 André Gide and Paul Valéry: *Correspondance*, 1890–1942, Paris, 1955, p. 358. Letter of 19 October 1899.

39 Claude Debussy: 'De quelques superstitions et d'un opéra. Monnsieur Croche et les Barbares de Saint-Saëns': *La Revue Blanche*, 15 November 1901.

40 Cf. the article, which created a sensation at the time, by Emile Vuillermoz in the *Mercure musical* of 15 June 1906, attacking the methods of teaching at the *Schola Cantorum*. This article gave rise to the quarrel between 'Debussystes' and 'd'Indyistes' which lasted several years.

41 Norbert Dufourcq: *César Franck*, Paris, 1949, p. 109.

42 Charles Oulmont: *Musique de l'amour. Ernest Chausson et la 'bande à Franck'*, Paris, 1935, vol. I, p. 44.

43 Claude Debussy: 'Ballade de Fauré' in *Le Gil Blas*, 9 March 1903.

44 Out of 157 candidates (38 boys and 119 girls) only 39 (8 boys and 31 girls) were admitted. At the end of the academic year Marmontel notes in his class book, with reference to Debussy: 'Charming child, a real artistic temperament – will become a distinguished musician with a big future before him'.

45 Paul Verlaine: *Confessions*, Paris, 1895.

46 The researches carried out by Marcel Dietschy have thrown a new light upon this period in the life of the composer; see *La Passion de Claude Debussy*, Neuchâtel, 1962. Edward Lockspeiser's two-volume work, *Debussy, his Life and Mind*, New York-London, 1962–6, has also brought to light fresh details, especially with regard to the composer's early years.

47 Letter to André Poniatowski in: Prince André Poniatowski: *D'un siècle à l'autre*, Paris, 1940, p. 307.

48 Cf. Maurice Emmanuel: *Pelléas et Mélisande*, Paris, 1930, pp. 18–19. This explains why he was so eager to grasp every opportunity of escaping from the Conservatoire, and also from the Villa Medici in Rome later on. Apart from material considerations, sometimes pressing, it was essential for him to breathe the air of freedom – the air of another world no matter where or of what nature – whether that of the 'powerful' or that of the 'accursed ones'.

49 Raymond Bonheur: 'Souvenirs et impressions d'un compagnon de jeunesse', in *La Revue Musicale*, May 1926, p. 3.

50 Cf. Charles Baudelaire, *Oeuvres Complètes*, coll. Pléiade, Paris, 1956, p. 291: 'Who amongst us has not, in his ambitious days, dreamed of the miracle of a poetic prose – musical without rhythm and without rhyme, flexible enough and sufficiently accented to correspond to the lyrical impulses of the spirit and to the undulations of the world of dreams'. Compare this with what Debussy says in his letter to Vasnier, of 19 October 1886: 'As to the kind of music I want to make, I would like it to be flexible enough and sufficiently accented to correspond to the lyrical impulses of the spirit and to the capriciousness of dreams'. (*La Revue musicale*, May 1926, p. 39.) It seems astonishing that no one until now has ever been struck by this similarity of outlook.

51 *Op. cit.*, vol. 1, p. 144.

52 Cf. Paul Delsemme: *Un théoricien du symbolisme, Charles Morice*, Paris, 1958, p. 252. In his *Notes quotidiennes* Morice records, on the 24 May 1912: 'Called on Debussy. Very friendly; told me that he owed more to me than to anyone else for having helped to shape his intellectual development'. None of Debussy's biographers have ever mentioned this before.

53 'Claude Debussy: textes et documents inédits'; see *La Revue de musicologie*, special no., 1962, pp. 99–100: letter from Paul Vidal to Henriette Fuchs, 12 July 1884.

54 Cf. John Rewald: *Post-Impressionism. From van Gogh to Gauguin*; New York, 1956.

55 Robert Godet: 'En marge de la marge', *La Revue Musicale*, May 1926, pp. 63–4.

56 Cf. Léon Daudet: *Souvenirs; op. cit.*, pp. 637 and 646.

57 André Gide: 'Souvenirs littéraires et Problèmes actuels', in *L'Arche*, nos. 18–19, 1946, pp. 4–6.

58 Cf. among others, Thadée Natanson: 'A Valvins, in Mallarmé's company', in *La Nef*, February 1949. Thadée Natanson was the brother of the founder and editor of *La Revue bleue*, Alexander Natanson, the barrister who defended Félix Fénéon in the famous trial of the thirty anarchists, and was the first husband of Missia Godebska (later, Missia Sert).

59 Paul Landormy: *La Musique Française de Franck à Debussy*, Paris, 1943, p. 211.

60 Claude Debussy: *Lettres à deux amis*, Paris, 1942, pp. 120–21.

61 Prince Poniatowski, *op. cit.*, p. 241.

62 See Claude Debussy: *Lettres à son éditeur*, Paris, 1927, p. 58.

63 Cf. Marcel Dietschy: *La Passion de Claude Debussy*, p. 80.

64 Robert Brussel: 'Claude Debussy et Paul Dukas', in *La Revue musicale*, May 1926, p. 101.

65 *Monsieur Croche, anti-dilettante*, 1945, p. 21.

66 Quoted from Maurice Denis: *Henri Lerolle et ses amis*, Paris, 1932, p. 30. Letter to Henri Lerolle, 28 August 1894.

67 *Correspondance inédite de Claude Debussy et Ernest Chausson*, in *La Revue Musicale*, December 1925, p. 126. Letter of February 1894.

68 *La Revue Musicale S.I.M.*, 15 February 1913.

69 'Considérations sur le Prix de Rome au point de vue musical', *Musica*, May 1903.

70 *Le Gaulois*, 8 January 1911.

71 *Monsieur Croche, anti-dilettante*, p. 19.

72 'Est-ce une renaissance de la musique religieuse?', *Excelsior*, 11 February 1911. Interview with Henri Malherbe after the production of *Le Martyre de Saint Sébastien*.

73 *Revue musicale S.I.M.,* November 1913.

74 *Le Gil Blas,* 16 February 1903.

75 *Comoedia-Charpentier,* 18 October 1941.

76 Paul Valéry: *Lettres à quelques-uns.* Letter to Mallarmé, 18 April 1891.

77 Cf. M. Malingue: *Lettres de Gauguin,* Paris, 1949; Gauguin to Schuffnecker in a letter of 14 January 1885 (no. 11).

78 'L'Etat actuel de la musique française', in *La Revue bleue,* 2 April 1904, p. 422.

79 Léon Vallas: *Les idées de Claude Debussy,* Paris, 1927, p. 30.

80 'L'Etat actuel de la musique française', *op. cit.*

81 *Revue musicale S.I.M.,* February 1913, p. 48.

82 *Ibid.,* November 1913, p. 44.

83 *Ibid.,* December 1912, p. 52.

84 *La Revue blanche,* 15 May 1901. Report on *The Storm* by Alfred Bruneau.

85 *Le Gil Blas,* 1 June 1903.

86 André Fontainas: *Mes souvenirs du symbolisme,* Paris, 1928, pp. 92-3.

87 Maurice Emmanuel: *Pelléas et Mélisande,* 1930, p. 34.

88 *Comoedia,* 4 November 1909.

89 *Le Gil Blas,* 6 April 1903.

90 *Ibid.,* 19 January 1903.

91 All the above quotations are from *Le Gil Blas* of January, June and April 1903.

92 *Mercure de France,* January 1903.

93 'A propos de Charles Gounod', *Musica,* July 1906, p. 99.

94 *Revue Blanche,* 15 May 1901.

95 *Le Gil Blas,* 17 February 1903.

96 Léon Vallas: *Les idées de Claude Debussy,* p. 144.

97 *Ibid.,* pp. 145-6.

98 *Comoedia-Charpentier,* 8 October 1941. Interview with G. Ricou in April 1902.

99 *Revue Blanche,* 15 May 1901.

100 Maurice Emmanuel: *op. cit.,* pp. 35-36.

101 *Revue musicale S.I.M.,* 15 January 1913.

102 'Que faire au Conservatoire', *Le Figaro,* 14 February 1909.

103 *Le Gil Blas,* 2 February 1903.

104 'A propos d'*Hippolyte et Aricie*', *Le Figaro,* 8 May 1908.

105 *Revue bleue,* 2 April 1904.

106 André Fontainas: *op. cit.,* pp. 92-3.

107 *Lettres à son éditeur,* p. 55. Letter to Durand of 3 September 1907.

108 Léon Vallas: *Claude Debussy et son temps,* 1058, p. 364.

109 *Revue blanche,* 1 May 1901.

110 *Musica,* October 1902, p. 5. 'Réponse à l'enquête sur l'orientation musicale'.

111 Charles Baudelaire: *Oeuvres complètes,* p. 1192.

112 Oswald Spengler: *Le Declin de l'Occident,* Paris, 1948, vol. I, p. 211.

113 *Revue blanche,* 1 May 1901.

114 Bernard Dorival: *Les Etapes de la peinture française contemporaine,* Paris, 1948, vol. I, pp. 108-110.

115 *Comoedia-Charpentier*, 8 October 1941. Conversation with G. Ricou, quoted above (note 102).

116 Léon Vallas: *op. cit.*, p. 39.

117 *Le Gil Blas*, 2 March 1903.

118 *Ibid.*, 19 January 1903.

119 'Musik im Raum', *Die Reihe*, Heft v, 1959, pp. 59–73.

120 *Corréspondance de Claude Debussy et de Pierre Loüys*, 1945, p. 45.

121 René Lenormand: *Etude sur l' Harmonie moderne*, Paris, 1913 (Monde Musical xxiv).

122 Léon Vallas: *op. cit.*, p. 356. Letter to René Lenormand, 25 July 1912.

123 *Revue Musicale S.I.M.*, 15 February 1913.

Chapter 5
THE MUSIC OF DEBUSSY

1 Stefania Lobaczewska (in Polish): 'La musique de Claude Debussy de la première période', *Kwartalnik Muzyczny*, no. 5, 1929, p. 56.

2 *Musica:* Reply to a questionnaire on the connection between music and poetry; March 1911.

3 Quoted by Alfred Cassagne: *La Théorie de l'art pour l'art en France*, Paris, 1906 p. 451.

4 Léon Vallas: *Achille-Claude Debussy*, 1944, p. 88.

5 Heinrich Strobel: *Claude Debussy*, Paris, 1952, p. 31.

6 It will not be forgotten that Maurice Ravel wrote his *Trois poèmes de Stéphane Mallarmé* in 1913, the same year as Debussy; for the first two he had chosen the same poems (*Soupir* and *Placet futile*), for the third, *Surgi de la croupe et du bond*.

7 See *La Revue musicale*, 1926.

8 Cf. Oswald d'Estrade-Guerra: 'Les manuscrits de *Pelléas et Mélisande* de Claude Debussy' in *La Revue Musicale*, no. 235, 1957, pp. 10–11.

9 See *La Revue musicale*, May 1926, p. 29.

10 Ed. Durand, 1905.

11 See bars 10–13, Ed. Durand, *Douze Chants*, 1906.

12 Cf. *Société Générale de Librairie Catholique*. I owe this information to M. d'Estrade-Guerra.

13 Verlaine's anagram in the *Poètes maudits*.

14 See *L'Echo de Paris*, 27 August 1900.

15 *Le Balcon*, Ed. Durand, bars 122–125.

16 *Comoedia-Charpentier*, 18 October 1941. Interview in April 1902.

17 *La Revue musicale S.I.M.*, February 1914.

18 Boris de Schloezer: *Igor Stravinsky*, Paris, 1929, p. 41.

19 *Monsieur Croche anti-dilettante*, op. cit., p. 10.

20 Author's underlining. R. Paoli: *Debussy*, Florence 1951, p. 204; letter of 6 October.

21 *Ségalen et Debussy*, Monaco, 1962, p. 107. Interview of 17 December 1908.

22 Claude Debussy: *Lettres inédites à André Caplet*, Monaco; 1957, p. 47. Letter dated 25 November 1910.

23 Cf. Maurice Denis: *Henri Lerolle et ses amis*, p. 30. Letter to Henri Lerolle 28 August 1894.

24 *Ségalen et Debussy*, p. 108.

25 Herbert Eimert: 'Debussy's *Jeux*', *Die Reihe*, no. 5, 1959, p. 18.

26 Françoise Gervais: 'La notion d'arabesque chez Debussy', *La Revue musicale*, no. 241, 1958, pp. 14–15.

27 Andréas Liess: 'L'Harmonie dans les oeuvres de Claude Debussy', *La Revue musicale*, January 1931, p. 45.

28 Cf. Gaston Bachelard: *L'Eau et les rêves*, Paris 1942, pp. 1, 31, 202.

29 Letter to Ernest Chausson, 2 October 1893.

30 Letter to Pierre Louÿs of 17 July 1895.

31 'Claude Debussy et Eugène Ysaÿe: Lettres inédites', *Les Annales politiques et littéraires*, 26 August 1933, p. 226. Letter of 13 October 1896; and Letter to Henri Lerolle quoted above. Cf. Maurice Denis, *op. cit.*

32 Vladimir Jankélévitch: *Debussy et le mystère*, Neûchâtel, 1949, p. 136. I owe more than one idea and suggestion to this fine work.

33 André Michel: *Psychanalyse de la musique*, Paris, 1952, p. 221.

34 *Revue bleue*, 2 April 1904; interview with Paul Landormy.

35 Vladimir Jankélévitch: *La musique et l'Ineffable*, Paris 1961, p. 164.

36 Vladimir Jankelévitch: *Debussy et le mystère*, pp. 14–16.

37 G. Courty: 'Dernières années de Debussy', *Revue des deux mondes*, 15 May 1958. Letter to Courty of 18 June 1916.

38 Marie Bonaparte: *Edgar Poe: Etude psychanalytique*, Paris, 1833, p. 367.

39 Letter to Jacques Durand, of 18 June 1908.

40 Letter to Jacques Durand, 8 July 1910.

41 Letter to André Caplet, of 22 December 1911.

42 Letter to Robert Godet, 4 January 1916.

43 *L'Enfance de Pelléas. Lettres de Claude Debussy à André Messager*, Paris, 1938, p. 74. Letter of 12 September 1903.

44 Vladimir Jankélévitch: *Debussy et le mystère*, p. 119.

45 *Ibid.*, p. 149. A recent study, *La vie et la mort dans la musique de Debussy*, Neuchâtel, 1968, by the same eminent author develops in brilliant style the principal theme that pervades the whole of Debussy's *oeuvre*. I sincerely regret not having known this book while I was writing mine.

Chapter 6
DEBUSSY AND THE MUSIC OF THE TWENTIETH CENTURY

1 *Relevés d'apprenti*, Paris, 1966, p. 35.

2 *Debussy et Edgar Poe*, Monaco, 1962, p. 40. Letter to Gabriel Mourey of 10 February 1902.

3 Theodor W. Adorno: *Philosophie de la nouvelle musique*, Paris, 1962, p. 183.

4 *Op. cit.*, p. 115.